College
NAMES
OF THE
GAMES

MIKE LESSITER

CB

CONTEMPORARY
BOOKS

CHICAGO · NEW YORK

MW00425876

Library of Congress Cataloging-in-Publication Data

Lessiter, Mike.
    The college names of the games : the stories behind the nicknames
of 293 college sports team / by Mike Lessiter.
        p.   cm.
    Includes index.
    ISBN 0-8092-4476-4
    1. College sports—United States—History.   2. Athletic clubs—
United States—Names—History.   I. Title.
GV351.L47   1989
796'.06073—dc19   88-39124
                                                                          CIP

Published by Contemporary Books, Inc.
180 North Michigan Avenue, Chicago, Illinois 60601
Manufactured in the United States of America
International Standard Book Number: 0-8092-4476-4

Published simultaneously in Canada by Beaverbooks, Ltd.
195 Allstate Parkway, Valleywood Business Park
Markham, Ontario L3R 4T8 Canada

It is with great pride that I dedicate this book to my father, Frank Lessiter. Without his support, guidance, and friendship, this book would never have become a reality. Thanks, Dad.

Contents

Introduction

AFTER WRITING and seeing the success of my first book, *The Names of the Games*, I had many people ask me how their college alma mater obtained its own wacky nickname. And the more unusual the nickname, the more questions I got. So I decided to tackle the exciting and enjoyable game of uncovering the mysteries behind all of the NCAA Division I basketball and football nicknames. You can take it from me, there are many school nicknames that at first seem a little off the wall—as you will see when you read this book.

Whether you're a true sports trivia junkie or simply interested in your alma mater's nickname, you will find this book interesting and complete as to all school name details. You'll find many interesting stories and anecdotes in the following pages. As an example, see if you can answer these puzzling questions:

- Which college's nickname was named after a pair of rubber-soled athletic shoes? (See page 322.)

- Which school named its teams after the chief product of a businessman who bailed them out of a financial disaster? (See page 300.)

- Which school literally adopted its mascot after it attacked the referee during a football game? (See page 165.)

- What college mascot first came over with Columbus in 1493? (See page 273.)

- Which school acquired its nickname because several football players had summer jobs working in the wheat fields? (See page 190.)

- What nickname was selected in honor of a popular regional dish served within the state's borders? (See page 21.)

- Which school obtained its nickname when an opposing team accused its coach of "having something up his sleeve?" (See page 173.)

- What school adopted its nickname after an agriculture professor slew a tiger in India? (See page 208.)

- Which school selected its nickname only to find out shortly afterward they had chosen a totally different animal? (See page 289.)

- Which school received its nickname because of its football players' long hair? (See page 18.)

All of the teams in this book are part of the National Collegiate Athletic Association (NCAA), the organization through which the nation's colleges and universities speak and act on athletic matters at the national level. It is a voluntary association of more than 1,000 institutions, conferences, organizations, and individuals devoted to the sound administration of intercollegiate athletics.

Ironically, it was football's flying wedge, the major offense at the time, which spurred on the formation of the NCAA in 1905. Because numerous injuries and deaths resulted from the mass formations and gang tackling which typified early-day football's rugged nature, many institutions decided to drop the popular sport from their athletic curriculum. Others felt that football should be either reformed or abolished from intercollegiate athletics.

President Theodore Roosevelt, who was an avid sports fan, summoned college athletic leaders to two White House conferences to encourage reforms in an effort to save the sport. In December 1905, New York University Chancellor Henry M. MacCracken convened a meeting of 13 institutions to initiate key changes in football's playing rules. At a later meeting on December 28 in New York City, the Intercollegiate Athletic Association of the United States was born with 62 schools as charter members.

The IAAUS was officially constituted on March 31, 1906, and took its present name in 1910. For several years, the NCAA served only as a discussion group and rule-making body. In 1921, however, the first NCAA national championship was held, the National Collegiate Track and Field Championships. Gradually, more rules committees were formed and more championships were held.

Besides supervising college athletics on a national scale, the NCAA also administers 76 championships in 21 sports for member institutions. More than 18,000 men and women student athletes compete annually in these events for national titles.

National Collegiate Athletic Association
Nall Avenue at 63rd Street
P.O. Box 1906
Mission, KS 66201

Southwestern Louisiana Ragin' Cajuns

1

American South Conference

American South Conference
P.O. Box 4348
New Orleans, LA 70178

Number of Schools: 6
Year Founded: 1987
Charter Members: Arkansas State, Lamar, Louisiana Tech, New Orleans, Pan American, and Southwestern Louisiana
Current Members: Same as charter members
Division I Sports: Baseball, Basketball, Cross-Country, Golf, Indoor Track, and Track and Field

Arkansas State Indians

Arkansas State University
State University, AR 72467

School Colors: Scarlet and Black
Year Founded: 1909
Basketball: Convocation Center
(11,000)
Football: Indian Stadium (18,709)

ARKANSAS STATE UNIVERSITY of Jonesboro, Arkansas, took on its current nickname because of the great fighting history of Indian tribes living in the area.

The school's first nickname, the Aggies, was dubbed in 1911 because ASU was the only agricultural school in eastern Arkansas. The name Farmers was later used interchangeably with the Aggies title.

In 1925, the nickname was changed to Gorillas, but that wasn't accepted too readily by the students and faculty since they felt it did not represent the school's athletes in a favorable light. Warriors was tagged as the nickname in 1930, and one year later it evolved into the current name, Indians.

The name Indians is taken from a part of Arkansas's state heritage—the Osage Indian tribe, which roamed the northern part of the state before any settlers arrived. During the 1700s, the Osage were constantly at war with most other plains tribes as well as the Woodland Indians.

For that reason, ASU selected the name with pride and hoped to instill the same fighting spirit in its athletic teams as the Osage had enjoyed 200 years earlier.

The ASU mascot is a trio of students attired in Indian clothing and popularly known as the Indian family. Chief Big Track, the legendary chief of the Osage, is the head of the family. The chief, a princess, and a brave all take the field on horseback at football games.

The expensive costumes worn by the family are styled after the Osage Indians' dress, and Chief Big Track's costume is valued at more than $1,000. The costume, which consists of 495 parts, required 800 yards of thread just to sew the eagle feathers to the headdress.

Lamar Cardinals

Lamar University
P.O. Box 10066
Beaumont, TX 77710

School Colors: Red and White
Year Founded: 1923
Basketball: Montagne Center (10,080)
Football: Cardinal Stadium (17,150)

LAMAR UNIVERSITY originated as South Park Junior College in 1923. In its first season, the football team went seven games without a nickname before Spike Cooper of the Beaumont *Enterprise* unofficially tagged the players as the Scholastics.

The following season, after South Park won its first four games, the students assembled to select a school nickname. By unanimous decision, the students came up with the unusual name Brahmas, which means bull, as their official moniker. The Brahmas wore red jerseys that season, shedding the green and white colors they had adopted the previous year. This was a most interesting combination of animals and colors since it is a widely accepted belief that bulls hate anything red.

The Beaumont campus underwent a big change in 1932. The school was renamed Lamar University, football was reinstated after a six-year absence, and Cardinals became the new official nickname.

School officials say they wanted a more down-to-earth nickname—one people could better relate to. Otto Plummer, who played baseball and basketball for the former South Park Junior College from 1925 to 1927, won a scholarship for his younger brother, Wesley, by coming up with the name Cardinals.

Louisiana Tech Bulldogs

Louisiana Tech University
Ruston, LA 71270

School Colors: Red and Blue
Year Founded: 1894
Basketball: Thomas Assembly Center
(8,000)
Football: Aillet Stadium (30,500)

LOUISIANA TECH school officials have no known record as to why Bulldogs evolved as the official nickname. However, it is believed the name was first used in the early 1920s after it was coined by local sportswriters.

The bulldog is a very popular and a traditional mascot in collegiate athletics and is a good choice for any school's team name.

In the 1930s sportswriters suggested changing the school name to something a little less common. They felt the name Bulldogs was far too abundant in collegiate athletics and suggested unusual names such as Parrots and Light Brigades to put Louisiana Tech in a class of its own. But a change was never made, and the official school nickname has been Bulldogs since the first athletic team was fielded.

In 1974, when women's basketball was introduced as a varsity sport, the head coach refused to let the press refer to her team as Bulldogs. She thought the name was demeaning and not feminine. Ever since, the successful women's basketball team has been known as the Lady Techsters.

New Orleans Privateers

University of New Orleans
Lakefront Arena
New Orleans, LA 70148

School Colors: Royal Blue and Silver
Year Founded: 1956
Basketball: Lakefront Arena (10,000)

IT TOOK FOUR ELECTIONS during the 1964–1965 school year before New Orleans approved the Privateer as the school mascot.

After a student referendum narrowed a list of nickname proposals to five, an election was held, in December 1964, with the name Panthers prevailing over Dolphins and Privateers. (School officials don't remember what the other two proposed names were.)

Because students protested that Panthers didn't receive a large enough plurality in the first vote and had nothing to do with New Orleans history or the school's location on Lake Ponchartrain, another election was scheduled. This time Dolphins was declared the winner over Privateers and Panthers. But the students were still unhappy. In a final head-to-head election in March, Privateers defeated Dolphins by a 16 percent margin.

A privateer, according to the dictionary, is "the commander or one of a crew of an armed private ship commissioned to cruise against the commerce or warships of an enemy." One of the most famous privateers in U.S. history was Jean Lafitte, who carried letters of marque (commissions) from several governments in order to prey upon the shipping of other countries' goods. Lafitte's hideaway was located on Barataria Bay, south of New Orleans. Lafitte's cannoneers were also instrumental in helping defeat the British forces in the Battle of New Orleans in 1815. Because of Lafitte's association with New Orleans, the name seemed a logical choice.

Other names originally considered were Cajuns, Mariners, Marlins, Ospreys, Pelicans, Seagulls, and Tigers.

UNO's women's teams were known as the Lady Privateers until the 1980–81 season when Joey Favaloro, the new women's basketball coach, suggested a change to the name Buc-kettes. Favaloro's proposal was approved immediately by the school's athletic and academic administration.

Pan American Broncs

Pan American University
1201 West University Drive
Edinburg, TX 78539-2999

School Colors: Green and White
Year Founded: 1927
Basketball: Pan American University
Field House (5,000)

PAN AMERICAN'S sports teams have been nicknamed the Broncs since 1927 when the institution was founded as Edinburg Junior College.

Legend says the Broncs were born because Edinburg Junior College's first coach came from Southern Methodist University, whose teams were nicknamed the Ponies (Mustangs). Because he wanted to stay with the horse imagery, the Broncs, a wild horse of the West, was adopted as the official Pan American nickname.

Southwestern Louisiana
Ragin' Cajuns

University of Southwestern Louisiana
201 Reinhardt Drive
Lafayette, LA 70506-4297

School Colors: Vermillion and White
Year Founded: 1898
Basketball: Cajundome (12,000)
Football: Cajun Field (31,000)

THE RAGIN' CAJUNS of Southwestern Louisiana are the only university teams in the nation to have this unique nickname.

The original teams were called the Bulldogs, a common name among colleges and universities. The name was first used in 1908 during USL's inaugural football season.

The Ragin' Cajuns' nickname originated in 1961 with the arrival of a new football coach. Sports information director Bob Henderson is credited with providing the unique name. Because more than 90 percent of the football team was composed of Louisiana high school players, many with French-speaking Acadian backgrounds, Henderson felt the name would suit the team. The nickname stuck, and all Southwestern Louisiana teams are known today as the Ragin' Cajuns.

Western Illinois Fighting Leathernecks

2

Association of Mid-Continent

Universities

Association of Mid-Continent Universities
2127 South Oneida Street
Green Bay, WI 54304

Number of Schools: 8
Year Founded: 1982
Charter Members: Cleveland State, Eastern Illinois, Illinois-Chicago, Northern Iowa, Southwest Missouri State, Valparaiso, Western Illinois, and Wisconsin–Green Bay
Current Members: Same as charter members
Division I Sports: Baseball, Basketball, Cross-Country, Golf, Indoor Track, Soccer, Swimming, Tennis, and Track and Field

Cleveland State Vikings

Cleveland State University
2451 Euclid Avenue
Cleveland, OH 44115

School Colors: Forest Green and
White
Year Founded: 1964
Basketball: Woodling Gymnasium
(3,000)
Convocation Center
(13,000)

WHEN CLEVELAND STATE UNIVERSITY was built in 1964, in downtown Cleveland on what had been Fenn College, it was decided that a more
appropriate nickname for the institution should be found.

Fenn College, a private institution, had fielded all its athletic teams under
the name Foxes since 1929. Since Foxes did not fit nearly as well phonetically with the new school name as with the old, a contest was held to select
a new moniker.

Favored nicknames included Lakers, since the campus is just a few
blocks from Lake Erie, and Foresters, since Cleveland was known for many
decades as the Forest City. But somehow, Vikings was the runaway winner.

No one is quite sure of the reason, but there was a strong suspicion that a
large contingent of St. Joseph High School graduates at CSU, whose teams
were known as the Vikings, had conducted a quiet, efficient, and successful
campaign to help their alma mater's nickname graduate to the collegiate
level.

Cleveland State's mascot was dubbed Viktorius Viking, and his cherubic
countenance has served as CSU's athletic symbol since the early days. In
1983, however, the university reached an agreement with cartoonist Dik
Browne and King Features Syndicate to adopt the character Hagar the
Horrible as its mascot. Ever since, the gnarled red-bearded Viking has been
a popular symbol of Cleveland State athletics, sharing the spotlight with
Viktorius.

Eastern Illinois Panthers

Eastern Illinois University
Old Main 109
Charleston, IL 61920

School Colors: Blue and Gray
Year Founded: 1895
Basketball: Lantz Gymnasium (6,500)
Football: O'Brien Stadium (12,000)

IN 1930, the *Teachers College News* decided it would be more appropriate and handy to have an official nickname for Eastern Illinois rather than the drab Blue and Gray title they had been using for 35 years.

In conjunction with the Fox Lincoln Theater, five dollars in theater tickets were offered to the winner of a contest to name Eastern's athletic teams.

Athletic director and football coach Charles Lantz, football captain Gene Kintz, and *News* sports editor Irvin Singler were chosen to select the winning entry. The judges considered several names with Indian backgrounds including Kickapoos, Ellini, and Indians itself. Also considered were names associated with the school colors such as Blue Racers, Blue Boys, Blue Battlers, and Greyhounds. On October 16, 1930, Panthers was announced as the official nickname.

Harland Baird, Paul Birthisel, and Thelma Brock all submitted the winning Panthers name and each received one-third of the five-dollar movie ticket prize.

Illinois-Chicago Flames

University of Illinois at Chicago
Box 4348
Chicago, IL 60680

School Colors: Indigo and Flame
Year Founded: 1896
Basketball: UIC Pavilion (10,000)

ON SEPTEMBER 1, 1982, the Chicago Circle and Medical Center campuses of the University of Illinois were consolidated to form the University of Illinois at Chicago.

Chicago Circle's former nickname Chicas, which means "little girls" in Spanish, was not popular with school officials. With a new campus name, they felt it was only fitting that UIC athletic teams have a new nickname.

An athletic advisory board studied a number of suggestions and put up Skyscrapers and Clout for the student vote. The students were unhappy with the choices, though, and organized a write-in campaign.

Because the great Chicago fire of 1871 had begun only a short distance from the campus, Flames was the winner in the May election. The Flames' moniker has been popular with UIC students ever since.

Northern Iowa
Purple Panthers

University of Northern Iowa
NW Upper UNI-Dome
Cedar Falls, IA 50614-0314

School Colors: Purple and Old Gold
Year Founded: 1876
Basketball: UNI-Dome (11,000)
Football: UNI-Dome (16,000)

IN 1931, STUDENTS OF Iowa State Teachers College (later to become the University of Northern Iowa) had finally had enough of their pacifist nickname Tutors. In the fall of that year, the *College Eye* and the men's physical education department sponsored a contest to change the school nickname.

The name Purple Panthers was the one that caught the college's eye and has guided the UNI athletic teams ever since. Burl Berry, the football team's most valuable player, who submitted the name, won a briefcase from Berg Drug Company for his suggestion. The runner-up received an alarm clock.

Northern Iowa students today should be glad school officials didn't choose the third-place suggestion. If they had, UNI athletic teams would be known today as the Purple Grackles. And that would have really been for the birds!

Southwest Missouri State Bears

Southwest Missouri State University
901 South National
Springfield, MO 65804

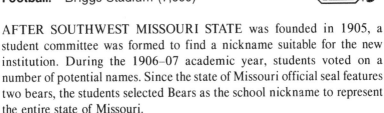

School Colors: Maroon and White
Year Founded: 1905
Basketball: Hammons Student Center
          (8,858)
Football: Briggs Stadium (7,000)

AFTER SOUTHWEST MISSOURI STATE was founded in 1905, a student committee was formed to find a nickname suitable for the new institution. During the 1906–07 academic year, students voted on a number of potential names. Since the state of Missouri official seal features two bears, the students selected Bears as the school nickname to represent the entire state of Missouri.

The school logo features a ferocious, attacking bear coming through the block U underneath the SMS arch.

Valparaiso University Fighting Crusaders

Valparaiso University
Valparaiso, IN 46383

School Colors: Brown and Gold
Year Founded: 1859
Basketball: Athletics-Recreation
          Center (4,500)
Football: Brown Field (5,000)

VALPARAISO'S CURRENT NICKNAME, the Fighting Crusaders, evolved during World War II. The original symbol of Valparaiso University was a uhlan. The uhlan was a member of a medieval German cavalry and was armed with a lance. This symbol had been selected because it represented Valparaiso as a German Lutheran institution.

But during World War II, the uhlan was regarded with dislike because anti-Nazi sentiment discouraged any German association. The Crusader's mascot emerged from the uhlan name, and today the plumed knight with his "dukes" up represents the VU student body. The athletic teams eventually took on the unofficial moniker Fighting Crusaders.

Western Illinois Fighting Leathernecks

Western Illinois University
900 West Adams
Macomb, IL 61455

School Colors: Purple and Old Gold
Year Founded: 1899
Basketball: Western Hall (6,000)
Football: Hanson Field (15,000)

WITH THE EXCEPTION of the three service academies, Western Illinois University is the only nonmilitary institution in the nation to have its nickname attributed to a branch of the military service.

Coach Ray Hanson was instrumental in the selection of WIU's unique nickname when he became Western's athletic director and head football coach in 1927. Prior to that time, all Western Illinois athletic teams had been known as the Pedagogues or Fighting Teachers.

Hanson, who had been an officer in the Marine Corps during World War I, received special permission from the U.S. Navy Department to use the marines' official seal and Bulldog mascot along with the Fighting Leathernecks nickname. Leatherneck is the slang term used to refer to U.S. Marines.

Hanson retired from Western Illinois in 1964 and held the rank of colonel in the Marine Corps Reserve until his death in 1982 at the age of 86.

However, the marines tradition lives on at Western Illinois. The official Marine Corps band frequently performs at Western Illinois football games, and several school mascots, all named Colonel Rock, have been provided by the U.S. Marine Corps.

Wisconsin–Green Bay Fighting Phoenix

University of Wisconsin–Green Bay
2420 Nicolet Drive
Green Bay, WI 54311-7001

School Colors: Forest Green, Phoenix Red, and White
Year Founded: 1968
Basketball: Brown County Veterans Memorial Arena (5,800)

GREEN BAY ATHLETIC TEAMS carry their distinctive nickname Phoenix as a result of a student-sponsored contest in the spring of 1970.

UW–Green Bay had just concluded its first year of intercollegiate athletics under the nickname Bay Badgers. This name was generally disliked because it implied that UWGB was a diminutive offshoot of the University of Wisconsin at Madison, whose nickname is Badgers. The name also inspired newspaper headlines such as "Offspring Bay Badgers Host Pappa Bucky in Soccer Tilt." It was decided the most democratic way to select a new nickname would be with a student vote. Phoenix won over several contenders.

The phoenix legend describes the bird as looking much like an eagle, only larger and more graceful. According to the myth, only one phoenix lives at a time, in cycles of 500 years each. When the time of death approaches, the bird builds a nest of branches and incense. The nest is ignited by the sun and the flames engulf the bird. A young phoenix then arises from the ashes of the old and leads all birds to the land of the gods.

One of the reasons the name Phoenix, which is singular, was selected was because it emphasizes the closeness of the students, faculty, and athletic teams. Today, UWGB teams are known as the Fighting Phoenix.

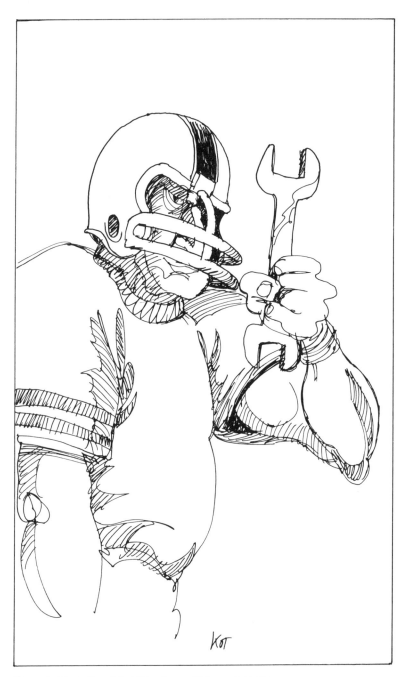

Georgia Tech Ramblin' Wrecks or Yellow Jackets

3

Atlantic Coast Conference

Atlantic Coast Conference
P.O. Box 29169
Greensboro, NC 27429-9169

Number of Schools: 8
Year Founded: 1953
Charter Members: Clemson, Duke, Maryland, North Carolina, North Carolina State, South Carolina, and Wake Forest
Current Members: Clemson, Duke, Georgia Tech, Maryland, North Carolina, North Carolina State, Virginia, and Wake Forest
Division I Sports: Baseball, Basketball, Cross-Country, Football, Golf, Indoor Track, Lacrosse, Soccer, Swimming, Tennis, Track and Field, and Wrestling

Clemson Tigers

Clemson University
P.O. Box 31
Clemson, SC 29633

School Colors: Purple and Burnt
Orange
Year Founded: 1889
Basketball: Littlejohn Coliseum
(11,820)
Football: Frank Howard Memorial
Field (79,854)

YOU WON'T FIND MANY universities who obtained their nickname because of the football players' long hair. Clemson, however, is one of them.

William J. Latimer, class of 1906, did some research on the subject and came up with the answer as to why Clemson's nickname is Tigers. "Due to the lack of helmets and head protection, the players wore long hair. These long manes might have gained them the name of Lions had it not been for the orange and purple striped jerseys and stockings that resembled tigers. The latter nickname seemed to stick."

The Clemson teams were dubbed the Tigers early in the 1900s, and the name has followed the teams ever since.

In 1970, in order to "upgrade" the image of the university, Pres. R. C. Edwards decided to hire an advertising agency to design a new Tigers insignia. The agency wrote to all the schools in the nation who had a tiger as mascot, asking for copies of each school's logo.

After viewing all of the tiger logos in America, it was decided that a tiger is a tiger and that there is nothing extraordinary or distinctive about the animal. So after many weeks of banging their heads together, an astute ad agent came up with an idea that soon made Clemson unique among schools with a Tiger nickname and mascot.

He suggested a Tiger Paw be developed as the insignia, and a request was sent to the Museum of Natural History in Chicago to get a plaster mold of a tiger's paw. Today, the Clemson Tiger Paw is one of the most recognized symbols in the nation—and it looks like President Edwards truly accomplished what he set out to do.

Duke Blue Devils

Duke University
135 Cameron Indoor Stadium
Durham, NC 27706

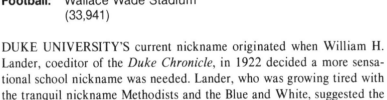

School Colors: Royal Blue and White
Year Founded: 1839
Basketball: Cameron Indoor Stadium
  (8,564)
Football: Wallace Wade Stadium
  (33,941)

DUKE UNIVERSITY'S current nickname originated when William H. Lander, coeditor of the *Duke Chronicle*, in 1922 decided a more sensational school nickname was needed. Lander, who was growing tired with the tranquil nickname Methodists and the Blue and White, suggested the school adopt the name Blue Devils.

Beginning with the first issue of the 1922–23 school year, he and fellow editor Mike Bradshaw insisted that all Duke teams be referred to as Blue Devils in the newspaper.

The Blue Devil nickname is derived from the French Blue Devils, a first-class Alpine corps, which wore a striking blue uniform with a blue beret.

However, the Blue Devils' name did not achieve instant popularity with the Duke student body that year. The university news bureau didn't pick it up, cheerleaders stayed away from it, and the school yearbook staff ridiculed the name. But through sheer repetition in the *Chronicle*, the name eventually caught on all over campus as Duke's nickname.

Georgia Tech Yellow Jackets or Rambling Wrecks

Georgia Institute of Technology
150 Third Street NW
Atlanta, GA 30332

School Colors: Old Gold and White
Year Founded: 1885
Basketball: Alexander Memorial
Coliseum (10,000)
Football: Grant Field (46,000)

UNLIKE MOST SCHOOLS, Georgia Tech recognizes two entirely unrelated mascots as its unofficial nickname.

The school's first nickname, the Yellow Jackets, did not grow out of the six-legged insect that serves as its mascot, but rather the mascot grew out of the nickname. The first reference to the Yellow Jackets was in the Atlanta *Constitution* in 1905, when the word was used to describe Tech supporters who attended athletic events. Fans were decked out in yellow coats and jackets, and the yellow swarm in the stands prompted newspapers to refer to the teams as yellow jackets.

Other common nicknames used to refer to Georgia Tech teams were Engineers, which is still in use today by some writers; Techs, the school's first known nickname; and Blacksmiths, which was used sparsely just after the turn of the century. Another school nickname, the Golden Tornado, was created by sportswriters when coaching great John Heisman led Tech to its first football national championship in 1917.

The school's second currently used nickname, the Ramblin' Wrecks, originated at a September 30, 1961, football game against Rice University. The Rambling Wreck, a restored 1930 Model A Ford Sport Coupe, was unveiled at the game while leading the Tech football team onto the field. This practice quickly developed into a great tradition, and the Wreck has led the team onto the field at every home game ever since.

The famous Ramblin' Wreck fight song was first sung by Tech students during the school's first two academic years. When almost the entire student body traveled to Athens to see Tech's baseball team defeat Georgia, the famous words "I'm a Ramblin' Wreck from Georgia Tech and a hell of an engineer" were sung for the first time.

Maryland Terrapins

University of Maryland at College Park
P.O. Box 295
College Park, MD 20740

School Colors: Red, Black, and Gold
Year Founded: 1856
Basketball: Cole Field House (14,000)
Football: Byrd Stadium (45,000)

THE UNIVERSITY OF MARYLAND'S historic nickname, the Terrapins, is a product of a fine dish served within Maryland's borders.

A terrapin is a North American turtle of the testudo genus found in both sea and fresh water and used for food. Terrapin soup has been native to Maryland's cuisine for decades, although it almost vanished from the salt marshes in the 19th century when terrapins were in high demand by restaurant owners.

Maryland president H. C. "Curley" Byrd adopted the diamondback terrapin as the school mascot in 1933, feeling that it was a good representation of Maryland's culture. Soon after, the Baltimore and Washington media shortened the name to Terrapins or Terps for use in headlines.

The class of 1933 presented the university with Testudo, a bronze statue of the new mascot. But Testudo was constantly "turtle-napped" by rival colleges before athletic events. In early 1949, after school officials grew tired of chasing the statue down, Testudo was filled with cement to thwart further attempts to steal it. Fittingly, the 500-pound statue now stands proudly behind H. C. Byrd Stadium, named after the man who first brought the Terrapins to Maryland.

Today the Terrapins are represented at sporting events by a Maryland student dressed in a $2,000 turtle suit. The terrapin is seen bobbing, wiggling, dancing, jumping, and turning cartwheels during time-outs and halftimes at Maryland athletic events.

North Carolina State Wolfpack

North Carolina State University
Case Athletics Center Box 8501
Raleigh, NC 27695-8501

School Colors: Red and White
Year Founded: 1887
Basketball: William Neal Reynolds
Coliseum (12,400)
Football: Carter-Finley Stadium (53,500)

NORTH CAROLINA STATE first was dubbed the Wolfpack in an insulting remark from a fan. However, for some reason the school liked it and kept the name.

In the early days of intercollegiate competition, State's teams were known as the Farmers and Mechanics, the Aggies, the Techs, and most frequently the Red Terrors.

In 1922, the football department received a letter from a disgruntled fan. After a poor season with three wins, three losses, and three ties, he complained to athletic officials that State would never have a winning program as long as the players "behaved like a wolfpack."

Students initially laughed at the comparison but eventually adopted the name Wolfpack for the football team. At first, the other sports remained under the Red Terrors moniker, but in time they also adopted the new name.

The label stuck for more than 20 years before chancellor J. W. Harrelson began a campaign for a new mascot in 1946. He reasoned the Wolfpack name put the university in an unfavorable light.

"The only thing lower than a wolf is a snake in the grass," Harrelson said. He even went so far as to remind students that Nazi submarines were known as the wolfpack during World War II.

Shortly afterward, suggestions poured into Harrelson's office. Included in the entries were North Staters, Cardinals, Hornets, and Cultivators and Cotton Pickers; one alum even submitted Pinerooters, the slang term for pigs in parts of North Carolina.

Unfortunately for Harrelson, after the balloting was completed Wolfpack was still on top. As one old graduate explained, "The Wolf is a scrappy, tough animal—the spittin' image of our team."

North Carolina Tar Heels

University of North Carolina
P.O. Box 2126
Chapel Hill, NC 27514

School Colors: Carolina Blue and
                White
Year Founded: 1795
Basketball: Dean E. Smith Center
            (21,444)
Football: Kenan Memorial Stadium
           (50,000)

THE REASON that North Carolina athletic teams are known as the Tar Heels is because the school took the easy way out in selecting a nickname. Since North Carolina is the Tar Heel State, they simply adopted the famous name of their home state.

There are a number of different stories about how North Carolina acquired the state nickname. That the production of tar, pitch, and turpentine was for many years the state's principal industry provides a good background for the name.

The two most widely accepted explanations involve North Carolina's role in wars. One theory relates the nickname to the revolutionary war. According to the story, British general Charles Cornwallis's troops were marching through what is now known as the Tar River between Rocky Mount and Battleboro when they discovered tar had been dumped into the stream to thwart their crossing. When they finally reached the opposite riverbank, they found their feet completely black with tar. Their conclusion that anyone who waded through the rivers of North Carolina would acquire tar heels helped name the state.

A second explanation theorizes the nickname was acquired during the Civil War. During one of the war's fiercest battles, a battalion of supporting troops was driven from the battlefield. The men of North Carolina, who then took over and successfully fought the battle alone, happened to meet the regiment that had retreated to safety and were asked by the cowardly group, "Any more tar down in the old north state, boys?"

"No, not a bit," replied one of the North Carolinians. "Old Jeff's bought it all up," referring to Confederate president Jefferson Davis.

"Is that so? What's he going to do with it?" the flurried troops asked.

"He's going to put it on you'ns heels to make you stick better in the next fight," said a North Carolina soldier.

Upon hearing of the incident, Robert E. Lee chuckled and said to a fellow officer, "God bless the tar heel boys."

Because North Carolina teams are known as the Tar Heels, it might seem odd that their mascot is a ram. But there is a good explanation, offered by 1924 head cheerleader Vic Huggins.

"In 1924, school spirit was at a peak," Huggins explained. "But something was missing. One day it hit me. Georgia had a bulldog for a mascot and State, a wolf. What Carolina needed was a symbol."

Two years earlier, North Carolina had a bruising fullback named Jack Merritt, who was nicknamed the battering ram for the way he butted through the line. It seemed natural to Huggins to link a mascot with Merritt's exciting sobriquet.

Huggins was given $25 to purchase a mascot and Rameses the First was shipped from Texas in time for the UNC–Virginia Military Institute football game. For three quarters the game was scoreless; then late in the fourth quarter, when Carolina's Bunn Hackney was sent in to attempt a field goal, he stopped to rub Rameses's head for good luck. Seconds later, Hackney's 30-yard dropkick gave the Tar Heels a 3–0 victory and a heroic mascot was born.

The highlight of each season for Rameses and his fans is trying to outwit Duke fans who always attempt to "ram-nap" him before the traditional game against the Blue Devils.

Virginia Wahoos or Cavaliers

University of Virginia
P.O. Box 3785
Charlottesville, VA 22903

School Colors: Orange and Blue
Year Founded: 1819
Basketball: University Hall (8,200)
Football: Scott Stadium (42,000)

THE UNIVERSITY OF VIRGINIA has dual nicknames, the Cavaliers and Wahoos.

Wahoos was a term used to refer to any Virginia student following World War II. The nickname probably came to be associated with Virginia athletes as a result of a cheer, "Wah-hoo-wah," which made its debut in the early 1890s.

Supposedly, it was Washington and Lee baseball fans who stuck the Wahoos tag on Virginia during their fierce baseball rivalry. The cheer became part of "The Good Old Song" in 1893 and has served as the school alma mater ever since.

The name Cavaliers better represents the qualities of an athletic team. Although both nicknames are used interchangeably, Cavaliers is used much more frequently by the media.

The original school colors were red and gray, to commemorate the bloody uniforms worn by Confederate soldiers who died serving the South. But since these colors did not wear well on the muddy gridirons, a movement was started to change the school's colors.

The Virginia colors, orange and blue, were adopted at a mass student meeting in 1889. This combination was proposed by Allen Potts, class of 1889, who happened at the time to be wearing an orange and blue scarf, which he had brought back from a visit to Oxford University.

Wake Forest Demon Deacons

Wake Forest University
P.O. Box 7426
Winston-Salem, NC 27109

School Colors: Old Gold and Black
Year Founded: 1834
Basketball: Memorial Coliseum
　　　　　　　(8,200)
　　　　　　　Greensboro Coliseum
　　　　　　　(15,300)
Football: Groves Stadium (31,500)

WAKE FOREST UNIVERSITY obtained its nickname because of a reporter on the student newspaper who was in search of a more colorful name for the school.

The Tigers was the school's original nickname and mascot, but the student body was never overly enthusiastic with the name. The name did not stick, and by the early 1920s, the school's nicknames were Old Gold and Black or the Baptists.

While covering the 1922 Wake Forest–Duke basketball game, school newspaper reporter Mayon Parker wrote that the school needed a more "devilish" nickname that would better represent the fighting spirit of Wake Forest's teams. Parker's suggested choice of Demon Deacons was quickly picked up by athletic director Hank Garrity and news director Henry Belk and used extensively. Over the years, the name Demon Deacons has become a unique and very popular aspect of the Wake Forest athletic scene.

Jack Baldwin, class of 1943, was the original deacon mascot. In 1941, on a fraternity brother's dare, Baldwin led the team onto the field before the annual North Carolina game, dressed in top hat and tails, waving an umbrella, and riding the North Carolina Ram. Intended simply as a joke, the stunt has become a great Wake Forest tradition.

Many schools are represented by two nicknames: Army—Cadets and Knights; Brown—Bears and Bruins; Citadel—Bulldogs and Cadets; Murray State—Racers and Thoroughbreds; Pennsylvania—Quakers and Red and Blue; St. Bonaventure—Bonnies and Brown Indians; Virginia—Cavaliers and Wahoos; Virginia Tech—Gobblers and Hokies; and Yale—Bulldogs and Elis.

West Virginia Mountaineers

4

Atlantic 10 Conference

Atlantic 10 Conference
10 Woodbridge Center Drive
Woodbridge, NJ 07095

Number of Schools: 10
Year Founded: 1976
Charter Members: Duquesne, George Washington, Massachusetts, Penn State, Pittsburgh, Rutgers, Villanova, and West Virginia
Current Members: Duquesne, George Washington, Massachusetts, Penn State, Rhode Island, Rutgers, St. Bonaventure, St. Joseph's, Temple, and West Virginia
Division I Sports: Baseball, Basketball, Cross-Country, Golf, Soccer, and Tennis

Duquesne Dukes

Duquesne University
600 Forbes Avenue
Pittsburgh, PA 15282

School Colors: Red and Blue
Year Founded: 1878
Basketball: Palumbo Center (6,300)
Football: South High Stadium (6,000)

MOST PEOPLE WILL TELL you that the Duquesne University Dukes' nickname is just an abbreviation of Duquesne. However, don't believe them.

The reason behind the name Dukes dates back to when the school changed its name from University of the Holy Ghost to Duquesne University of the Holy Ghost in 1911. The name Duquesne was selected in honor of Marquis Duquesne, who built Fort Duquesne at The Point in Pittsburgh in 1754 and who was also the first man to bring Catholic observances to the city.

Since a marquis and a duke are similarly dressed, the unofficial symbol of the athletic teams became a man dressed in top hat, tails, and a royal sash worn across his breast. Because the term duke is more readily known than marquis, the name was officially assigned to the symbol and has stuck ever since.

George Washington Colonials

George Washington University
600 Twenty-second Street, NW
Washington, DC 20052

School Colors: Buff and Blue
Year Founded: 1821
Basketball: Charles E. Smith Center
(5,000)

GEORGE WASHINGTON UNIVERSITY'S logical nickname came from, you guessed it, George Washington's important role in the colonial movement for freedom.

The school was named after the first United States president and revolutionary war hero. Because the university itself is located in Washington, D.C., Colonials seemed the logical choice for the school's athletic teams. In fact, it is the only official nickname ever used by the school.

The Colonials' moniker fits in well with the George Washington tradition on the District of Columbia campus. The student newspaper is called *The Hatchet*, and the yearbook is known as *The Cherry Tree*. Both titles are taken from the legendary tale of George Washington's boyhood statement, "Father, I cannot tell a lie. I did it with my little hatchet."

Massachusetts Minutemen

University of Massachusetts
255 Boyden Building
Amherst, MA 01003

School Colors: Maroon and White
Year Founded: 1863
Basketball: Curry Hicks Cage (4,024)
Football: Warren McGuirk Alumni
Stadium (16,000)

UNIVERSITY OF MASSACHUSETTS'S athletic teams were formerly known as the Redmen. But because of pressure from American Indians, the name was changed. In the spring of 1972, a group of American Indians from New York wrote a letter to university officials asking if they were aware of the defamatory racial connotations of the term Redmen. They asked if the university would kindly abstain from using the word.

The administration quickly answered this request by asking all personnel, administrative staff, athletic personnel, and media to refrain from using the Redmen name as much as possible. The Student Senate reviewed the request and resolved that the nickname suggested a stereotype of violence and savagery and created a "false picture of American history."

The Student Senate then ran a poll for a new nickname and came up with three options: Minutemen, Statesmen, and Artichokes. Minutemen triumphed in the poll, and it has been Massachusetts's official moniker ever since.

Uniquely linked to the state, the name has a historical and patriotic relationship with Massachusetts. Without the famous Paul Revere and the Minutemen, who were ready to fight at a moment's notice, America might still be under British rule today.

Penn State Nittany Lions

Penn State University
234 Recreation Building
University Park, PA 16802

School Colors: Blue and White
Year Founded: 1855
Basketball: Rec Hall (7,200)
Football: Beaver Stadium (83,370)

PENN STATE'S athletic mascot, chosen by the students in 1906, is a mountain lion once believed to have roamed the mountains of central Pennsylvania.

After seeing the Princeton Tiger on a Penn State baseball trip, H. D. "Joe" Mason, a member of the class of 1907, started a one-man campaign to choose a school mascot. The student newspaper sponsored the campaign, and Penn State is believed to be the first college to adopt a lion as its mascot.

Since Penn State is located in the heart of the Nittany Valley at the foot of Mount Nittany, the mascot was designated as the Nittany Lion.

The origin of the school colors is also interesting. In 1887, the Penn State football team was looking for bright colors to wear for the first game. The team didn't want to wear orange and red, the most common colors. Black and cerise (a very deep pink) were the first choice, and in 1880 this color combination was quickly accepted by the students.

But after a few weeks' exposure to the sun, the dazzling uniform colors faded to black and white. The official colors were soon changed to blue and white, and this combination has remained with Penn State ever since.

Rhode Island Rams

University of Rhode Island
207 Keaney Gymnasium
Kingston, RI 02881

School Colors: Blue and White
Year Founded: 1888
Basketball: Keaney Gymnasium
(5,000)
Football: Meade Stadium (10,000)

THE UNIVERSITY OF RHODE ISLAND mascot, the Ram, evolved out of the school's agricultural history; the doors were first opened as the Rhode Island College of Agriculture and Mechanic Arts in 1892.

Rhode Island students officially adopted the Rams as their nickname on March 8, 1923, and the first live ram mascot arrived on the scene on November 21, 1929. These popular mascots from the mountains were housed on campus until the 1960s when it was no longer practical for the students to care for a live ram.

Although the live ram tradition was "butted out" of Rhode Island athletics for many years, it was reinstated at football games in 1983.

Rutgers Scarlet Knights

Rutgers University
P.O. Box 1149
Piscataway, NJ 08854

School Color: Scarlet
Year Founded: 1766
Basketball: Louis Brown Athletic
Center (9,000)
Football: Rutgers Stadium (23,000)

RUTGERS UNIVERSITY officials changed their Chanticleer nickname in 1956 due to some unfortunate implications and remarks that some folks said were in bad taste.

The Chanticleer—a proud fighting cock—bore bad modern connotations. In fact, the concern over the problem finally grew to the point where a campus-wide effort was made to find a new mascot.

English professors required all composition students to write essays about a new choice. An enterprising sophomore named Oscar Karl Huh conceived and promoted the Scarlet Knight, equipped with a shield and a trusty steed named Duke. Huh and Duke rode forth for the first time against Lafayette on November 3, 1956.

St. Bonaventure Brown Indians

St. Bonaventure University
St. Bonaventure, NY 14778

School Colors: Brown and White
Year Founded: 1856
Basketball: Reilly Center (6,000)

ST. BONAVENTURE'S NICKNAME, the Brown Indians, emerged when two entirely different objects were condensed into one team name.

The name Indians came about because the St. Bonaventure campus is located in southwestern New York, where Indian heritage was once quite prevalent and still exists to some extent today. Salamanca, St. Bonaventure's neighbor to the west, is the home of the Seneca National Indian reservation.

The Franciscan Friars, who run St. Bonaventure, are easily identified by their brown hooded robes—thus the name Brown Indians.

Another commonly used school nickname is the Bonnies, a short derivation of Bonaventure that emerged in the late 1960s. This is the most common nickname used to describe St. Bonaventure athletic teams today.

St. Joseph's Hawks

St. Joseph's University
5600 City Avenue
Philadelphia, PA 19131

School Colors: Crimson and Gray
Year Founded: 1851
Basketball: Alumni Memorial
Fieldhouse (3,200)
The Palestra (8,722)

PRIOR TO 1929, St. Joseph's University athletic teams were dubbed by the press as the Saints or City Liners, referring to the school's location along the border of western Philadelphia's city limits. But in 1929, yearbook editor Charlie Dunn decided to initiate a contest among the student body to come up with a school symbol.

Almost 100 nicknames were suggested and after the names were narrowed down to two, the students voted for their official mascot. Hawks won by a slim margin over Grenadiers, a name describing World War I soldiers who specialized in throwing grenades at the Germans.

The name Hawks was submitted by John Gallagher, class of 1931, who explained the name's significance as "suggestive of the aerial attack which made our football team famous." However, football was dropped by the athletic board following the 1939 season.

The Hawks' mascot flaps his wings nonstop from pregame warmups until the final buzzer sounds at every basketball game. The hawk tradition has continued since the first student donned the costume in 1956.

Temple Owls

Temple University
McGonigle Hall 047–00
Philadelphia, PA 19122

School Colors: Cherry and White
Year Founded: 1884
Basketball: McGonigle Hall (3,900)
Football: Veterans Stadium (66,592)

THE STORY HAS IT that the Owls was initially adopted as Temple's nickname in 1887 because the University originally began as a night school. Temple University was the first United States school to adopt the owl as its mascot.

Even today, Temple University officials are proud of their nickname, though the school is now much more than just a night classroom. Accepted as a universal symbol for wisdom and knowledge, the owl makes an excellent symbol for any center of higher learning. It must also be remembered that the owl was the symbol of Athena, who was not only the goddess of wisdom, arts, and skills, but also the goddess of warfare.

The owl also makes an excellent choice to represent athletic teams because of its other attributes. Besides being perceptive, resourceful, quick, and courageous, the owl is a very fierce fighter—as are Temple's athletic teams.

West Virginia Mountaineers

West Virginia University
P.O. Box 877
107 Coliseum
Morgantown, WV 26507

School Colors: Gold and Blue
Year Founded: 1867
Basketball: WVU Coliseum (14,000)
Football: Mountaineer Field (63,500)

SINCE ATHLETICS first began at West Virginia University, the teams have been called the Mountaineers. The nickname was derived from the state motto *Montani semper liberi*, which means "mountaineers are always free." Because of its topography, West Virginia's state nickname is the Mountain State. So when it came time to name West Virginia University's athletic teams, it was only natural for them to be called the Mountaineers.

WVU's official mascot is a mountaineer dressed in buckskin garb and sporting a coonskin hat. He represents the outstanding courage and ruggedness of the school's athletes.

Connecticut Huskies

5

Big East Conference

Big East Conference
321 South Main Street
Heritage Building
Providence, RI 02903

Number of Schools: 9
Year Founded: 1979
Charter Members: Boston College, Connecticut, Georgetown, Providence, St. John's, Seton Hall, and Syracuse
Current Members: Boston College, Connecticut, Georgetown, Pittsburgh, Providence, St. John's, Seton Hall, Syracuse, and Villanova
Division I Sports: Basketball, Cross-Country, Golf, Swimming and Diving, Indoor Track, Tennis, and Track and Field

Boston College Eagles

Boston College
Roberts Center 206
Chestnut Hill, MA 02167

School Colors: Maroon and Gold
Year Founded: 1863
Basketball: McHugh Forum (8,500)
Football: Alumni Stadium (32,000)

IT TOOK BOSTON COLLEGE almost 60 years to come up with a nickname. But thanks to the help of a faculty priest, it finally happened.

Since a suitable nickname was never chosen for the men of the Heights, a local cartoonist took it upon himself to depict Boston College as a large cat following their 1919 Intercollegiate Track Championship.

Rev. Edward McLaughlin, S.J., felt it was time Boston College had a school nickname. He didn't like the cat, so he petitioned through the student newspaper, *The Heights*, for the eagle (accipitridae) as the Boston College symbol.

The name went over well with the students, and in 1920 the Eagles was officially adopted as the school nickname.

Connecticut Huskies

University of Connecticut
2111 Hillside Road
Box U-78
Storrs, CT 06268

School Colors: Blue and White
Year Founded: 1881
Basketball: UConn Field House
(4,600)
Hartford Civic Center
(16,016)
UConn Sports Complex
(8,028)
Football: Memorial Stadium (16,200)

SOME PEOPLE TEND to believe that the husky was selected as the University of Connecticut's mascot because of the nickname UConn, which has a close-sounding relationship to the homeland of its Yukon mascot. However, this was not a factor in naming the school's athletic teams, as the school was known as Connecticut State College at the time and the name UConn was not yet born.

On November 9, 1934, at the annual football game against arch rival Rhode Island State College, the editor of the student newspaper noticed Rhode Island's ram and realized that Connecticut had no mascot. He soon appealed to the student body for the adoption of a mascot and the Alumni Association agreed to take a poll. Undoubtedly, the frigid hills of the Storrs campus made at least one person suggest the Alaskan husky as the perfect mascot.

The first mascot, a brown and white husky pup, was named Jonathan after Connecticut's first governor, Jonathan Trumbull. This first Connecticut mascot featured pedigree royalty, as he boasted a great grandfather who journeyed to the North Pole with Admiral Robert E. Peary in 1909. Unfortunately, only one year after the pup arrived, he was struck by a car while playing on Storrs Road. Jonathan was buried on campus next to the steps of old Whitney Hall across from Storrs Church.

Several new dogs who served as mascots were also known by the name Jonathan. In 1947, Jonathan III arrived, another imperial husky who traveled with Admiral Richard E. Byrd in the Antarctic.

Over the years, the image of the UConn Husky has changed from a two-tone color to the current pure white dog. But the principle behind Connecticut's mascot has not veered from its original goal. Jonathan the husky dog symbolizes cheerful survival of frigid New England winters, a determined spirit, and doglike loyalty to this master—the University of Connecticut.

Georgetown Hoyas

Georgetown University
Thirty-Seventh and O Street, NW
Washington, DC 20057

School Colors: Blue and Gray
Year Founded: 1789
Basketball: Capital Centre (19,035)
Football: Kehoe Field (3,000)

WHENEVER GEORGETOWN athletics are mentioned, at least one curious person will ask, "What's a Hoya?" Unfortunately, the question is not an easy one to answer, as the name came from an incoherent combination of two entirely different languages.

Many years ago, there was a team at Georgetown known as the Stonewalls. Supposedly, a student applied the Greek and Latin terms and created the cheer *hoia saxa*, "what rocks!"

Although no one seems to know exactly under what circumstances the term *hoya saxa* was first used at Georgetown, there seems to be little doubt about the derivation of the words. *Hoya* is from the Greek word *hoios* meaning "such a" or "what a." The neuter plural of this word is *hoia* which agrees with the neuter plural of the Latin word *saxa* meaning "rocks." Thus we have hoya, substituting y for i.

Around the turn of the century, Georgetown had its first mascot, an enormous canine of unspecified breed belonging to the Reverend William Carrol, S.J. The hound's name was Hoya. Unfortunately, he took the rivalry with the college team a bit too seriously. He was banished to St. Thomas Manor for biting the opposing team's running backs.

After World War I, a succession of Boston bull terriers followed the list of mascots. The first and most famous was Hoya I (whose real name was Jazz Bo), recruited from Green Bay, Wisconsin, by Paul Van Laanen, class of 1926.

Hoya I soon became a sidekick of the Reverend Vincent McDonough, S.J., who was prefect of discipline and moderator of athletics. While "Father Mac" kept his eye on the athletes, Hoya would work on his famous halftime routine—nudging a football around the field—that had become a tradition a few years earlier.

Al Phillip Kane, class of 1928, remembers the spectators cheered just as loudly for Hoya as they did for the team. Kane also pointed out that it was during Hoya I's reign that newspapers began to refer to the team as the Hoyas rather than Hilltoppers or the Blue and Gray. It seems the team was named for the dog, who was in turn named for the traditional cheer.

Pittsburgh Panthers

University of Pittsburgh
P.O. Box 7436
Pittsburgh, PA 15213

School Colors: Blue and Gold
Year Founded: 1787
Basketball: Fitzgerald Field House
(6,798)
Pittsburgh Civic Arena
(16,290)
Football: Pitt Stadium (56,500)

THE UNIVERSITY OF PITTSBURGH officially adopted the panther (*felis concolor*) as its mascot at a student-alumni meeting held in the early autumn of 1909.

The idea for the famous name is credited to the newly graduated George M. P. Baird, class of 1909. According to Baird, the name was chosen for the following reasons:

1. The panther was the most formidable creature and was once indigenous to the Pittsburgh region.

2. It had ancient, heraldic standing as a noble animal.

3. The happy accident of alliteration with the institution's name.

4. The close approximation of its hue to the old gold of the university's colors (old gold and blue), hence its easy adaptability in decoration.

5. The fact that no other college or university then employed the panther as a symbol.

Providence Friars

Providence College
River and Eaton Streets
Providence, RI 02918

School Colors: Black and White
Year Founded: 1917
Basketball: Providence Civic Center (13,100)

PROVIDENCE COLLEGE'S NICKNAME, the Friars, is a fitting tribute to the Dominican fathers who founded the university in 1917.

The school's proud Roman Catholic tradition was carried over to athletics sometime in the early 1920s when the original Friars logo was pictured on posters, programs, and brochures.

The Friars' moniker suits the school very well even to this day, as the fathers still wear the long rope-tied cassocks they wore when they first arrived at the school.

The official school colors may very well coincide with the Friar's own legacy, as they are black and white—the traditional colors of the priest.

St. John's Redmen

St. John's University
Grand Central and Utopia Parkways
Jamaica, NY 11439

School Colors: Red and White
Year Founded: 1870
Basketball: Alumni Hall (6,000)
Football: St. John's Field (2,000)

CONTRARY TO POPULAR belief, St. John's University's nickname, Redmen, has nothing to do with Indians.

The name dates back to 1923 when Ray Lynch, a Holy Cross graduate and former football star, became the first layman to hold the office of athletic director. Lynch started football at St. John's that same season.

When Lynch searched for team equipment, he got a special deal on red uniforms. These uniforms were all red—including shoes, socks, pants, jerseys, and helmets.

When St. John's ran over Stevens Tech that first season in a 30–12 triumph, the Brooklyn *Eagle* referred to the St. John's squad as the big red team. The name quickly caught on and was soon shortened to Redmen for headline use. The nickname Redmen has been St. John's symbol ever since.

Prior to the *Eagle's* dubbing of Redmen, St. John's had gone by the name of Brooklyn Vincentians, which was too long for headline use, or the Johnnies, which left something to be desired in a nickname and was the "butt" of a lot of jokes.

Years later, a cigar store Indian was adopted as the official mascot and dubbed Chief Blackjack. Although the Redmen nickname had no relationship whatsoever to Indians, someone thought the chief could appropriately represent the athletes of St. John's.

Seton Hall Pirates

Seton Hall University
400 South Orange Avenue
South Orange, NJ 07079

School Colors: Blue and White
Year Founded: 1856
Basketball: Meadowlands Arena
(20,149)
Walsh Gymnasium (3,600)

SETON HALL UNIVERSITY athletic teams are known as the Pirates, not because of any relationship to the sea but because of the way a sportswriter described one of Seton Hall's teams.

In the April 24, 1931, edition of the Newark *Evening News*, a story recounted Seton Hall's five-run ninth inning that beat Holy Cross of Worcester, Massachusetts. The *News* article read, "One of the sportswriters was so excited by the turn of events that he exclaimed with disgust, 'That Seton Hall team is a gang of pirates.' "

Although the intentions of the name were not originally good ones, the name Pirates has remained with Seton Hall ever since.

Syracuse Orange or Orangemen

Syracuse University
Manley Field House
Syracuse, NY 13244-5020

School Color: Orange
Year Founded: 1870
Basketball: Carrier Dome (33,000)
Football: Carrier Dome (33,000)

SYRACUSE UNIVERSITY'S two nicknames, the Orange and Orangemen, are obviously taken from the official school color.

The first thing to establish here is that the founders of Syracuse had no thoughts of the citrus fruit or even liked the color orange when selecting their school colors. The original school colors were adopted by the school's trustees on June 24, 1872, as rose pink and pea green. This combination was selected because they represented the colors of dawn as seen in midstate New York.

However, these colors were constantly ridiculed, and opposing teams and fans frequently poked fun at Syracuse athletes. Apparently, the last straw was dropped on the athlete's backs after they beat Hamilton College in a track meet in Clinton, New York, in May 1889. After several humiliating comments were heard about the pink and green of the visiting athletes, the track team returned to Syracuse determined to change the school colors.

When a committee looked into the dilemma, they found that orange, a primary color, had not been adopted as a single color by any college or university in the country. As a result, the committee submitted their choice of orange as the sole school color.

The color orange idea was passed through the student body, the faculty, and the trustees before finally being approved by the Alumni Association on June 24, 1890, as the official school color.

One alumnus suggested orange was chosen because the House of Orange, founding family of Holland, was responsible for the first colonization of the state of New York. This same graduate, William van Allen, noted that the motto of Dutch royalty was *oranje booen*, which he translated as "orange over all."

Early football teams at Syracuse were known as the Orioles, alluding to the male American oriole's orange and black plumage. But generally, the Syracuse teams were known as the Orange or Orangemen.

Two earlier nicknames, Bill Orange and Saltine Warriors, were both popularized by two members of a student theatrical society. Harry Lee, who played the banjo by ear, wrote a song titled "Bill Orange," which was an instant success and still is a Syracuse tradition today.

Another Syracuse legend is explained by one of Lee's lyrics, "Last night, the sun set orange." It is believed that when the sun sets orange before a game, Syracuse will win.

Sam Darby wrote "The Saltine Warrior," which was plugged into a student minstrel show in 1911. It might be guessed that the author was inspired by the fact that Syracuse was the Salt City in 1911, as the citizens of Galeville were boiling salt in the town at the time.

Darby called his warrior "a bold, bad man and his weapon was a pigskin ball." Somewhere down the line, the Saltine Warrior and Bill Orange evolved into an Indian.

In 1939, the color was depicted by a human mascot who performed at football and basketball games. A Syracuse student dressed in a suit of orange with extra long trousers was continually on the loose at athletic events. This character, known as Bill Orange, stood 10 feet tall on stilts.

The first Orangemen were members of a Protestant society founded in Ireland in 1795. Today, the athletes of Syracuse proudly wear the Orangemen name every time they set out for victory.

Villanova Wildcats

Villanova University
Villanova, PA 19085

School Colors: Blue and White
Year Founded: 1842
Basketball: John E. duPont Pavilion
    (6,500)
    The Spectrum (18,060)
Football: Goodreau Stadium (13,400)

VILLANOVA UNIVERSITY selected Wildcats as its official nickname in a contest held in the mid-1920s.

The name Wildcat was adopted by the Villanova University student body after a contest in search of a suitable name was conducted by the class of 1926. Wildcats was suggested by assistant football coach Edward Hunsinger.

According to the May 1926 issue of *The Villanovan*, "The name (Wildcats) is meant to convey the fighting spirit, alertness and skill of the animal chosen in vanquishing its enemies. This is the spirit of the Villanova athletic teams, whether upon the gridiron, diamond, or track. In victory or defeat the dogged determination to win is always present, with the fighting spirit and alertness of the (Wildcat.)"

It can really get confusing when several schools in a conference use the same nickname. But it can happen when a school has used a nickname for years and then moves into a new conference.

In the Southeastern Conference, Auburn and Louisiana State are both known as the Tigers. Georgia and Mississippi State go by the name Bulldogs. In the Southwestern Conference, it is even worse. The name Tigers is used by a trio of schools—Jackson State, Grambling State, and Texas State.

Oklahoma Sooners

6

Big Eight Conference

Big Eight Conference
600 East Eighth Street
Kansas City, MO 64106

Number of Schools: 8
Year Founded: 1907
Charter Members: Iowa, Kansas, Missouri, Nebraska, and
Washington University–St. Louis
Current Members: Colorado, Iowa State, Kansas, Kansas State,
Missouri, Nebraska, Oklahoma, and
Oklahoma State
Division I Sports: Baseball, Basketball, Cross-Country,
Football, Golf, Gymnastics, Indoor Track,
Swimming, Tennis, Track and Field, and
Wrestling

Colorado Buffaloes

University of Colorado
Campus Box 368
Boulder, CO 80309

School Colors: Silver, Gold, and
                     Black
Year Founded: 1876
Basketball: Events/Conference Center
                  (11,199)
Football: Folsom Field (51,463)

THE UNIVERSITY OF COLORADO has one of the most unusual mascots found in intercollegiate athletics, a real buffalo named Ralphie.

Prior to the 1934 football season, Colorado teams were referred to as the Silver and Gold. For the final game that season, Colorado students rented a buffalo calf, and Colorado stomped over Utah in a 7–6 victory. The buffalo was an immediate hit with the fans, and from that moment on, university athletic teams have been known as the Buffaloes.

The live buffalo mascot leading the football team out on the field at the start of each half has been a tradition at Colorado ever since. It is one of the truly special sights that exists anywhere in college or professional sports, especially for the opposing team, which often stops dead in their tracks watching the massive buffalo round the end zone and charge directly at its sideline.

Iowa State Cyclones

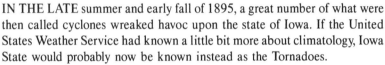

Iowa State University
129 Olsen Building
Ames, Iowa 50011

School Colors: Cardinal and Gold
Year Founded: 1858
Basketball: James H. Hilton Coliseum
            (14,020)
Football: Cyclone Stadium/Jack Trice
            Field (54,066)

IN THE LATE summer and early fall of 1895, a great number of what were then called cyclones wreaked havoc upon the state of Iowa. If the United States Weather Service had known a little bit more about climatology, Iowa State would probably now be known instead as the Tornadoes.

The same fall the cyclones first hit, the Cardinals, as ISU teams were so named at the time, played in Evanston against the heavily favored Northwestern Wildcats. ISU, the underdog, posted a shocking 36–0 rout over Northwestern, and the next morning's Chicago *Tribune* headline read, "Iowa Cyclone Devastates Evanston." Ever since, Iowa State teams have been known as the Cyclones. However, as a concession to history, Iowa State still uses the cardinal as its mascot and logo.

Kansas Jayhawks

University of Kansas
202 Allen Field House
Lawrence, KS 66045

School Colors: Crimson and Blue
Year Founded: 1866
Basketball: Allen Field House (15,800)
Football: Memorial Stadium (51,000)

THE JAYHAWKS' history in Kansas dates back to a band of pioneers who crossed through the territory in 1849. This party, who called themselves the Jayhawkers of '49, are believed to have taken the name of two birds familiar in the West, the blue jay and the hawk. It is believed these settlers were the first in the area to use the name Jayhawks.

In 1861, when Doc Jennison was commissioned as a colonel by Kansas governor Charles Robinson to raise a cavalry regiment, he named his group after those early settlers. Jennison's regiment, the Independent Mounted Kansas Jayhawkers, was the first Kansas cavalry.

During the Civil War, the name Jayhawks became associated with the spirit of comradeship and the courageous efforts of Kansas soldiers to keep the state free. Following the war, Kansans were proud to be known as Jayhawks. By 1886, the University of Kansas had adopted the mythical bird as their own mascot.

Kansas State Wildcats

Kansas State University
202 Ahearn Field House
Manhattan, KS 66506

School Colors: Purple and White
Year Founded: 1857
Basketball: Ahearn Field House
(11,220)
Football: KSU Stadium (42,000)

THE NICKNAME WILDCATS was given to the 1915 Kansas State University football team. Head coach Chief Bender named the team Wildcats because of the squad's intensity and fighting spirit.

Prior to use of the name Wildcats, the school's athletic teams were known as the Aggies because the primary field of study was agriculture. In 1916, the school nickname was changed back to an agriculture term, and Kansas State teams were renamed the Farmers.

However, Coach Charles Bachman switched the team name back in 1920 because he wanted to add more fight to his team. It has remained Wildcats ever since.

Missouri Tigers

University of Missouri
P.O. Box 677
Columbia, MO 65205

School Colors: Old Gold and Black
Year Founded: 1839
Basketball: Hearnes Center (13,143)
Football: Memorial Stadium/Faurot
Field (62,000)

THE UNIVERSITY OF MISSOURI selected its nickname because of a critical part of history that took place in Columbia during the Civil War.

Plundering guerrilla bands routinely raided small towns in the area during the war, and the people of Columbia were constantly in fear of an attack. But in an effort to curb this injustice, the community pulled together to form home guards and vigilance companies to fight off any possible raids.

Columbia's toughness discouraged the guerrillas from attacking their town, and they started to disband in 1854. However, it was later rumored that a guerrilla band led by the notorious Bill Anderson intended to pilfer the town. The citizens quickly organized, built a blockhouse, and fortified the old courthouse in the town square. This company was called the Missouri Tigers.

The marauders never showed up. The reputation of Columbia's Tigers somehow reached Anderson's gang and they stayed clear of Columbia on their plundering tour.

Soon after Missouri's first football team was organized in 1890, athletic officials adopted the nickname Tigers in official recognition of the fearless defenders of the city.

Nebraska Cornhuskers

University of Nebraska
116 South Stadium
Lincoln, NE 68588-0123

School Colors: Scarlet and Cream
Year Founded: 1869
Basketball: Bob Devaney Sports
              Center (14,478)
Football: Memorial Stadium (73,650)

PRIOR TO 1900, Nebraska football teams were known by such unusual names as the Old Gold Knights, Antelopes, and—get this—Bugeaters.

However, sportswriters grew tired of referring to the Nebraska football team as Bugeaters. Lincoln writer Charles S. "Cy" Sherman, who later helped originate the Associated Press football ranking poll, was one of them and decided to do something about it.

According to Nebraska officials, Iowa athletes were frequently called the Cornhuskers, and the name appealed to Sherman. Iowa supporters seemed to prefer the name Hawkeyes, so Sherman "borrowed" the name Cornhuskers from Nebraska's neighbor to the east. Sherman was the first to refer to Nebraska athletic teams as Cornhuskers in 1900, and the name quickly caught on.

Nebraska's newest logo is Herby Husker, who evolved out of Nebraska's 1974 trip to the Cotton Bowl. Artist Dirk West of Lubbock, Texas, designed the character for the Cotton Bowl press headquarters. West's concept of Nebraska football was appropriate—a burly, rugged, and confident fellow who is proud of both the athletic and agricultural traditions of the University of Nebraska.

Oklahoma Sooners

University of Oklahoma
Memorial Stadium
Norman, OK 73019

School Colors: Crimson and Cream
Year Founded: 1890
Basketball: Lloyd Noble Center (10,871)
Football: Memorial Stadium (75,004)

THE SOONERS of the University of Oklahoma were named after settlers who posted illegal claims before they were allowed in Oklahoma Territory, which was strictly an Indian settlement from the 1820s to the 1880s. The federal government restructured the territory and announced that in 1889 it would become a white settlement.

In an effort to attract eastern settlers, land runs were to be held that would allow settlers to stake their claim on any free land in Oklahoma. The first land run, called the Old Oklahoma Run, would take place in 1889.

The land runs consisted of settlers assembling on the borders of Oklahoma under army supervision. When the opening gunshot was fired, the run officially began and thousands of settlers—men, women, and children—dashed to sections of land they wished to claim as their own.

However, some settlers did not wish to wait for the sound of the pistol. They illegally slipped into the territory a day early, eluding army patrols and hiding out near choice pieces of land. When the land run officially began, these settlers just waltzed up to the prime land they wanted, threw a stake in the ground, and it was theirs. These settlers were known as sooners since they came into the territory before the land run officially began.

Sooners was not immediately taken as Oklahoma's nickname. The athletic teams were first known by two nicknames: Rough Riders and Boomers. The current nickname emerged in 1908 but was actually derived from a 1908 student pep club called the Sooner Rooters.

Oklahoma State Cowboys

Oklahoma State University
202 Gallagher-Iba Arena
Stillwater, OK 74078-0300

School Colors: Orange and Black
Year Founded: 1890
Basketball: Gallagher-Iba Arena
          (6,700)
Football: Lewis Stadium (50,440)

OKLAHOMA STATE UNIVERSITY adopted its current nickname in honor of an old gunman who roamed the Stillwater campus.

When Oklahoma A&M, as it was then known, fielded its first intercollegiate team in 1901, two faculty members who happened to be Princeton grads suggested their alma mater's nickname and colors. The teams were first known as the Tigers, and the official colors were orange and black, which still reign as the school colors today.

But because it was an agriculture school, it was only natural to call the team Aggies, and in 1925 the name Aggies was officially adopted.

By 1930, area sportswriters had taken it upon themselves to use Cowboys interchangeably with Aggies in their articles. However, the official change to Cowboys did not occur until 1956, when the school name was changed to Oklahoma State University.

Because the school no longer was known by its agricultural name, school officials decided a new nickname was in order. At this time there was a legendary gunman, Frank Eaton, better known as Pistol Pete, who resided in nearby Perkins and liked to walk the Stillwater campus. He carried his pistol with him everywhere he went, a habit he picked up after shooting five of his father's murderers. He often stopped in on classes and would demonstrate his great skill with his pistol. He was even known to shoot a hole in a classroom wall from time to time.

Since Pistol Pete was such a popular figure on campus, school officials decided to adopt the school nickname of Cowboys. Pistol Pete became the school's official mascot and someone dressed to represent him still fires his pistols at all OSU athletic events.

It should be noted that New Mexico State also appointed Pistol Pete as its official mascot in honor of his courageous efforts in avenging his father's death.

Frank Eaton, better known as Pistol Pete, helped name two schools—New Mexico State and Oklahoma State.

Northern Arizona Lumberjacks

7

Big Sky Conference

Big Sky Conference
P.O. Box 1736
106 North Sixth Street, Suite 200
Boise, ID 83702

Number of Schools: 9
Year Founded: 1963
Charter Members: Idaho, Idaho State, Montana, Montana State, and Weber State
Current Members: Boise State, Eastern Washington, Idaho, Idaho State, Montana, Montana State, Nevada-Reno, Northern Arizona, and Weber State
Division I Sports: Basketball, Cross-Country, Indoor Track, Tennis, and Track and Field

THE BIG SKY CONFERENCE name originated from the 1947 novel *The Big Sky*, written by A. B. ("Bud") Guthrie of Great Falls, Montana. Former Montana advertising director Jack Hollowell first promoted the Big Sky theme, and on February 20, 1963, Harry Missildine of the Spokane *Spokesman-Review* called for the new conference to be named the Big Sky Conference. Only five days later at a meeting in Spokane, the five school presidents officially swore in the Big Sky Conference.

Boise State Broncos

Boise State University
1910 University Drive
Boise, ID 83725

School Colors: Blue and Orange
Year Founded: 1932
Basketball: BSU Pavilion (12,200)
Football: Bronco Stadium (21,500)

BOISE STATE UNIVERSITY acquired its Broncos' nickname one year after the school was founded, when students at what was then Boise Junior College held an election to select the official school nickname, colors, and mascot.

The nickname Broncos won out over all other suggestions and became the official school nickname and mascot. There is no pinpointed reason behind the name, other than that it was extremely popular on the Boise campus.

The name Broncos represents Idaho and the spirit of the West. Many rodeos are still held in the Boise area, and they play a major role in the state's heritage and culture. Being a horse, the bronco is also one of the most noble, respected animals on earth.

Eastern Washington Eagles

Eastern Washington University
MS-66
Cheney, WA 99004

School Colors: Red and White
Year Founded: 1882
Basketball: Reese Court (5,000)
Football: Albi Stadium (33,891)

IN A BIND to determine which nickname to use, Eastern Washington University officials were saved by the campus ROTC unit.

In the early 1920s, when nicknames first became popular, Eastern Washington was known as the Savages. The nickname remained until 1974 when the trustees, without receiving any requests from any lobbyist group, decided on their own that the name cast an unfavorable ethnic connotation on the school.

In order to stay away from problems with American Indians and other activist groups, a campus contest was held to select a new nickname. Apparently, the students did not want to change names, as the voter turnout was very low and most of the suggested names were considered frivolous. The name Savages, although not on the ballot, received by far the most votes. In second place was Lakers, which was actually just the best of the rest.

While the administration was puzzling over what to do, the university's very active army ROTC unit, which was known as the Screaming Eagles, formally suggested that school officials adopt the moniker Eagles. Following the leadership of the ROTC unit, the name was adopted.

Idaho State Bengals

Idaho State University
741 South Seventh
Pocatello, ID 83209

School Colors: Orange and Black
Year Founded: 1901
Basketball: Holt Arena (7,938)
Football: Holt Arena (12,000)

WHEN THE ACADEMY OF IDAHO was founded in 1901, its athletic teams were burdened with the unfavorable nickname of Bantams. As Merrill D. Beal notes in his *History of Idaho State College*, "As neither their size nor behavior conformed with the name, it was never very popular."

Despite disapproval, the term stuck until 1921, when Ralph H. Hutchinson, a Princeton graduate, was named director of education and athletics. Hutchinson noticed the name Bantams wasn't readily accepted by the student body and immediately formed an organization of athletes, which eventually adopted the Princeton Bengal tiger as the school's mascot.

Undoubtedly, Hutchinson had some doing in the athletes' decision to adopt his alma mater's mascot.

Though numerous changes in the school's name have taken place over the years, the Bengal tiger has stuck as the official mascot.

Idaho Vandals

University of Idaho
Kibbie Activity Center
Moscow, ID 83843

School Colors: Silver and Gold
Year Founded: 1889
Basketball: Kibbie-ASUI Dome
(10,000)
Football: Kibbie-ASUI Dome (16,000)

SINCE 1918, Joe Vandal has served faithfully as the unique mascot for University of Idaho athletic teams.

The name Vandals was first used in the late teens when the basketball team was making shambles of the opposition and were tagged "the wrecking crew" by the local media.

Dean Edward M. Hulme of the College of Liberal Arts thought the Idahoans were like the old Norsemen and sports editor Lloyd ("Jazz") McCarty of the student newspaper, the *Aqronaut* agreed.

In 1921, the Vandals officially became the nickname of all Idaho athletic teams. The nickname provides the team with a unique, exciting, and mischievous name. At any rate, school officials hoped Idaho teams would do some damage to their opponents.

Montana Grizzlies

University of Montana
Adams Field House
Missoula, MT 59812

School Colors: Copper, Silver, and
Gold
Year Founded: 1893
Basketball: Dahlberg Arena (9,057)
Football: Washington-Grizzly Stadium
(14,089)

WHEN THE UNIVERSITY OF MONTANA fielded its first football team in 1897, the sideliners dubbed the pioneer 11 as the Varsity. Although the name showed no imagination whatsoever, it lasted for 10 years. In 1909, someone suggested the name Bruins, and this stuck as a replacement for Varsity. But it too was destined to be short lived.

In the coverage of the 1912 Montana-Utah football contest, a Salt Lake City sportswriter coined the name Grizzlies for the marauders from Montana. Until the mid-1920s, the teams were known as the Grizzlies, Bruins, or Bears.

However, when Montana joined the Pacific Coast Conference, the names became confusing, as the University of California, Berkeley and UCLA both had bear mascots. More important, the California schools wanted the confusing name situation cleared up.

It was then that each school officially took on only one nickname. Berkeley became the Golden Bears, UCLA became the Bruins, and Montana adopted the Grizzlies.

The grizzly is the most feared, strongest, and smartest of the bears. The name seems appropriate, too, since Montana has more grizzly bears than any other state, counting more than 400 out of only about 700 of this endangered species found in the world today.

Montana State Bobcats

Montana State University
114 Hamilton Hall
Bozeman, MT 59717

School Colors: Blue and Gold
Year Founded: 1893
Basketball: Worthington Arena (7,848)
Football: Reno H. Sales Stadium
       (15,197)

FROM THE SCHOOL'S INCEPTION in 1893 until 1916, Montana State was without an appropriate nickname. Early Montana State teams were known as the Aggies, Bozeman Farmers, Farmer Boys, and more often simply as the State College Team. But after the persuasion and determination of the students, in 1916 the school finally had a nickname they could be proud to call their own.

Sensing the great need for a Montana State nickname, the *Weekly Exponent* and the *Montanan* joined forces in 1915 to select one. They offered a free copy of the yearbook to the student submitting the best name, and Fred Bullock, class of 1917, won the prize for his entry, Bobcats.

The campus was ecstatic. The January 7, 1916, *Exponent* wrote, "There is more fight and pep in a Bobcat than there is in all the rest of the animal kingdom. He is not big, but is highly respected by his enemies. As for being wild, there is nothing wilder than a Bobcat. . . . He does not depend on strength alone but upon headwork and cunning."

Today, Montana State University is proudly represented by that wily, independent little fighter of the western mountains, who is always ready for a battle with any antagonist and always fights hardest when the odds are against him.

Nevada-Reno Wolf Pack

University of Nevada at Reno
Reno, NV 89557

School Colors: Silver and Blue
Year Founded: 1864
Basketball: Lawlor Events Center
            (13,303)
Football: Mackay Stadium (14,322)

THE HISTORY behind the Nevada-Reno Wolf Pack's nickname is, at best, sketchy.

As early as 1918, Reno's athletic teams were known as the Sagebrush Warriors after the grayish-green shrub that is common to the Reno area. In an effort to add more flair to their athletic image, the name was officially changed to Nevada Wolves in 1923.

Over the years, and probably with some help from the media, the name was gradually modified to the University of Nevada at Reno Wolf Pack. It is believed this nickname belongs to only two schools: Reno and North Carolina State University, which spells its nickname as one word.

Northern Arizona Lumberjacks

Northern Arizona University
Box 15400
Flagstaff, AZ 86011-5400

School Colors: Blue and Gold
Year Founded: 1899
Basketball: J. Lawrence Walkup
            Skydome (9,000)
Football: J. Lawrence Walkup
            Skydome (15,000)

NORTHERN ARIZONA UNIVERSITY received its nickname because of a contest held on school grounds during the summer of 1909 when the university was still known as Northern Arizona Normal School.

Harold P. Blome, a freshman that year, recalled, "I first attended NANS in 1909, at which time we had three sawmills. On the Fourth of July, we had celebrations on the grounds which are now the football field. The events included bronco riding by local cowboys and sawing logs against time by men who worked in several logging camps.

"The saws were six- or seven-foot cross saws with one man working each end. These men were called lumberjacks. It was phenomenal how fast the two lumberjacks cut a big log in two. From this, the athletic teams adopted the name of Lumberjacks."

Weber State Wildcats

Weber State College
3750 Harrison Boulevard
Ogden, UT 84408-2701

School Colors: Royal Purple and
White
Year Founded: 1889
Basketball: Dee Events Center
(12,000)
Football: Wildcat Stadium (17,500)

NO ONE KNOWS for sure where Weber State's nickname Wildcats actually originated, but like many other school monikers, the press seems to be mainly responsible for its origin.

The name is believed to have emerged from a 1928 newspaper clipping in which Weber State athletes were described as being "scrappy as wildcats." From that time on, Weber State teams have been known as the Wildcats.

In 1964, Dean Hearst was asked to design a wildcat cartoon character to represent the WSC football team. The fun, animated character was named Waldo Wildcat and is still a favorite among collegiate mascots.

"He wasn't necessarily furious, because I thought of him as being more than just athletically oriented," said Hearst. "He is a student, an athlete, and a scholar."

Since he was first drawn, Waldo the Wildcat has been sketched and photographed hundreds of times, doing everything from skiing to parachuting to dancing. Regardless of his sport or recreational activity, he is loved by the students on the Weber State campus.

Campbell Fighting Camels

8

Big South Conference

Big South Conference
P.O. Box 2099
203 Main Street
Conway, SC 29526

Number of Schools: 7
Year Founded: 1983
Charter Members: Augusta, Baptist, Campbell, USC Coastal
Carolina, and Winthrop
Current Members: Augusta, Baptist, Campbell, Coastal
Carolina, North Carolina–Asheville, Radford,
and Winthrop
Division I Sports: Baseball, Basketball, Cross-Country, Golf,
Soccer, and Tennis

Augusta Jaguars

Augusta College
2500 Walton Way
Augusta, GA 30910

School Colors: Blue and White
Year Founded: 1925
Basketball: Augusta/Richmond Civic
Center (7,500)
Augusta College
Gymnasium (1,200)

THE AUGUSTA COLLEGE JAGUARS' nickname evolved not from any catlike animal but from the initials of the original name of the institution.

When the Augusta campus opened in 1925, the name of the school was Junior College of Augusta. The idea for the Jaguars' nickname came from *Ju*nior College of *Aug*usta.

Ironically, the first team to carry the school name was the football team, which was the first and last time a football program existed at the Augusta school. After the squad posted a three wins, three losses record, it was evident that the school had fallen upon hard times.

"There is simply not enough money to finance both football and basketball teams," James Lister Skinner sadly explained in the school newspaper. After one season, football was dropped because it dragged down the relatively inexpensive, longer established basketball program.

Baptist Buccaneers

Baptist College
P.O. Box 10087
Charleston, SC 29411

School Colors: Indigo and Gold
Year Founded: 1965
Basketball: Baptist College
Fieldhouse (2,500)

BECAUSE THE STUDENTS at Baptist College weren't very fond of the nickname that school officials wanted to adopt, they changed the officials' minds with great school spirit.

Since Baptist College is affiliated with the Southern Baptist Convention, school officials were searching for religious sobriquets, such as Crusaders or Christians, as school nicknames. However, according to athletic director Howie Bagwell, the students wanted something a "little more rambunctious."

Bagwell recalled that at the start of the school's first academic year, athletes were still without their own nickname. For some unknown reason, at every athletic event during that first year, groups of students dressed up like buccaneers with eye patches, swords, bandannas, pirate hats, and painted faces. These students attracted much attention around campus, and the religious nicknames were soon forgotten.

At the end of the year, students voted on an official nickname for the school's athletic program. Buccaneers was elected as the winner, and students today are very proud of their "rambunctious" nickname.

Campbell Fighting Camels

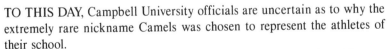

Campbell University
P.O. Box 10
Buies Creek, NC 27506

School Colors: Orange and Black
Year Founded: 1887
Basketball: Cumberland County
Memorial Arena (5,500)
Carter Gymnasium
(1,500)

TO THIS DAY, Campbell University officials are uncertain as to why the extremely rare nickname Camels was chosen to represent the athletes of their school.

As far back as 1920 there are records of teams using the nickname Hornets. The name Hornets dates back to the revolutionary war, when British general Charles Cornwallis wrote to the king of England in his battle report from North Carolina that "this place is like fighting in a hornet's nest."

Even in the early days, there were a number of other references to the school's athletic squads. As a variation, Campbell teams were often called the Campbells or the Campbellites.

There is no explanation as to why the nickname was changed to Camels; the only information known is that the change took place in late 1933 or 1934. However, it is logical to assume the name came about because it sounded phonetically correct when used with Campbell University.

Coastal Carolina Chanticleers

Coastal Carolina College
P.O. Box 1954
Conway, SC 29526

School Colors: Scarlet and Black
Year Founded: 1954
Basketball: Kimbel Gymnasium
(1,900)

WHEN COASTAL CAROLINA COLLEGE, a branch of the University of South Carolina system, was founded in 1954, the school board was expected to develop a take-off nickname on South Carolina's Fighting Gamecocks.

While searching for an appropriate name, one of the members pulled out Geoffrey Chaucer's *Canterbury Tales*, a collection of British short stories. In "The Nun's Priest Tale," one of the main characters is a sly, crafty chanticleer, or gamecock.

The feared and respected chanticleer was described as follows: "For crowing there was not his equal in all the land. His voice was merrier than the merry organ that plays in the church, and his crowing from his resting place was more trustworthy than a clock. His comb was redder than fine coral and turreted like a castle wall, his bill was black and shone like a jet, and his legs and toes were like azure. His nails were whiter than lily and his feathers were like burnished gold."

The school board thought the name Chanticleers would fit well with South Carolina's Gamecock, as well as providing Coastal Carolina's athletes with uniqueness. But today's real students of history still recognize it as a takeoff on the mother university's Gamecock's nickname.

North Carolina at Asheville Bulldogs

University of North Carolina at Asheville
One University Heights
Asheville, NC 28804-3299

School Colors: Royal Blue and White
Year Founded: 1927
Basketball: Justice Center (2,500)

NORTH CAROLINA–ASHEVILLE school officials really have no clue as to why Bulldogs was chosen as its official nickname. The school was founded in 1927 and went a fairly long time without any official nickname.

Sometime in the late 1940s, the school decided to adopt a nickname. Asheville sports information director Mike Gore believes that when it came time to select a name, school officials just jumped on the bandwagon and chose one of the more popular college nicknames at the time, the Bulldogs.

Bulldogs is popular among collegiate athletic teams because it has many distinct qualities teams would like to have. Bulldogs have the reputation as one of the most tenacious, strongest breeds of dog. The toothy snarl that generally accompanies the pug-nosed animal has been known to strike fear in the hearts of many a passerby.

Radford Highlanders

Radford University
P.O. Box 5760
Radford, VA 24142

School Colors: Red, Navy, and Forest
                   Green
Year Founded: 1910
Basketball: Donald N. Dedmon
               Center (5,000)

RADFORD UNIVERSITY'S nickname, the Highlanders, is a result of the influence of Scottish immigrants who settled in southwestern Virginia more than 300 years ago.

These settlers were characterized by "firmness of decision, resourcefulness, ardor in friendship, love of country, and a generous enthusiasm." Today, both Radford's athletic teams and the university band celebrate that heritage by proudly carrying the Highlander name into competition and performance.

In the spring of 1978, Radford's student body adopted the red, navy, and forest green colors woven into each and every tartan kilt worn by the Highlander band as the school's official colors.

Winthrop Eagles

Winthrop College
Winthrop Coliseum
Rock Hill, SC 29733

School Colors: Garnet and Gold
Year Founded: 1886
Basketball: Winthrop Coliseum
(6,100)

WINTHROP COLLEGE BEGAN its intercollegiate athletic program in 1969, at a time when the institution was an all-women's school. In 1974, males were admitted, and men's athletics were founded that same year.

During the spring of 1976, Student Government Association president Margaret Williamson called for an election to select a school mascot. More than 60 suggestions were made and the list was narrowed to 10 names before the ballots were cast.

The top vote getters were Eagles, Sandlappers, and Cardinals, but none of the three obtained a needed majority. In a run-off election, the name Eagles was selected as school mascot.

Because the prize for the winning entry was $100 and three students submitted the name, the money was divided among the three winners.

Prior to the 1976 election, each academic class had its own mascot—the Panthers, Tigers, Wildcats, and Bulldogs. Today, the student body rallies around one mascot, the Eagle, rather than four different ones.

Wisconsin Badgers

9

Big Ten Conference

Big Ten Conference
111 Plaza Drive, Suite 600
Schaumburg, IL 60173-4990

Number of Schools: 10
Year Founded: 1895
Charter Members: Chicago, Illinois, Michigan, Minnesota, Northwestern, Purdue, and Wisconsin
Current Members: Illinois, Indiana, Iowa, Michigan, Michigan State, Minnesota, Northwestern, Ohio State, Purdue, and Wisconsin
Division I Sports: Baseball, Basketball, Cross-Country, Football, Golf, Gymnastics, Indoor Track, Swimming, Tennis, Track and Field, and Wrestling

THE BIG TEN CONFERENCE was born on January 11, 1895, when President James H. Smart of Purdue University called a meeting of seven midwestern university presidents to discuss regulation and control of intercollegiate athletics.

One year later, representatives from Chicago, Illinois, Michigan, Minnesota, Northwestern, Purdue, and Wisconsin met at the Palmer House in Chicago to establish standards for the league. The representatives designated themselves as the Intercollegiate Conference of Faculty Representatives.

Indiana and the State University of Iowa were admitted in 1899, and after Ohio State became a member in 1912, the popular titles Big Ten and Western Conference emerged.

Michigan withdrew from the conference in 1908, but resumed membership in 1917.

Ironically, the Big Ten carried only nine schools for three years following World War II. Chicago withdrew from the conference in 1946, and the Big Ten had an empty room in the house until 1949, when Michigan State was admitted.

Illinois Fighting Illini

University of Illinois
115 Assembly Hall
Champaign, IL 61820

School Colors: Orange and Blue
Year Founded: 1867
Basketball: Assembly Hall (16,153)
Football: Memorial Stadium (70,563)

BECAUSE THERE is very limited information on record at the University of Illinois regarding the Illini nickname, school officials really don't know how the name was formed.

All University of Illinois sports information officials can say on the subject is that in 1874 the student newspaper changed its name from *The Student* to *The Daily Illini*. The name of the newspaper is the first known reference to the name Illini.

The mascot, Chief Illiniwek, was born in 1926 at the suggestion of head football coach Robert Zuppke. Assistant band director Ray Dvorak came up with the idea of having an Indian do a war dance at the Pennsylvania-Illinois football game in 1926. Donning a homemade Indian costume, Lester Leutwiler, a student keenly interested in Indian lore, performed the first dance.

For more than 60 years, the dramatic war dance of Chief Illiniwek has been among the most colorful and memorable traditions associated with collegiate athletics. The Chief's energetic halftime dance has long been a highlight of Illinois football and basketball games.

The second chief, Webber Borchers, another student who shared an interest in Indian lore, initiated a campaign to raise money to purchase a costume.

Since the Depression was in full force, students contributed only $15 to Borcher's fund drive. However, a Champaign merchant donated the remainder of the needed money. Borchers then set out for South Dakota to purchase the costume.

"In the summer of 1930, I went at my own expense to the Pine Ridge Reservation in South Dakota," he said in a later letter to the university. "I hitchhiked out, called on an Indian agent, and explained my mission. He and an Indian trader called in an older Sioux Indian woman, and she and two younger women made the suit. While I stayed a month, the suit was not finished when it became necessary for me to return home for the fall term.

"The regalia was not ready for the first few games, but was ready in time for me to wear in the Army-Illinois game in Yankee Stadium in New York City on November 8, 1930."

Since that time, five different costumes have been worn by Chief Illiniwek. The most recent is an authentic, elaborately beaded costume that includes moccasins, blanket, peace pipe, pouch, breastplate, and a war bonnet with 90 eagle feathers bought from a 93-year-old Sioux Indian chief.

Names of the more than two dozen Illinois students who have been Chief Illiniwek since 1926 are recorded on the tail of the Chief's war bonnet.

Indiana Hoosiers

Indiana University
Seventeenth Street and Fee Lane
Bloomington, IN 47405

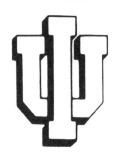

School Colors: Cream and Crimson
Year Founded: 1820
Basketball: Assembly Hall (17,357)
Football: Memorial Stadium (52,354)

INDIANA'S NICKNAME, Hoosiers, is unique and one the people of Indiana take a certain pride in. However, it seems everyone in the state has a different idea about its origin.

One of the more plausible theories cites a Samuel Hoosier, who in 1825 was a contractor building the Louisville and Portland (Ohio Falls) Canal. He found the men from the Indiana side of the river were much better diggers, and his preference for them eventually resulted in a force made up mostly of Indiana men. These men were first known as the Hoosier men and later as Hoosiers. When it came time to call it quits, they carried the name back home.

A large number of explanations deal with the linguistics and phonetics of the word Hoosier. According to one story, a Polish officer who served under Napoleon and later settled in Indiana gave lectures on the courage and endurance of the Hussars, which he incorrectly pronounced as Hoosiers. The people of Indiana apparently liked the story and claimed it for themselves.

Indiana governor Joseph Wright claimed that the term was derived form the Indian word *hoosa*, which means corn, and that the Indiana flatboaters utilizing the Ohio and Mississippi rivers came to be known as hoosa men. The only problem with this theory is that no one has ever been able to come up with such an Indian word.

There are a few more explanations, which deal with misinterpretations of the English language. Some say it originated from the habit of travelers shouting out their greeting when they passed cabins as night approached. The cautious pioneer, before unlatching the door, would call out, "Who's thar?" Somehow this reply evolved into hoosier.

Along the same lines, author James Whitcomb Riley had his own version of how the name originated. According to Riley, early Indiana settlers were not only vicious fighters who scratched and gouged their opponents but from time to time would also bite off noses and ears.

As the story goes, a settler who saw an ear on the barroom floor after a bad night, and who had grown accustomed to this sort of behavior, pushed it aside and asked, "Whose ear?"

There are also quite a few derogatory explanations about the word's origin, but Indianaians never seem to own up to any of them. One such tale deals with the word *hoose*, which is a disease common to calves. Symptoms of the disease were staring eyes, a rough coat with hair turned backward, and hoarse wheezing.

Some say it derives from an old Saxon word *hoo* meaning a hill dweller. Former sports information director Tom Miller pointed out, "In case you don't recognize it, it is an obtuse way of saying hillbilly."

At any rate, the people of Indiana can be proud that they have such a unique name. And if they really do know what it means, they aren't telling anyone.

Army, Navy, Air Force, Marines. Oh, yeah; who are the Marines? Answer: Western Illinois University. See the whole story on how the Fighting Leathernecks' name came about in the Association of Mid-Continent Universities.

Iowa Hawkeyes

University of Iowa
205 Carver-Hawkeye Arena
Iowa City, Iowa 52242

School Colors: Gold and Black
Year Founded: 1847
Basketball: Carver-Hawkeye Sports
              Arena (15,500)
Football: Kinnick Stadium (67,000)

THE HAWKEYES'S NICKNAME, which was first known as the nickname of the state of Iowa, comes from a popular 19th century novel.

The name Hawkeye originally belonged to a hero in James Fenimore Cooper's 1826 fictional novel *The Last of the Mohicans.* Cooper came up with the name Hawkeye for the hero by getting in touch with the Delaware Indians.

Judge David Rorer suggested to newspaper editor James Edwards that Iowa be known as the Hawkeye State. Edwards wrote about this proposal in his newspaper, the Ft. Madison *Patriot*, on March 24, 1838. The two men began a campaign to popularize the name, and their work paid off.

During the fall of 1838, territorial officials, including Gov. Robert Lucas, formally met and recommended the name Hawkeye for the territory. The recommendation was accepted, and the nickname has stuck ever since.

Edwards really believed in the name. When he moved the newspaper to Burlington in 1843, he renamed it the Burlington *Hawk-Eye.* The state's nickname was later adopted as the official University of Iowa name.

The mascot of the university originated in 1949 when Herky the Hawk was born. Herky is a little guy with a big beak, expressive features, and short wings and tail, along with active legs that enabled him to participate as an all-sport performer.

Herky became known to many as the football forward passer, a basketball player with an "overwing" hook shot, a baseball player with a big bat, a fancy diver, a powerful wrestler flexing his muscles, a discus thrower, a wielder of a tennis racket, and a putting golfer. He even donned a military uniform during the Korean War and became the insignia for the 124th Fighter Squadron.

Michigan State Spartans

Michigan State University
116 Linton Hall
East Lansing, MI 48824-1044

School Colors: Green and White
Year Founded: 1855
Basketball: Jack Breslin Student
                Events Center (15,000)
Football: Spartan Stadium (76,000)

MICHIGAN STATE COLLEGE replaced the name Michigan Agricultural College in 1925. In addition, the nickname Aggies was dropped at that time and Michigan Staters was the winning entry in a contest conducted among students and alumni.

But the new school nickname Michigan Staters was distinguished by a short career that would last only a few months. The school's new name would actually have its beginning many miles away from the East Lansing campus in Fort Benning, Georgia, during the university's first southern baseball training tour.

In rewriting baseball game leads from Fort Benning in the spring of 1926, George S. Alderton and Dale Stafford, sportswriters for the Lansing *State Journal* and Lansing *Capitol News*, respectively, found the school name too dull. So they set out to find a better nickname.

Among names rejected in the initial contest had been Spartans, a name submitted by former athlete Perry J. Fremont.

In the spring of 1926, however, the two writers began to refer to the baseball team as Spartans. Alderton first used the new name sparingly in copy dealing with the baseball team, then ventured into using it in newspaper headlines as well. (Incidentally, after two days of spelling the name incorrectly with an *o*, he changed it to the correct spelling on a tip from a close friend.)

"No student, alumnus or college official had called up the editor to complain about our audacity in giving the old school a new name, so we ventured into headlines with it," said Alderton. "Happily for the experiment, the name took. It began appearing in other newspapers and when the student publication used it, that clinched it."

Standing at the entranceway to Michigan State's athletic facilities is Sparty, a huge statue. Designed in 1945 by a member of the school's art department, the statue stands $10\frac{1}{2}$ feet tall and is mounted on a $5\frac{1}{3}$ foot diameter brick-and-concrete base. Weighing three tons, it is one of the largest freestanding ceramic figures in the world.

Proudly displayed by students on the campus, the statue serves as a tribute to all athletes who have worn the green and white over the years for the Spartans.

Michigan Wolverines

University of Michigan
1000 South State Street
Ann Arbor, MI 48109-2201

School Colors: Maize and Blue
Year Founded: 1817
Basketball: Crisler Arena (13,609)
Football: Michigan Stadium (101,701)

ALTHOUGH THE University of Michigan borrowed its nickname from the state, it is a serious misnomer.

According to a study by former football coach Fielding H. Yost, a wolverine may never have crossed through any part of the Michigan territory in the entire history of the state.

Dr. Lee R. Dice, associate professor of zoology at Michigan, stated in a 1943 issue of *Michigan History* magazine, "There is no authenticated evidence that a live wolverine was ever in Michigan." So why does Michigan have the nickname the Wolverine State?

Yost felt the state obtained the name because of the extensive trading in wolverine pelts brought from Canada but sold at Sault Ste. Marie in Michigan's Upper Peninsula for many years. Some traders assumed the pelts were from Michigan and hence the name Michigan Wolverines. Undoubtedly, the state nickname transferred over to the university.

In 1923, Yost began a quest to locate a Michigan wolverine for football games. The University of Wisconsin carried live badgers as mascots, and he felt Michigan deserved a live mascot as well. However, his extensive efforts did not pan out. He contacted trappers and tradesman all over upper and lower Michigan and came away with nothing—no one had ever seen a wolverine.

But through determination, hard work, and the help of a Detroit alumnus, Yost finally obtained 10 live wolverines from Alaska. The wolverines were placed on exhibition at the Detroit Zoo and brought to Ann Arbor to be carried around the field in cages on big football days. Or perhaps so the people of Michigan could see their state animal for the first time?

However, Yost was not as good at working out wolverine strategies as he was calling football plays. The beasts treated their handlers in such an unfriendly way that the wolverines no longer were welcome at the football games.

Minnesota Golden Gophers

University of Minnesota
516 Fifteenth Avenue, SE
Minneapolis, MN 55455

School Colors: Maroon and Gold
Year Founded: 1851
Basketball: Williams Arena (16,991)
Football: Hubert H. Humphrey
           Metrodome (62,000)

THE UNIVERSITY OF MINNESOTA also swiped their school nickname from their home state.

The state of Minnesota first received its dubbing as the Gopher State after the "five million dollar loan" was submitted by the legislature on February 24, 1858. The bill, which would provide a loan for the building of railroads in Minnesota, was bitterly opposed. As a humorous break from the monotonous hearings, someone passed around a satirical cartoon showing a "gopher train" pulled by nine striped gophers with human heads. This humorous drawing permanently labeled Minnesota with the nickname Gopher State.

Under the direction of Coach Bernie Bierman, the Gophers of the 1930s were busy establishing themselves as national football champions. During those championship seasons, the press described the Minnesota teams as the "golden-shirted horde" and the "golden swarm" in reference to the team switch to golden colored jerseys. Thus the new name, Golden Gophers, was born.

Northwestern Wildcats

Northwestern University
1501 Central Street
Evanston, IL 60208

School Colors: Purple and White
Year Founded: 1851
Basketball: Welsh-Ryan Arena (8,117)
Football: Dyche Stadium (49,256)

THE NORTHWESTERN UNIVERSITY football team was tagged Wild-cats by a sportswriter following a memorable victory in 1924.

The words of Wallace Abbey of the Chicago *Tribune* officially named the team. After the 1924 Northwestern-Chicago game, which heralded the start of a new era for Northwestern football, he wrote, "Football players had not come down from Evanston; Wildcats would be a name better suited to (Coach) Thistlethwaite's boys. . . . Stagg's boys, his pride, the 11 that had tied Illinois a week ago, were unable to score for 57 minutes. Once they had the ball on the nine-yard line and had been stopped dead by a purple wall of wildcats."

Northwestern officials obviously had a liking for Abbey's suggestion, as their athletic teams have used the Wildcats name ever since.

Ohio State Buckeyes

Ohio State University
141 St. John Arena
410 Woody Hayes Drive
Columbus, OH 43210-1166

School Colors: Scarlet and Gray
Year Founded: 1873
Basketball: St. John Arena (13,320)
Football: Ohio Stadium (85,339)

LIKE MANY OTHER Big Ten teams, Ohio State University took its nickname from the state. According to historians, the Ohio territory and its inhabitants may have been known as the Buckeyes as early as 1788. The buckeye tree, which is native to Ohio, belongs to the same family as the horse chestnut tree. The great number of trees scattered across the state prompted early settlers to refer to the area as the Buckeye State.

The buckeye leaf has been a part of the university's seal since 1871, and in October 1953, a bill was passed adopting the buckeye as Ohio's official tree.

Purdue Boilermakers

Purdue University
Mackey Arena, Room 10
West Lafayette, IN 47907

School Colors: Old Gold and Black
Year Founded: 1869
Basketball: Mackey Arena (14,123)
Football: Ross-Ade Stadium (67,861)

PURDUE UNIVERSITY received its nickname as a result of a name-calling spree by a bunch of sore losers after the 1889 Purdue-Wabash football game.

Located just 30 miles from West Lafayette, Wabash College teams were bitter rivals of Purdue in that day. Following Purdue's victory over Wabash, the students of the small liberal arts school felt inclined to hurl derogatory remarks at the cultural backgrounds of the Purdue athletes, who represented a school devoted to the practical arts of engineering and farming.

However, the name Boilermakers struck the fancy of the Purdue players, who had grown accustomed to being called names such as Cornfield Sailors, Blacksmiths, Pumpkin Shuckers, Hayseeds, Farmers, and Rail Splitters.

Wabash College's anger may be explained, however. There was a story going around in the late 1880s that Purdue enrolled eight boilermakers from the shops of the Monon Railroad just in time to suit up for football season.

Wisconsin Badgers

University of Wisconsin
1440 Monroe Street
Madison, WI 53706

School Colors: Cardinal and White
Year Founded: 1848
Basketball: Wisconsin Field House
          (11,895)
Football: Camp Randall Stadium
          (76,293)

BUCKY BADGER, the University of Wisconsin mascot, was actually borrowed from the state of Wisconsin nickname. Wisconsin was named the Badger State due to its association with the lead miners of southwestern Wisconsin in the 1820s.

During this time, hundreds of settlers from Missouri, Tennessee, Kentucky, and Illinois began prospecting at mine sites already discovered in the area by Indians.

It was because of this mining boom, not the number of animals in the state, that the Badgers' name evolved. In fact, the badger is rarely seen in Wisconsin. The name came from the miners who had not built houses when winter began and had to "live like badgers" in holes tunneled into the hillside and abandoned mine shafts.

Badgers are quick tempered and can be savage fighters when cornered. Pound for pound, a badger is as tough and courageous as any other wild animal. Badgers have been known to chase off full-grown bears who invaded and challenged the badger's territory.

The university's badger mascot—sporting a cardinal and white striped Wisconsin letter sweater, strutting with fists clenched and lips curled defiantly—was first drawn in 1946 or 1947 by either a Madison-based artist or a decal artist in Iowa.

Soon after the badger became the official mascot, badgers were brought to the football games and were cared for by several fraternities. After a live badger squirmed out of his leash and chased a Northwestern wildcat halfway up the goal post, it was decided that for the safety of the players and fans, the badgers would retire to Madison's city zoo.

The name Bucky was officially given to the Badger mascot in 1949, a result of a contest held before that fall's homecoming football game. Though none of the contestants submitted the name Bucky, the name that contest organizers preferred, the mascot was christened Buckingham U. Badger—Bucky for short—at a pregame pep rally.

While football games traditionally last four quarters, there is a special fifth quarter at all Wisconsin home games. Win or lose, the nationally known University of Wisconsin marching band performs for a half hour or more on the field following the game.

It is an amazing sight to see, as band members play their instruments, polka, and basically tear around the field having a great time. Songs such as the alma mater "Varsity," "Tequila," the Budweiser song, and "On Wisconsin" have been favorites for many years. Wisconsin supporters love it; 55,000 fans are often still singing, clapping, and stomping their feet 30 minutes after the game is over.

Camp Randall, the grounds where Wisconsin plays football, basketball, and indoor track, was once a Civil War camp used for training soldiers to defend the Union.

The Atlantic Coast and Big Ten Conferences have the most unusual nicknames of any conferences in Division I basketball.

Richmond Spiders

10

Colonial Athletic Association

Colonial Athletic Association
5707 Grove Avenue, Suite 200
Richmond, VA 23226

Number of Schools: 8
Year Founded: 1985
Charter Members: American, East Carolina, George Mason, James Madison, United States Naval Academy, North Carolina–Wilmington, Richmond, and William and Mary
Current Members: American, East Carolina, George Mason, James Madison, North Carolina–Wilmington, Richmond, United States Naval Academy, and William and Mary
Division I Sports: Baseball, Basketball, Cross-Country, Golf, Soccer, Swimming, and Tennis

American Eagles

American University
4400 Massachusetts Avenue
Washington, DC 20016

School Colors: Red, White, and Blue
Year Founded: 1893
Basketball: Bender Arena (5,000)

AMERICAN UNIVERSITY, recognized as a United States national institution, patriotically adopted the nation's symbolic eagle as its nickname.

American University, located in our nation's capital, was created by an
official act of the U.S. Congress in 1893. In appreciation of its founding,
American selected the bald eagle, the national mascot, as its official
nickname and mascot. School officials also adopted the red, white, and blue
colors of the American flag as school colors.

East Carolina Pirates

East Carolina University
Scales Field House
Greenville, NC 27858-4353

School Colors: Purple and Gold
Year Founded: 1907
Basketball: Minges Coliseum (6,500)
Football: Ficklen Stadium (35,000)

THE PIRATE, a symbol of East Carolina University and its athletic teams,
was adopted from the numerous legends and lore of coastal North Carolina.

During the colonial period, the fierce and colorful pirates were prominent and roamed the state's outer banks. Pirates found these ocean banks to
be ideal as hideouts for their treasure and many had homes and families
located in small villages along the coast.

One of the most well-known and feared pirates was Edward Teach, best
known as Blackbeard, who was a resident of eastern North Carolina. He

had a house at Ocracoke on the Outer Banks and an inland home at Bath along the Pamlico River.

In 1934, East Carolina's football team was known as the Teachers, a sorry band of athletes who won only two games in three seasons of existence. The student body's interest in pirates and sea lore quickly resulted in changing the name to capture the romantic appeal of the high seas adventures.

The change to Pirates brought so much enthusiasm that during the 1935 season, the Pirate football team won three of its six games—matching as many total victories as they had enjoyed during the previous three seasons.

George Mason Patriots

George Mason University
4400 University Drive
Fairfax, VA 22030

School Colors: Green and Gold
Year Founded: 1957
Basketball: Patriot Center (10,000)

KEEPING UP WITH THE GREAT patriotic tradition around Washington, D.C., the George Mason University athletic director selected Patriots as the school's official nickname in 1968.

The institution was formed in 1957 as a branch of the Virginia higher education system. The university itself is named after the great patriot George Mason, an American colonial leader born in 1725 in Virginia's Fairfax County.

Mason was very influential in establishing the Constitutional Convention, the Declaration of Independence, and the Virginia Constitution. He was also recognized as one of the first southerners to speak out against the evils of slavery.

The Patriots' nickname was born in 1968 when 23-year marine veteran Raymond "Hap" Spuhler, athletic director and coach of many sports at George Mason, sponsored a contest. Spuhler offered a prize radio to the person who submitted the winning suggestion. He received 10 entries and selected Patriots as the winner. Spuhler also selected the school colors of green and gold at a later date.

James Madison Dukes

James Madison University
South Main
Harrisonburg, VA 22807

School Colors: Purple and Gold
Year Founded: 1908
Basketball: JMU Convocation Center
             (7,612)
Football: JMU Stadium (15,000)

YOU MAY THINK the Dukes' nickname was chosen because of ties to royalty. However, it was named after one of the university's early presidents.

James Madison University was founded in 1908 as a women's institution. Men were admitted after World War II and then only as daytime students. The men's intercollegiate athletic program began in 1947.

The Dukes' cognomen was selected as a tribute to James Madison's second president, Dr. Samuel P. Duke, who served from 1919 to 1949. The first intercollegiate athletic program was developed during his tenure.

Although the nickname is in honor of a school president, James Madison proudly takes advantage of the royalty theme. The colors are purple and gold and the bulldog was selected as mascot, as Dukes often kept bulldogs as pets. The Bulldog wears a crown with a purple and gold cape.

The university itself is named after the fourth United States president, James Madison.

North Carolina at Wilmington Seahawks

University of North Carolina at
Wilmington
601 South College Road
Wilmington, NC 28403

School Colors: Green and Gold
Year Founded: 1947
Basketball: Trask Coliseum (6,100)

WHILE THE INFORMATION ON the source of Wilmington's Seahawks'
name is sketchy, the strong mascot and nickname have represented the
school well since the early days of its athletic program.

According to Adrian Hurst, one of the original instructors at the school,
an early Wilmington Junior College basketball player named Huck Moore
is responsible for coming up with the name. Other sources claim the name
was derived from the Iowa Seahawks, a famous United States Naval Service
football team of the 1940s.

Although no one knows the exact origin of the nickname, it was well
liked and was officially bestowed upon UNCW athletes by the student
body following a campus-wide contest.

Richmond Spiders

University of Richmond
Robins Center
University of Richmond, VA 23173

School Colors: Red and Blue
Year Founded: 1830
Basketball: Robins Center (9,171)
Football: University of Richmond
Stadium (22,500)

THE UNIVERSITY OF RICHMOND is the only school in the country that sports the nickname Spiders—a title Richmond's athletes earned while playing as if they were all arms and legs.

The original school nickname was the Colts, in the days when Richmond was dubbed for playing "as an energetic group of young colts."

The name Colts remained until the 1890s, when a baseball team comprised of Richmond athletes and city residents used the name Spiders in a summer league. Star pitcher Puss Ellyson's lanky arms and stretching kick confused batters to such an extent that Richmond *Dispatch* reporter Ragland Chesterman exercised the clever, creeping, name Spider to fit all Richmond team members.

United States Naval Academy Midshipmen

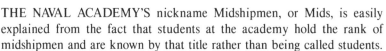

United States Naval Academy
Ricketts Hall
Annapolis, MD 21401

School Colors: Navy Blue and Gold
Year Founded: 1845
Basketball: Halsey Field House
            (5,000)
Football: Navy–Marine Corps
            Memorial (30,000)

THE NAVAL ACADEMY'S nickname Midshipmen, or Mids, is easily explained from the fact that students at the academy hold the rank of midshipmen and are known by that title rather than being called students.

The name is used in much the same way as Army's students are known as cadets. However, there was a period when the terms Cadet, Cadet Midshipman, and Naval Cadets were all used at the same time in Annapolis. But on July 7, 1903, the use of Midshipmen in referring to Navy's students became permanent.

Naturally, the name Midshipmen carried over to the school's athletic teams, and the name has remained as a tradition since Navy's first football game was played against the Baltimore Athletic Club in 1879.

William and Mary Tribe

College of William and Mary in Virginia
P.O. Box 399
Williamsburg, VA 23187-0399

School Colors: Green and Gold
Year Founded: 1693
Basketball: William and Mary Hall
            (10,000)
Football: Cary Field (15,000)

THE COLLEGE OF WILLIAM AND MARY acquired its nickname from the first British colony in North America, founded in 1607 as Jamestown, which is located only three miles from the Williamsburg campus. The college, founded in 1693, was named after King William III and his wife, Mary, who took over as England's king and queen in 1688.

Hundreds of years ago, the exact site of the William and Mary campus was an Indian settlement. Without the help of the Indians during those first few years, the Jamestown colony surely would have failed. The British colonists owed their survival to the neighboring tribes who helped them through the tough winters.

In honor of those Indians, the College of William and Mary selected the nickname the Tribe. It has been used ever since the athletic department was founded in 1898.

Hofstra Flying Dutchmen

11

East Coast Conference

East Coast Conference
c/o Drexel University
Building 14
Philadelphia, PA 19104

Number of Schools: 8
Year Founded: 1974
Charter Members: American, Bucknell, Delaware, Drexel, Hofstra, Lafayette, La Salle, Lehigh, Rider, St. Joseph's, Temple, and West Chester
Current Members: Bucknell, Delaware, Drexel, Hofstra, Lafayette, Lehigh, Rider, and Towson State
Division I Sports: Baseball, Basketball, Cross-Country, Golf, Indoor Track, Lacrosse, Soccer, Swimming, Tennis, Track and Field, and Wrestling

Bucknell Bison

Bucknell University
Lewisburg, PA 17837

School Colors: Orange and Blue
Year Founded: 1846
Basketball: Davis Gymnasium (2,100)
Football: Memorial Stadium (14,400)

IN THE EARLY 1900s, Bucknell University teams had no definite nickname. To remedy this situation, mathematics and astronomy professor William C. Bartol suggested the nickname Bisons in 1910.

Bartol's reasoning behind selecting the name Bisons was purely geographical. Bucknell's campus lies in the eastern end of the Buffalo Valley, which was one of the last stomping grounds of the American buffalo, or bison. At one time it is estimated that at least 10,000 bison roamed the Buffalo Valley ranges. As late as 1799, more than 300 were reported. The last buffalo was believed to have been shot in 1800 at Buffalo Crossroads, located within six miles of Bucknell's Memorial Stadium.

The name Bisons, which had great success, has been modified to Bison by writers and announcers.

Delaware Fightin' Blue Hens

University of Delaware
105 Delaware Field House
Newark, DE 19716

School Colors: Blue and Gold
Year Founded: 1833
Basketball: Delaware Field House
           (3,000)
Football: Delaware Stadium (23,000)

THE STORY BEHIND the University of Delaware's nickname involves a bit of history . . . even though some folks might think the school laid an egg when it selected this name.

Col. John Haslet's first Delaware regiment reported for duty near the outset of the American Revolution in January 1776. The brave regiment of men from the Diamond State were often referred to as the Fighting Delawareans.

The Blue Hen Chickens soon became the accepted sobriquet for all Delawareans. The name originated from a practice begun by the soldiers of Capt. Jonathan Caldwell's company, who carried with them gamecocks of the Kent County blue hen breed, which was celebrated for its fighting qualities.

Undoubtedly, these birds were brought along to entertain the men during boring times on the front. The regiment acquired a considerable reputation for its own fighting prowess in engagements with the British at Long Island, White Plains, Trenton, and Princeton.

It is with an understanding of this tradition and proud heritage that Delaware's teams continue to attempt to justify their right to the title the Fightin' Blue Hens. It should also be noted that Delaware's state bird is the blue hen chicken.

Drexel Dragons

Drexel University
Thirty-third and Market Streets
Philadelphia, PA 19104

School Colors: Navy Blue and Gold
Year Founded: 1891
Basketball: Physical Education
Athletic Center (2,500)

UNFORTUNATELY, THERE IS NOTHING written in the Drexel University history books that fully explains the origin of its nickname, the Dragons.

Drexel University, which was founded in 1891 by Anthony J. Drexel, went by the nickname Engineers until the autumn of 1928. The Engineers was a sensible choice, as the school was then known as the Drexel Institute of Technology.

In September 1928, the school president appointed William J. Stevens to the newly formed position of graduate manager of athletics.

Stevens became the first Drexel official to be in charge of unifying and supervising the entire athletic program. Stevens's term coincided with the second year of Walter Halas's era as football coach. Halas put very skilled teams on the field year in and year out, and they soon represented the new athletic tradition at Drexel.

Brian DePasquale, Drexel's current sports information director, believes that between Stevens and Halas, the Dragons' moniker was created to elevate the visibility of athletics at the university. Although no written documents have been found, it is said to have been chosen because the name is quite rare and the two men were looking for something that would make Drexel stand out among schools across the country.

At any rate, Stevens and Halas hoped to "fire up" their players with the new mascot.

Hofstra Flying Dutchmen

Hofstra University
Hempstead Turnpike
Hempstead, NY 11550

School Colors: Blue, White, and Gold
Year Founded: 1935
Basketball: Physical Fitness Center
              (3,900)
Football: Hofstra Stadium (7,500)

HOFSTRA UNIVERSITY selected its nickname in honor of the school's founder Willie Hofstra, a Dutch shipbuilder.

The name Flying Dutchmen, which was adopted before World War II, originated from the legendary flying ghost ship. However, it fits well with the university since Hofstra was a ship builder, the campus is located within 10 miles of the sea, and much of the surrounding community's residents are of Dutch descent.

Another version of the origin of the Flying Dutchmen's name is not as popular with school officials. Supposedly during a basketball game in the late 1930s, one of Hofstra's tallest players was a great jumper and also of Dutch descent. Watching him play on the court, someone was prompted to say, "Look at the Flying Dutchman."

Lafayette Leopards

Lafayette College
Easton, Pa 18042

School Colors: Maroon and White
Year Founded: 1826
Basketball: Allan P. Kirby Field House
(3,500)
Football: Fisher Field (13,750)

THERE IS NO steadfast explanation as to why the Leopards' name became the symbol of Lafayette College's athletic teams.

The first time the name was used at Lafayette was October 7, 1927, in a story in the student newspaper. George Parkman, then sports editor of *The Lafayette*, recalled that a number of the school's opponents had animal nicknames and someone thought Lafayette should also have one.

Perhaps the name Leopards was used because it flowed well with Lafayette. Prior to 1927, Lafayette teams had been referred to simply as the Maroon.

Lehigh Engineers

Lehigh University
436 Brodhead Avenue
Bethlehem, PA 18015

School Colors: Brown and White
Year Founded: 1865
Basketball: Stabler Athletic and
Convocation Center
(5,800)
Football: Murray H. Goodman
Stadium (14,000)

ALTHOUGH THERE IS NO CONCRETE evidence as to why Lehigh University is known as the Engineers, director of sports information Ron Ticho reveals some rumors involving the name's origin.

The institution was founded in 1865 by Asa Packer, who also founded the Lehigh Valley Railroad. Between 1865 and 1890, the railroad greatly helped the financial status of the university and provided students with free tuition. Because of Packer's close relationship with both the school and the railroad, it seemed only natural to dub the teams the Engineers, a takeoff on the operators of the railroad cars.

Another story states that because Lehigh was primarily a technical school in the 1880s, the athletes were called engineers. Today, school officials prefer the first account since the university is no longer a single-school institution.

Ticho also relates the entertaining but undocumented anecdote about the origin of the school's colors. On February 9, 1876, a meeting was to be held to elect official school colors. In those days, ladies wore stockings with alternating stripes of different hues. As students chatted outside the meeting place, the breeze lifted the dress of a woman from a nearby women's school. The wind revealed the shapely legs and attractive brown and white stockings of this woman. At the meeting, many of the young men who witnessed this event immediately proposed the colors brown and white. So it was actually a woman's legs that decided Lehigh's official school colors.

Rider Broncs

Rider College
2083 Lawrenceville Road
Lawrenceville, NJ 08648-3099

School Colors: Cranberry and White
Year Founded: 1865
Basketball: Alumni Gym (2,200)

IN 1928, THE LEGENDARY Clair F. Bee came to Rider College as athletic director to organize the varsity athletic program.

Prior to Bee's arrival, athletes were referred to as Riderites. The football, men's and women's basketball, and baseball teams were all coached by Bee, and he soon dubbed his players the Rough Riders. Following Bee's action, the student newspaper renamed itself the *Rough Rider* the same year.

Bee designed the athletic logo, which is still in use today. Actually, creativity was nothing new to Bee. Besides coaching, he was the author of the famous Chip Hilton series of sports books, which many teenagers faithfully read in the '40s, '50s, and '60s.

The name Rough Riders was used until the late 1940s, when the term

Little Broncs was given to the junior varsity basketball team. Trenton newspapers, feeling that Rough Riders was too long for a headline, began substituting Broncs and Broncos. By 1950, Rider College used both Rough Riders and Broncs to refer to its athletes. Since the 1960s, Rider teams have been known almost exclusively as the Broncs.

Unlike the professional Broncos of Denver, who feature a horse as their mascot, Rider players are the Broncs with the roughrider (cowboy) riding the horse. The person is the mascot.

During the 1987–88 school year, school colors were changed from purple and gold to the current cranberry and white, as a tribute to Andrew J. Rider. Rider, known as the Cranberry King, owned cranberry bogs in south Jersey and was said to be the first to introduce the fruit to Europe.

Towson State Tigers

Towson State University
Towson Center
Towson, MD 21204

School Colors: Black and Gold
Year Founded: 1866
Basketball: Towson Center (5,200)
Football: Minnegan Stadium (5,000)

THE NICKNAME TIGERS IS one of the most common school monikers used in the United States. Although Towson State is aware of the name's tremendous popularity, that is not the reason it was adopted.

When Towson State was a two-year normal school, the Baltimore media dubbed their teams the Teachers. As the school grew into a four-year program, the Baltimore papers granted Towson State athletes full tenure and called them Professors, which was eventually shortened to Profs. Later, it was changed again to Schoolmasters.

The Indians and Golden Knights were other short-lived nicknames. The story goes that a soccer contest settled the issue once and for all.

One autumn afternoon a local sportswriter was covering the Towson State soccer team's uphill battle against the competition. The next day, the local newspaper printed that although the team lost the game, "they played like tigers." The soccer team was so appreciative of the comments that they soon adopted Tigers as their nickname. Enthusiasm for the new name quickly spread over the campus and it soon became the official mascot of Towson State.

New Hampshire Wildcats

12

ECAC North Atlantic

ECAC North Atlantic
P.O. Box 69
Orono, ME 04473

Number of Schools: 10
Year Founded: 1979
Charter Members: Boston University, Canisius, Colgate, Holy Cross, Maine, Niagara, New Hampshire, Northeastern, Rhode Island, and Vermont
Current Members: Boston University, Canisius, Colgate, Hartford, Maine, New Hampshire, Niagara, Northeastern, Siena, and Vermont
Division I Sports: Basketball, Cross-Country, Golf, Soccer, Tennis, and Track and Field

Boston Terriers

Boston University
285 Babcock Street
Boston, MA 02115

School Colors: Scarlet and White
Year Founded: 1869
Basketball: Walter Brown Arena
          (4,200)
Football: Nickerson Field (17,369)

BOSTON UNIVERSITY students selected their nickname shortly after the football team received official university recognition back in 1917.

The students came up with the name Terriers. The terrier is one of the few breeds of dogs originally bred in the United States. Interestingly enough, it was 1869, the year the university was incorporated, that a well-known Boston dog breeder came up with this American favorite when he crossed an English terrier with a bulldog.

Although quite small, the terrier was used to pursue prey into its burrow. Boston University officials selected the name to hopefully frighten opposing teams and maybe even scare them back into their locker rooms.

Canisius Golden Griffins

Canisius College
2001 Main Street
Buffalo, NY 14208

School Colors: Blue and Gold
Year Founded: 1870
Basketball: Koessler Athletic Center
          (1,800)
          Memorial Auditorium
          (16,476)
Football: War Memorial Stadium
          (41,897)

ACCORDING TO CANISIUS OFFICIALS, the time and place of the griffin's reign as King Herald of the Canisius College coat of arms is not easily settled, but the source is quite clear.

The griffin, a creature that was half lion and half eagle, flew to the Canisius campus from the bow of LaSalle's lost Griffon, the Flying Dutchman boat of the Great Lakes. The vessel vanished after making a safe voyage from the Niagara River to the Strait of Detroit.

Research studies imply that the griffin first became a Canisius symbol in 1933. The school paper assumed the title later that year, and athletic teams were soon dubbed the Griffins.

Steve Weller, in the January 22, 1962, edition of the *Canisius News*, analyzed the Griffins' sporting utility: "You can have your Chihuahuas, Piranhas, Horned Frogs, and Iguanas. The best all-around athletic mascot in business today has to be the beast adopted by Canisius College—the Golden Griffin.

"The Griffin is a creature with the head and wings of an eagle, which is patriotic; the torso of a lion, which gives the student body a feeling of security; and most important, the changeable personality of a chameleon which keeps the coach from getting complacent."

Colgate Red Raiders

Colgate University
P.O. Box 338
Hamilton, NY 13346

School Colors: Maroon and White
Year Founded: 1819
Basketball: Cotterrell Court (3,000)
Football: Andy Kerr Stadium (8,800)

COLGATE UNIVERSITY'S nickname, the Red Raiders, was coined in 1932 by Colgate sports publicity director Dexter Hoyt Teed.

Teed came up with this name because the football team had just bought new game uniforms featuring maroon pants and white jerseys with maroon trim. Topped with the traditional Colgate white helmet, the team's natty appearance prompted Teed's phrase the Red Raiders.

The designation of the 1932 football squad stuck and was carried over to all Colgate athletic teams. That first Red Raider football team of 1932 went on to the remarkable feat of finishing unbeaten, untied, unscored upon, yet uninvited to any postseason bowl games.

Hartford Hawks

University of Hartford
312 Bloomfield Avenue
West Hartford, CT 06117-0395

School Colors: Scarlet and White
Year Founded: 1877
Basketball: Hartford Civic Center
(16,014)

HILLYER COLLEGE, now known as the University of Hartford, came up with the nickname Hawks in the late 1940s. At that time, Hillyer athletic teams were known as the Fighting Hawks.

No one is quite sure exactly how the Hawks' nickname became associated with Hillyer, but the modifier "fighting" was obviously installed due to the fighting, never-give-up, aggressive nature of the school's athletic teams.

One possibility as to the source of the Hawks' name is that spectators had to climb four flights of stairs in the old Chauncey Harris School, or the Hawk's Nest as it was often called, to watch basketball and wrestling events.

In 1947, a live mascot known as Harry the Fightin' Hawk made his debut at Hillyer. The hawk lived at student Judd William's game farm in East Hartford. Harry had excellent attendance at all athletic events, especially basketball and other social gatherings at the school.

When the University of Hartford was chartered in 1957, "fighting" was dropped and the university nickname became simply Hawks.

Maine Black Bears

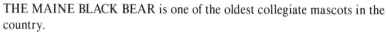

University of Maine
Gymnasium Drive
Orono, ME 04469

School Colors: Columbia Blue and
                     White
Year Founded: 1865
Basketball: Memorial Gym (1,800)
                  Bangor Auditorium (7,000)
Football: Alumni Field (8,500)

THE MAINE BLACK BEAR is one of the oldest collegiate mascots in the country.

The history of the bear mascot started in 1914 when a cub named Jeff was presented to the University of Maine by an Old Town Indian guide. When the cub entered the auditorium for his first official appearance, the crowd gave him a rousing reception. The cub's response was to stand on his head. According to the story, the crowd went "bananas" over the tiny cub's antics.

The bear cub, however, was not the school's first mascot. In 1903 a group of students "borrowed" an elephant from a real-life advertising promotion in nearby Bangor. The Great Bolivar, as they named him, was marched onto the football field and helped Maine beat its opponent.

But it was Jeff who stole the hearts of the Maine football fans. In 1914 he was credited with bringing about an upset victory over Colby; because of his heroism and inspiration the Maine athletic teams have been called the Black Bears ever since.

Since Jeff there have been a number of bear mascots who have all answered to the name Bananas. Maine's bears have been asked for interviews and to perform at other schools' games; and in 1921 a Maine mascot even accepted a role in a feature film, *Rider of the King Log*.

Bananas VI is credited with inspiring a stunning come-from-behind victory over the Bowdoin football team in 1923. Bowdoin was ahead at the half, and the Black Bears' spirits were low. When the Bowdoin mascot, the husky, and his trainer came out on the field at the half, Bananas and his trainer went out to greet them. Tempers flared and a skirmish occurred. The husky dashed back to the Bowdoin sideline with its tail between its legs, dragging his trainer on the ground behind the chain. The crowd's spirits soared and, spurred by the inspiration of Bananas, the Black Bears came back to defeat Bowdoin 28–6.

In 1966, after the death of Cindy Bananas, Maine outlawed the practice of using a live animal as a mascot. But in 1969, the Sigma Xi chapter of Alpha Phi Omega fraternity volunteered to provide the school with a human mascot—and the human form of the legendary black bear has been a part of Maine athletic events ever since.

New Hampshire Wildcats

University of New Hampshire
Field House
Durham, NH 03824

School Colors: Blue and White
Year Founded: 1866
Basketball: Lundholm Gymnasium
          (3,000)
Football: Cowell Stadium (13,000)

NEW HAMPSHIRE received its first school mascot after three university students traveled 50 miles to retrieve a live mascot for the 1926 homecoming football game. Earlier in 1926, a local newspaper stated that the UNH football team played as viciously as wildcats. This description eventually led to the adoption of the school nickname.

That fall, Cupe Osgood, Eddie K. Simpson, and Gill Reed learned that a farmer near Meredith, New Hampshire, had captured a wildcat and had placed it in a local zoo. Because of the article, Osgood decided to bring it back and asked his two friends to accompany him on his trip to make it more exciting. If it was excitement Osgood was looking for, he would not have needed his two friends along.

When they got to Meredith, the farmer stuffed the cat into a wooden box, nailed some slats on top, and put the box in the back seat of Osgood's car. A few miles down the road the cat started raising havoc in the box and produced some frightening sounds. The three students were soon terribly apprehensive about the stability of the box.

A short time later, one of the three happened to look back just in time—the cat had chewed through one of the slats and was already halfway out of the box. Simpson and Reed quickly renailed the box shut, tossed a blanket over the top, and hoped for the best.

Mischievous as college students often are, Reed couldn't pass up the opportunity for a great practical joke. While Osgood was driving, Reed reached around and jabbed Osgood in the neck, at the same time giving his best wildcat imitation. Osgood jumped on the brakes, leaped out of the car, and headed for a cornfield as the other two rolled around on the ground laughing hysterically. To say the least, it was very quiet the rest of the way home.

The three students took the cat to each game that season, but the cat didn't like the sound of the band very much. Every time an instrument was played, the wildcat buried his head in his paws.

Hopefully the band has improved over the years!

Niagara Purple Eagles

Niagara University
Niagara University, NY 14109

School Colors: Purple, White, and Gold
Year Founded: 1856
Basketball: John J. "Taps" Gallagher Center (3,200)

THE NIAGARA UNIVERSITY nickname is derived from the official seal of the university.

Pictured at the top of Niagara's seal is a purple and white wreath with an eagle perched atop it. This part of the seal represents the location of Niagara University, which is on Monteagle Ridge overlooking the Niagara gorge.

The full nickname is Purple Eagles because the eagle bears a purple diamond displaying a silver heart, symbolizing St. Vincent dePaul. St. Vincent founded the Congregation of the Mission (Vincentian) in 1625. His philosophy served as the inspiration for the Vincentian tradition, the essential foundation for Niagara's mission statement.

Northeastern Huskies

Northeastern University
360 Huntington Avenue
Boston, MA 02115

School Colors: Red and Black
Year Founded: 1898
Basketball: Matthews Arena (6,500)
Football: Edward S. Parsons Field
            (7,000)

NORTHEASTERN UNIVERSITY officially adopted its Huskies' nickname in 1927, after the first Alaskan husky—bred from a line of sled dog royalty—appeared on campus on March 4 of that year.

When the husky arrived by train from Alaska, classes were cancelled so students could greet the dog at Boston's North Station. More than 1,000 students and the university band were there to welcome the tired husky that afternoon. He was even provided with a police escort for the four-mile drive back to campus.

The husky, whose real name had been Sapsut, was presented with an honorary degree by the university president and renamed King Husky. King Husky's father was Noonok of Marly, the lead dog on Leonard Seppala's famous team that rushed diphtheria vaccine 700 miles from Nenna to Nome, Alaska, in 1925 to save the stricken village.

King Husky's first athletic event was a track meet in which Northeastern set three school records and was the decisive victor. The current King Husky is part of the proud dynasty representing the energetic working student, symbolic of all Northeastern undergraduates.

Siena College

Siena College
Loudonville, NY 12211

School Colors: Green and Gold
Year Founded: 1937
Basketball: Alumni Recreation Center
(4,000)
Football: Siena Field (300)

SIENA COLLEGE, at the time this book was written, was without an athletic nickname.

When the school was founded in 1937, Golden Warriors was the title used to refer to the school's athletes. The Golden Warriors' nickname was a takeoff on the school's colors as well as a tribute to the Indian tribes that occupied upstate New York. These tribes included the Iroquois, Mohican, Mohawk, Tuscarora, and many others.

However, Golden Warriors was found difficult to use for publicity purposes because of its length, and it was nearly impossible for use in headlines. Hence, the name was shortened to Indians, a moniker that served Siena College faithfully for many years. In 1988, however, the college, conscious of minority concerns, opted to change its nickname in an effort to eliminate cultural stereotypes. The Student Senate governed the process of the nickname selection and a decision will be reached in time for the 1989–90 school year. Siena College competed during the 1988–89 school year without a nickname.

Vermont Catamounts

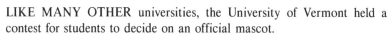

University of Vermont
Burlington, VT 05405

School Colors: Green and Gold
Year Founded: 1791
Basketball: Vermont Gymnasium
          (3,200)

LIKE MANY OTHER universities, the University of Vermont held a contest for students to decide on an official mascot.

In 1926, the students went to the polls to elect a mascot, and a longshot came away as the winner. The students were in search of a wild mountain cat–type nickname because of the campus location near the Green Mountains.

The ballot listed Lynx and Wildcat as well as provided a place for write-ins. It is not known specifically what type of campaign took place, but when the votes were counted, "a longshot from left field pulled the upset of upsets," and the Catamount was the student's choice.

The 1926 baseball team was the first to officially play under the name Catamounts, which has stuck with the school ever since.

Nicknames describing people are popular at many schools. These names include 49ers, Boilermakers, Buccaneers, Colonels, Cowboys, Dons, Dutchmen, Engineers, Explorers, Gauchos, Gentlemen, Governors, Hoosiers, Jaspers, Lumberjacks, Mavericks, Miners, Mountaineers, Pirates, Privateers, Rebels, Toreros, Vandals, Vikings, and Volunteers.

Yale Bulldogs

13

Ivy League

Ivy League
70 Washington Road, Room 22
Princeton, NJ 08540

Number of Schools: 8
Year Founded: 1954
Charter Members: Brown, Columbia, Cornell, Dartmouth, Harvard, Pennsylvania, Princeton, and Yale
Current Members: Same as charter members
Division I Sports: Baseball, Basketball, Cross-Country, Fencing, Football, Golf, Hockey, Indoor Track, Lacrosse, Rowing, Soccer, Squash, Swimming, Tennis, Track and Field, and Wrestling

Brown Bears or Bruins

Brown University
485 Elmgrove Avenue, Box 1932
Providence, RI 02912

School Colors: Seal Brown, Cardinal
Red, and White
Year Founded: 1764
Basketball: Marble Gymnasium
(3,000)
Football: Brown Stadium (20,000)

THE BIRTH DATE OF THE Brown Bear is January 20, 1904, when he was introduced to the university by Senator Francis Green, class of 1887.

"The Brown Bear is truly American and, most important of all, he embodies and suggests those qualities we want to emphasize," the senator said in his speech. "While somewhat unsociable, he is good-natured and clean. While courageous and ready to fight, he does not look for trouble for its own sake, nor is he bloodthirsty. He is not one of a herd but acts independently.

"He is intelligent and capable of being educated (if caught young enough!). Remember, an athlete can make Phi Beta Kappa. Furthermore, the bear's color is brown; and its name is Brown."

Bear cub mascots, which were presented by a nearby animal farm, appeared on the Brown sidelines for many years. In 1963, the live bear mascot was replaced by a costumed bear. Brown also uses the Bruins as its unofficial name.

Columbia Lions

Columbia University
Broadway and 116th Street
New York, NY 10027

School Colors: Columbia Blue and
                    White
Year Founded: 1754
Basketball: Levien Gymnasium
                 (3,408)
Football: Lawrence A. Wien Stadium
               (17,000)

COLUMBIA UNIVERSITY adopted the lion as its mascot via the Student Board in 1910, as a result of a unique banner that was presented to the institution.

A blue and white banner bearing a rampant lion, with the motto *Leo, Columbiae*, meaning "Lion of Columbia," was the gift of the Society of the Early Eighties. George Brokaw of the class of 1909 first suggested the adoption of the nickname Lions.

Columbia's school colors, Columbia blue and white, used as early as 1852, were appropriated from the campus Philoexian and Peithologian societies, whose official colors were blue and white, respectively. The early-day sports teams were known as the Blue and White, the most common school title until 1910.

The Columbia Lion logo, which was suggested by Howard Dietz of the class of 1917, eventually served as the basis for the famous Hollywood MGM lion, which is known for its fierce gnarl on the silver screen at the beginning and end of the firm's film productions.

Cornell Big Red

Cornell University
P.O. Box 729
Ithaca, NY 14851

School Colors: Carnelian and White
Year Founded: 1865
Basketball: Barton Hall (4,800)
Football: Schoellkopf Field (27,000)

AS LATE AS 1905, Cornell University still did not have a nickname. Quite by accident, a Cornell graduate's song lyrics emerged as the school nickname.

In 1905, Romeyn Berry, a recent graduate of Cornell, was composing the lyrics to a new football song. Because Cornell had no nickname, he referred to the Cornell squad as the big red team. The name caught on and was popularized by the song, and it was eventually adopted as the official school nickname.

Cornell's first mascot was a live bear that appeared in 1915 during Cornell's undefeated national championship football season. However, one of its successors, Touchdown IV, was never allowed on Schoellkopf Field. The bear was shipped by Cornell alumni to Columbus, Ohio, for the Ohio State–Cornell game. But before the bear even took the field, the Animal Protective League stepped in and declared the bear was to be let loose in the wilds of western Pennsylvania.

Since then, a Cornell undergraduate dressed as a bear has performed at all home football and hockey contests.

Dartmouth Big Green

Dartmouth College
Alumni Gym
Hanover, NH 03755

School Colors: Dartmouth Green and
                    White
Year Founded: 1769
Basketball: Leede Arena (2,100)
Football: Memorial Field (20,416)

ALTHOUGH THERE IS no written document on the subject, it is easy to speculate why Dartmouth College's teams are called the Big Green.

The nickname Big Green has been around for years. Undoubtedly, the name originated from the fact that the school color is Dartmouth green, a dark shade of forest green.

Dartmouth's teams were formerly known as the Indians, but the name was dropped in the mid-1970s when activist groups were lobbying against the use of Indians as school mascots.

To this day, no one knows exactly what a Big Green is, as there is no mascot or logo used by the school. The official symbol of athletics is a block-letter D.

Harvard Crimson

Harvard University
60 JFK Street
Cambridge, MA 02138

School Color: Crimson
Year Founded: 1636
Basketball: Briggs Cage (3,000)
Football: Harvard Stadium (37,289)

FOR HARVARD'S SELF-IMAGE, the most important date in athletic history may have been May 6, 1875. This is the date when Crimson was voted in as both the official school color and nickname. Had the vote gone the other way, we might refer to Harvard's teams today as the Magenta.

Former Harvard president Charles W. Eliot, class of 1853, recalled the adoption of crimson in the first *H Book*: "It was on the occasion of the regatta of June 19th, 1858, that red was first used as a distinguishing color for Harvard. The crews were in the habit of rowing in their ordinary underclothing, wearing miscellaneous hats or caps. When we heard that a large number of boats had been entered for the regatta, and that the crews of most of them were to wear uniforms, we agreed that we must have some distinguishing mark on the Harvard crew.

"Thereupon, B. W. Crowninshield, crew captain, and I went to the store of C. F. Hovey and Co. and bought six Chinese handkerchiefs of a handsome red hue, then called bandannas and often carried by men as pocket handkerchiefs. We were shown handkerchiefs of many hues—blue, orange, green, yellow, and red—but we two chanced to prefer the red ones. The crew tied these handkerchiefs around their heads and this was the only distinguishing mark."

The use of these red handkerchiefs at the regatta is believed to be the first recognized use of red as a Harvard color. In the spring of 1863, however, two players were appointed to select colors for the baseball squad. A local seamstress ignored the suggested crimson color and substituted the "more fashionable, prettier" magenta.

But in the 1875 vote, crimson was supported by a large majority and the controversy was settled. However, Harvard was still without an official mascot. It was not until 1950 that a member of the cheerleading squad donned puritan garb to represent John Harvard. The tradition continues and the Puritan still entertains fans at supporting events today.

Over the years, writers have also dubbed Harvard teams as the Johnnies (for John Harvard) and the Cantabrigians or Cantabs (from Cantabrigia, medieval Latin for Cambridge). Yet the official nickname has remained the Crimson.

Pennsylvania Red and Blue

University of Pennsylvania
235 South Thirty-third Street
Philadelphia, PA 19104-6322

School Colors: Crimson and Navy
                   Blue
Year Founded: 1740
Basketball: The Palestra (9,200)
Football: Franklin Field (60,546)

ALTHOUGH MOST SPORTS FANS know the University of Pennsylvania athletic teams as the Quakers, the official nickname is actually the Red and Blue.

However, somewhere down the line sportswriters tagged the teams as the Quakers. The name probably emerged because of William Penn, the famous Quaker, who was made full proprietor of the Pennsylvania land which carries his name today. Penn was instrumental in the beginnings of early Philadelphia, the home of the University of Pennsylvania.

The Quakers are an important part of Pennsylvania heritage. The Quakers were members of a Christian group called the Society of Friends, which refused to go to war or take oaths. Their clothes, lifestyles, and religious services were extremely simple.

The school mascot is a cheerleader dressed up in Quaker attire who represents Benjamin Franklin, founder of the university in 1740.

Princeton Tigers

Princeton University
P.O. Box 71
Princeton, NJ 08544

School Colors: Orange and Black
Year Founded: 1746
Basketball: Jadwin Gymnasium
              (7,550)
Football: Palmer Memorial Stadium
            (45,725)

IN 1880, THE PRINCETON FOOTBALL TEAM wore an orange and black striped jersey with alternating stripes on both the body and full sleeves. It was about this time that a local newspaper credited the men from Nassau Hall as having fight, like tigers.

The "Tiger Cheer" probably also played a role in selection of the new nickname. The cheer apparently was picked up during the Civil War years when the New York Seventh Regiment passed through the Princeton campus. Responding to the students' applause, the regiment gave a version of the cheer.

The cheer originally stemmed from the British navy's "three cheers and a tiger," which did not mean shouting "tiger" at the end but rather concluding the triple round of yells with a tigerlike roar. After the Princeton students heard the cheer, they substituted "Princeton" where the regiment name had been and officially adopted the cheer as their own.

In the 1920s, some undergraduates brought a live tiger to Princeton and exhibited the mascot at home football games. However, after realizing the total costs of keeping the feline, it was sent back to its previous home.

The university went nearly 20 years without a regular mascot at its football games until immediately following World War II. Then a cheerleader, who also happened to be an accomplished varsity diver, rented a tiger suit from a New York costume house. The tumbling cheerleader made the tiger an added attraction to fans, and the costumed Tiger has been around for years.

Yale Elis or Bulldogs

Yale University
P.O. Box 402A Yale Station
New Haven, CT 06520

School Colors: Yale Blue and White
Year Founded: 1701
Basketball: Payne Whitney
      Fieldhouse (3,100)
Football: Yale Bowl (70,896)

YALE UNIVERSITY WAS originally founded in 1701 as the Collegiate School of Branford, Connecticut, with a gift of 10 books from clergymen. In 1718, after it had been located in New Haven for two years, the institution was renamed Yale College after a generous benefactor, Elihu Yale. Thus the nickname Elis.

The famous bulldog mascots, all known as Handsome Dan, first came to Yale in 1889. The first dog was a significant specimen whose splendid face helped him win numerous awards. Today, his stuffed body is found in a sealed case in Yale's trophy room.

The Yale bulldog tradition is still carried on today as Handsome Dan prances proudly and cavorts joyously along the Yale sidelines at football games.

South Carolina Fighting Gamecocks

14

Metro Athletic Conference

Metro Collegiate Athletic Conference
One Ravinia Drive
Suite 1120
Atlanta, GA 30346

Number of Schools: 7
Year Founded: 1975
Charter Members: Cincinnati, Georgia Tech, Louisville, Memphis State, St. Louis, and Tulane
Current Members: Cincinnati, Florida State, Louisville, Memphis State, South Carolina, Southern Mississippi, and Virginia Tech
Division I Sports: Baseball, Basketball, Cross-Country, Golf, Swimming, Tennis, and Track and Field

Cincinnati Bearcats

University of Cincinnati
ML 21
Cincinnati, OH 45221-0050

School Colors: Red and Black
Year Founded: 1819
Basketball: Myrl Schoemaker
          Memorial Fieldhouse
          (13,500)
Football: Riverfront Stadium (59,754)
          Nippert Stadium (26,592)

THERE ARE THREE possible versions that explain the University of Cincinnati's adoption of the Bearcats' nickname, but no one knows for sure which is the real one.

One version holds that the nickname was prompted by a 1914 picture or cartoon of Cincinnati lineman Leonard K. "Teddy" Baehr standing on the gridiron next to a Stutz Bearcat car.

Another theory states the nickname was a result of a sports cartoon that appeared in a newspaper following the 1914 Cincinnati-Kentucky game showing the Kentucky Wildcat being harassed by a bearlike, catlike animal.

Still another explanation traces the moniker back to a 1912 newspaper account of a Cincinnati game in which *Enquirer* sports editor Jack Ryder stated that "the team played like bearcats."

The bearcat, a native animal of Southeast Asia, is a member of the viverrid suborder of carnivorous animals. Bearcats can be very ferocious and will eat just about anything, including opposing teams.

Florida State Seminoles

Florida State University
P.O. Box 2195
Tallahassee, FL 32316

School Colors: Garnet and Gold
Year Founded: 1857
Basketball: Leon County Civic Center
(12,500)
Football: Doak Campbell Stadium
(60,519)

FLORIDA STATE UNIVERSITY, founded in 1857, was originally a women's college. Because millions of veterans were returning after serving in World War II, the state of Florida, which at the time had very limited educational facilities, was caught in a bind. In 1946, the state's college system was swamped with applicants and received 2,200 more applicants than it could accommodate.

In this educational emergency, the women's college agreed to provide some instruction for the returning veterans. The new students were housed in the vacant air force training base, which became known as the Tallahassee Branch of the University of Florida.

In the spring of 1947, the legislature officially named the institution Florida State University and voted for it to remain coeducational. Immediately following this action, the students and the surrounding community helped form a football team, which would begin play the following year.

Between the first and second football games of the team's first season, the student body was asked to submit entries for the school nickname.

The suggestions were narrowed to six names: Golden Falcons, Statesmen, Crackers, Senators, Indians, and Seminoles. Seminoles prevailed as the nickname, eventually winning over the Statesmen name by 110 votes.

Florida State University was the first in the country to use the name Seminoles, which was chosen to represent Florida's Seminole Indians and their extravagant dress and exciting war dances.

Louisville Fighting Cardinals

University of Louisville
Louisville, KY 40292

School Colors: Cardinal and Black
Year Founded: 1798
Basketball: Freedom Hall (18,865)
Football: Cardinal Stadium (35,500)

THE UNIVERSITY OF LOUISVILLE originated in 1798 as Jefferson Seminary. It was later known as Louisville College, and in 1846 it received university status as a medical and law school.

Louisville's nickname came sometime after 1913 when the cardinal was chosen as the university's athletic symbol. The cardinal gave Louisville statewide identification, as it is the state bird of Kentucky. The team colors of cardinal and black were adopted at the suggestion of Mrs. John L. Patterson.

Sometime after 1921, Louisville's teams became known as the Fighting Cardinals, perhaps to instill the fierce, competitive attitude the university encourages.

Memphis State Tigers

Memphis State University
205 Athletic Office
Memphis, TN 38152

School Colors: Blue and Gray
Year Founded: 1912
Basketball: Mid-South Coliseum
                (11,200)
Football: Liberty Bowl Memorial
            Stadium (50,180)

MEMPHIS STATE UNIVERSITY first opened its doors to students in 1912 as West Tennessee State Normal School. Because it was a teacher's institution, the early athletic teams were called the Teachers.

After a successful 1915 football season, a spontaneous student parade took place. With banners flying and Normal yells and songs rending the atmosphere, the students in their exuberance shouted, "We fight like tigers," and a new nickname was born.

The name was immediately accepted around campus and in student publications. But the name did not catch on with the downtown Memphis newspapers, who continued to call the teams the Normals or the Blue and Gray.

In 1924, the Memphis papers finally began to use the name Tigers in print. But before the 1925 season began, the school was renamed West Tennessee State Teachers College and the players were once again referred to as the Teachers or Tudors.

In 1941, the school name was changed again—this time to Memphis State College—and the school retained the nickname Tigers once and for all.

South Carolina Fighting Gamecocks

University of South Carolina
1300 Rosewood Drive
Columbia, SC 29208

School Colors: Garnet and Black
Year Founded: 1801
Basketball: Carolina Coliseum (Frank McGuire Arena) (12,401)
Football: Williams-Brice Stadium (72,400)

THE UNIVERSITY OF SOUTH CAROLINA is the only major college athletic program in the country that uses Fighting Gamecocks as its official nickname and mascot.

Because South Carolina's athletic teams had struggled with poor records for more than a decade under numerous nicknames, the school's football team was unofficially dubbed the Game Cocks at the turn of the century. In 1903, Columbia's morning paper, *The State*, shortened the name to one word, and South Carolina teams have been the Gamecocks ever since.

Those early teams must have been a feisty and spirited group of men. A gamecock is a fighting rooster known for its spirit and courage. A cock fight, which was a popular sport throughout the United States in the 19th century, would last until the death of one of the combatants. This practice has been outlawed by most states for humanitarian reasons but is still held secretly in some areas.

The state of South Carolina has long been closely connected with the breeding and training of fighting gamecocks. One of the state's true heroes, Gen. Thomas Sumter, the famed guerrilla fighter of the revolutionary war, was known as the Fighting Gamecock.

Southern Mississippi Golden Eagles

University of Southern Mississippi
Southern Station, Box 5161
Hattiesburg, MS 39406

School Colors: Black and Gold
Year Founded: 1910
Basketball: Reed Green Coliseum
            (8,095)
Football: M. M. Roberts Stadium
            (33,000)

THE UNIVERSITY OF SOUTHERN MISSISSIPPI selected its current nickname as late as 1972.

Southern Mississippi's athletic teams prior to that year were known simply as the Southerners. The school nickname Golden Eagles was selected by the student body and active members of the alumni association and was officially announced during the school's homecoming festivities on November 11, 1972.

Virginia Tech Hokies

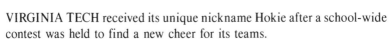

Virginia Polytechnic Institute and State
  University
P.O. Box 158
Blacksburg, VA 24060

School Colors: Chicago Maroon and
                   Burnt Orange
Year Founded: 1872
Basketball: Cassell Coliseum (10,000)
Football: Lane Stadium (51,000)

VIRGINIA TECH received its unique nickname Hokie after a school-wide contest was held to find a new cheer for its teams.

In 1896, senior O. M. Stull hollered his "hokie" yell and took first prize in the contest. Soon thereafter, the name Hokie was declared as the official nickname of the school and its students.

Stull's cheer is still performed at all Tech athletic events. When asked if hokie had any special meaning, Stull explained that the word was solely the product of his imagination and was used only as an attention getter for his cheer.

The official university colors, Chicago maroon and burnt orange, were also introduced in 1896. The colors were chosen because they made a unique combination and were not worn on any other campus at the time.

In 1912, team officials installed the Gobbler as the mascot for the football squad. The sight made such an impression on the fans and sports-writers that the name Gobblers also became an unofficial nickname for Tech athletic teams.

Manhattan Jaspers

15

Metro Atlantic Conference

Metro Atlantic Athletic Conference
One Lafayette Circle
Bridgeport, CT 06604

Number of Schools: 8
Year Founded: 1980
Charter Members: Fairfield, Fordham, Iona, Manhattan, St. Peter's, and U.S. Military Academy
Current Members: Fairfield, Fordham, Holy Cross, Iona, La Salle, Manhattan, St. Peter's, and U.S. Military Academy
Division I Sports: Baseball, Basketball, Cross-Country, Golf, Soccer, Swimming, and Tennis

Fairfield Stags

Fairfield University
Fairfield, CT 06430-7524

School Color: Cardinal Red
Year Founded: 1942
Basketball: Alumni Hall (3,022)

THE FAIRFIELD UNIVERSITY STAGS were named because of the beautiful environment in which the campus is located.

Fairfield is situated on a rolling, immensely wooded 200-acre campus overlooking Long Island Sound. When Fairfield's doors were opened in 1942, a school seal was designed featuring a deer leaping over a tumbling brook to represent the school's close ties with nature.

The name fits well as an athletic nickname because the stag is a good jumper and is spirited, fast, and agile, as Fairfield would like its players to be.

After seeing the school seal, the school's order of Jesuits selected Stags as the official nickname of Fairfield's athletic program.

Fordham Rams

Fordham University
East Fordham and Southern Boulevard
Bronx, NY 10458

School Colors: Maroon and White
Year Founded: 1841
Basketball: Rose Hill Gymnasium
            (3,200)
Football: Jack Coffey Field (10,000)

THE FORDHAM RAM is believed to have originated because of a school cheer that authorities thought was in bad taste.

Around the turn of the century at an Army-Fordham game in West Point, Army fans mocked a cheer the Fordham students were shouting. The short, expressive cheer was, "One dam, two dam, three dam, Fordham."

However, because school authorities objected to the language, it was later changed to "Ram! Ram! Ram! F-O-R-D-H-A-M! Fordham, Fordham, Fordham," a cheer that is still popular today.

The Ram has been Fordham's mascot since 1905 when the school introduced its first live ram mascot, Rameses. It has followed with the tradition ever since.

It is believed that Fordham and Harvard played a baseball game in New Haven, Connecticut, in 1874, to settle which school would get crimson and maroon as colors. Harvard won and picked crimson. Fordham therefore had to settle for maroon.

Holy Cross Crusaders

College of the Holy Cross
1 College Street
Worcester, MA 01610

School Color: Royal Purple
Year Founded: 1843
Basketball: Hart Center (4,000)
Football: Fitton Field (23,500)

THE NICKNAME CRUSADERS was first used at a Holy Cross athletic banquet in 1884, although it was not adopted as the official nickname until 41 years later.

Stanley Woodward, a sportswriter for the Boston *Herald*, is credited with reviving the name Crusaders in an article. Then on October 6, 1925, the Holy Cross student body elected Crusaders as their official nickname. The balloting was sponsored by the student newspaper, *The Tomahawk*, and the choice was virtually unanimous, winning over the other suggestions of Chiefs and Sagamores.

Chiefs was adopted by the school for a brief period, but its limited appeal led to its quick replacement. "Although interwoven with the Indian lore of Packachoag, it suggested nothing more than a whooping savage," commented *The Tomahawk*.

The formal adoption of Crusader as the school's nickname has suited the endeavors of Holy Cross athletes and students alike for generations.

Iona Gaels

Iona College
715 North Avenue
New Rochelle, NY 10801-1890

School Colors: Maroon and Gold
Year Founded: 1940
Basketball: Mulcahy Center (3,200)
Football: Memorial Field (10,000)

WHEN IONA COLLEGE was founded in 1940 by the Irish Christian Brothers, a tradition of strong Gaelic flavor was born on the campus. When the school began to participate in intercollegiate athletics two years later, it was natural that the Gaelic tradition continue.

Although it is not known exactly when and for what reason Gaels was chosen as the school's nickname, it is obvious it somehow emerged because of Iona's Gaelic history. Even today, most of the brothers are of Irish descent and all belong to the Irish Christian Brother order.

The original Iona logo featured a leprechaun twirling a basketball on one finger. Because this logo presented problems with sports such as football, hockey, and baseball, and because the Irish Christian Brothers felt the leprechaun was demeaning to the Irish, it was put to rest in 1987. In its place, a new logo featuring the interlocking school initials was developed.

La Salle Explorers

La Salle University
Hayman Hall
Philadelphia, PA 19141

School Colors: Blue and Gold
Year Founded: 1863
Basketball: The Palestra (9,200)

BECAUSE THERE IS no written document as to the origin of the La Salle Explorers' nickname, the university sports information department doesn't know its source.

However, Bob Lyons of the news bureau, who has been at La Salle for more than 30 years, remembered the story behind the name.

La Salle University itself was named after St. John the Baptist de La Salle, a French teacher who founded the Order of the Christian Brothers in the 1600s.

A newspaper writer covering a La Salle football game sometime between 1931 and 1941, when the school participated in the sport, is credited with naming the school teams. The sportswriter mistakenly assumed the name came from the French explorer La Salle, who navigated his way through the Ohio and Mississippi rivers, and dubbed the football team the Explorers.

The mistaken name stuck around the campus, and the school's sports teams have been known as the Explorers ever since.

Manhattan Jaspers

Manhattan College
Manhattan College Parkway
Riverdale, NY 10471

School Colors: Kelly Green and
White
Year Founded: 1853
Basketball: Draddy Coliseum (3,000)

MOST SPORTS FANS probably think that Manhattan's nickname, the Jaspers, comes from the tiny, opaque, crystalline quartz mineral. However, that's not the case at all.

The nickname is derived from Brother Jasper of Mary, a Christian Brother who first came to Manhattan in 1861. Appointed head of resident students, college archivers describe him as being "especially endowed for his work, having robust health and marvelous patience . . . a man of strict discipline, a man of vision and insight, a man worshipped by his students."

During his 31 years at Manhattan, Brother Jasper was responsible for initiating many cultural and athletic events. He organized a band, an orchestra, and a glee club; created literary clubs; and started an amateur talent night. He also introduced many sports to the campus, including baseball, which began in 1864.

But probably Brother Jasper's biggest accomplishment was that he established one of baseball's longest-standing traditions—the seventh-inning stretch.

At all Manhattan home games, Brother Jasper marched the entire student body to the field and seated them in the stands, telling them not to leave their seats if they wanted dinner that evening. Because he was both the coach and prefect of discipline, he had a tough time keeping all the students in line at once.

One hot, sticky day in the spring of 1882, Manhattan was playing the Metropolitans, a semipro club. It turned out the contest was a long, drawn-out affair. As the game passed the halfway mark, Brother Jasper noticed that the students were getting restless and unruly. So as the team came to bat in the seventh inning, he went over to the stands and told his pupils to stand, stretch, and move about for a minute or two. This eased the tension and unrest, and Brother Jasper repeated it in the rest of the games that season.

The student body soon made it a practice "to give it the old seventh-inning stretch." Since Manhattan played many of its games at the old Polo Grounds, the home of the Giants, it was soon passed on to the Giants and then the world of baseball.

This account of Brother Jasper's role in the seventh inning stretch is officially recognized by the Baseball Hall of Fame in Cooperstown, New York.

Because of his great loyalty and love for Manhattan College, school officials adopted the nickname Jaspers for all their athletic teams.

St. Peter's Peacocks

St. Peter's College
2641 Kennedy Boulevard
Jersey City, NJ 07306

School Colors: Blue and White
Year Founded: 1872
Basketball: Yanitelli Center (3,200)
Football: St. Peter's Field (3,200)

ST. PETER'S, the only school in the nation with the nickname Peacocks, chose its moniker for religious reasons.

According to the book *The Jesuit College in Jersey City* the peacock was selected as the school symbol by Father Gannon in December 1930. He chose the peacock for several reasons. The most important was because in mythology, the peacock committed itself to the flames of a funeral pyre and then was reborn with even more beauty.

To Father Gannon, there was a parallel between this myth and St. Peter's College, which practically had died in the flames of World War I. Then it rose again in blue and white, hopefully with more academic prowess and beauty.

The seal of the college was also designed in 1930. It was a peacock rising above a rock, two crossed keys, and the legend *in perpetuum*. The peacock is symbolic of the soul finding immortality after death, and the rock symbolizes the "rock" upon which the church is built. The keys represent the keys to heaven, and the words *in perpetuum* denote the hope of eternal life.

It should also be noted that the St. Peter's College nickname is altered for the female athletes, who are known as the Peahens.

United States Military Academy Black Knights

United States Military Academy
Howard Road, Building 639
West Point, NY 10996

School Colors: Black, Gold, and
              Gray
Year Founded: 1802
Basketball: Multi-Purpose Sports
              Facility (5,000)
Football: Michie Stadium (39,867)

THE UNITED STATES Military Academy's athletic team nickname, Black Knights, was chosen because of its relation to medieval times.

Many buildings on the West Point campus feature architecture of a medieval nature, with towering granite overlooking the green countryside.

The knight is a medieval soldier of high military rank. Because West Point is an institution where soldiers are "born," the name fits quite well. The Black Knight is dressed entirely in black and wears a black cape and helmet.

The formal nickname of the academy is the Black Knights of the Hudson, because of West Point's location on the river.

Although Black Knights is the official nickname for the academy's athletic teams, another school nickname is Cadets. The name Cadets is the term used to refer to all Army undergrads.

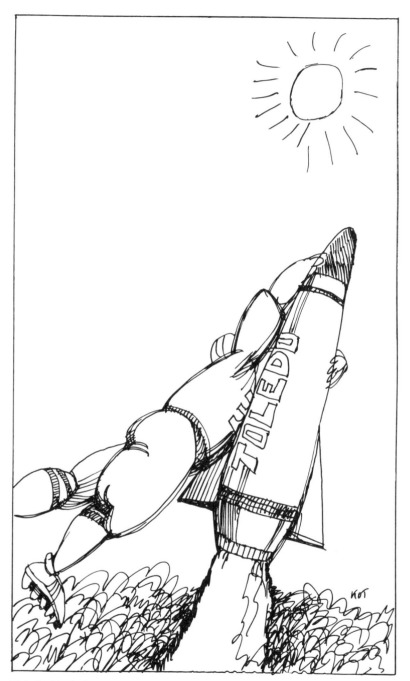

Toledo Rockets

16

Mid-American Conference

Mid-American Conference
Four Seagate, Suite 501
Toledo, OH 43604

Number of Schools: 9
Year Founded: 1946
Charter Members: Butler, Cincinnati, Ohio, Wayne State, and Western Reserve
Current Members: Ball State, Bowling Green, Central Michigan, Eastern Michigan, Kent State, Miami, Ohio, Toledo, and Western Michigan
Division I Sports: Baseball, Basketball, Swimming, Tennis, Track and Field, and Wrestling

Ball State Cardinals

Ball State University
Neely Avenue at North McKinley
Muncie, IN 47306

School Colors: Cardinal and White
Year Founded: 1918
Basketball: University Gymnasium
(7,000)
Health and Physical
Activity Complex (12,000)
Football: Ball State Stadium (16,319)

IN THE FALL of 1927, the students and faculty at Ball State Teachers College were growing tired of the drab Hoosieroons school nickname.

Shortly after, the school newspaper, *The Easterner*, sponsored a contest to select a new name and offered five dollars in gold to the person submitting the winning entry.

After careful analysis of all suggestions, the nine-student contest committee reported that no better school nickname had been found. Turned down were Indians, Ball Players, Flying Crimson, The Easterners, Braves, Scrappin' Teachers, and Ball Bullets.

A week later, Norman C. Wann and Coach Paul "Billy" Williams were talking about the nickname dilemma in the athletic office. Being a loyal fan of the St. Louis Cardinals baseball team, Williams commented that the Cardinal appearing on Rogers Hornsby's jersey was distinctive. Williams eventually submitted the name, and Cardinals became the new school nickname by a landslide over Indians, Delawares, and the former Hoosieroons nickname.

For submitting the winning entry, Coach Williams received the five-dollar gold prize.

Bowling Green State Falcons

Bowling Green State University
Bowling Green, OH 43403

School Colors: Brown and Orange
Year Founded: 1910
Basketball: Anderson Arena (5,000)
Football: Doyt L. Perry Field (30,599)

IN 1927, BOWLING GREEN *Sentinel Tribune* sports editor Doc Lake decided Bowling Green's nickname, Normal, was boring. So he decided to take this problem into his own hands.

Lake suggested that Bowling Green take on a new name. In one of his articles, he suggested that the school needed "something with a punch, something that represented power, courage, and skill . . . We will call [Bowling Green sports teams] the FALCONS!"

The new nickname took the campus by storm, and the fact that brown is both the color of the falcon and one of the school colors made Lake's suggestion even more appropriate. The falcon is very courageous and is known to be the best fighter of all birds. It is powerful, skillful, enduring, determined, and a natural-born fighter—just like Bowling Green expects its athletes to be.

Central Michigan Chippewas

Central Michigan University
122 Rowe Hall
Mount Pleasant, MI 48859

School Colors: Maroon and Gold
Year Founded: 1892
Basketball: Dan Rose Arena (6,000)
Football: Kelly/Shorts Stadium
            (20,086)

CENTRAL MICHIGAN UNIVERSITY sports teams were named after an Indian tribe located in the school's surrounding community.

The Chippewas are members of the Woodland Indians clan, located mainly in the Great Lakes area and Canada. The largest tribe of the Woodland Indians, the Chippewas were mainly a hunting and fishing tribe who also grew wild rice. Although not much is known of their exploits in battle, they did engage in many fierce revenge raids against other tribes.

A large Chippewa reservation is still located in the middle of the state, just east of Mount Pleasant.

Central Michigan's first official nickname was Dragons, which appeared in 1925. The student newspaper began calling the CMU athletes Bearcats three years later, and this name lasted until 1942, when student and faculty dissent finally led to the adoption of the name Chippewas.

The formal school name had changed more times than the nickname. It opened its doors as Central Michigan Normal and Business Institute in 1892 and was changed to Central Michigan Normal School in 1896 when students and athletes were then unofficially known as Normalites. The school has also been known as Central State Teachers College, Central Michigan College of Education, and Central Michigan College.

Eastern Michigan Hurons

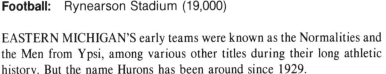

Eastern Michigan University
Bowen Field House
Ypsilanti, MI 48197

School Colors: Dark Green and
                                    White
Year Founded: 1849
Basketball: Bowen Field House
                        (5,600)
Football: Rynearson Stadium (19,000)

EASTERN MICHIGAN'S early teams were known as the Normalities and the Men from Ypsi, among various other titles during their long athletic history. But the name Hurons has been around since 1929.

The nickname first came into existence as a result of a contest held by the Men's Union. On October 31, 1929, a three-man committee of Dr. Clyde

Ford, Dr. Elmer Lyman, and Prof. Bert Peet selected the name Hurons from hundreds of entries. Finishing a very close second was Pioneers.

The winning entry was submitted by two students, Gretchen Borst and George Hanner. Hanner was working at the local Huron Hotel at the time of the contest and was no doubt influenced as much by his employer as by the Huron Indians of Michigan.

Kent State Golden Flashes

Kent State University
154 Memorial Gym
Kent, OH 44242

School Colors: Navy Blue and Gold
Year Founded: 1910
Basketball: Memorial Gymnasium
(6,034)
Football: Dix Stadium (30,520)

THE ORIGIN OF Kent State University's nickname has been a topic of debate for many years. Two possibilities are given for the source of this unusual nickname.

According to Phillip Shriver's book *The Years of Youth*, Merly Wagoner claims that the name change from Silver Foxes to Golden Flashes occurred in 1926, after the dismissal of Pres. John E. McGilvrey. McGilvrey owned a silver fox farm east of campus and thus the name Silver Foxes.

Following McGilvrey's departure, one of acting President T. Howard Winters's first tasks was to hold a contest to select a new nickname. With $25 offered as first prize, the suggestion Golden Flashes was chosen, although there was no special significance to the choice of the name. It was approved by the student body and faculty in time for the 1927 basketball season.

Another claim to the origin of the nickname came from Oliver Wolcott, a former football player who starred on the 1921 and 1922 teams. As sports editor of the Kent *Courier Tribune*, he felt the name Silver Foxes seemed too frail and tame for such a rugged group of athletes. So during the 1927 football season, he began referring to the team as the Golden Flashes.

Kent State's school colors of navy blue and gold came about purely by accident. When Kent State received its charter in 1910, the original colors were orange and purple. However, a local laundry service inadvertently changed the gawdy colors for them. The basketball jerseys, orange and purple when they went into the hot water, came back dark blue and gold.

Because money was tight in those days, the squad really had no choice but to wear the uniforms out on the floor. They soon got used to them, and the new combination drew such a great reception that the student body selected them as the official school colors.

Miami Redskins

Miami University
210 Millett hall
Oxford, OH 45056

School Colors: Red and White
Year Founded: 1809
Basketball: Millett Hall (9,800)
Football: Yager Stadium (25,183)

MIAMI UNIVERSITY'S nickname was taken from the school's close ties with the area Indians.

Miami University is named after the Miami Indian tribe who used to call the Oxford area home. Many surrounding areas are also named after the tribe, such as the Miami Valley, the Great Miami River, and the Little Miami River.

When athletics began at the university in the late 19th century, the school selected Redskins as its nickname in honor of the native tribes of the area.

In the early 1970s, some schools across the nation were forced to give up their Indian-related nicknames at the requests of Indians who thought it was demeaning to their culture. However, the Oxford campus received a document from the Miami Indian chief on the Oklahoma reservation stating that they were proud to allow Miami University to continue use of both the Miami and Redskins names.

Miami University's official mascot, Chief Miami, is portrayed by a student, often of Indian descent, who is sent to the Miami reservation in Oklahoma each summer to be educated in Miami war dances, folklore, and customs.

Ohio Bobcats

Ohio University
105 Convocation Center
Athens, OH 45701

School Colors: Kelly Green and
White
Year Founded: 1804
Basketball: Convocation Center
(13,000)
Football: Peden Stadium (20,000)

OHIO UNIVERSITY sports information officials have no records on why the name Bobcats was chosen. All they know is that the final decision was made via a contest.

In 1960, students in Lincoln Hall began the Bobcat mascot tradition. Strangely enough, 1960 marked the end of a 15-game winless streak against archrival Miami (of Ohio), highlighted by the appearance of Mr. Bobcat. He and his female counterpart, Bobkitten, can still be seen roaming the sidelines, boosting school spirit at Ohio basketball and football games.

In addition to the human mascots, Ohio University introduced a live bobcat to football fans in 1983. Sir Winsalot, as he was known, was owned by Ohio graduate Richard Widdis. Sir Winsalot entertained fans on football Saturdays and zoo goers in Columbus the rest of the week.

Ohio University's current athletic logo originated when athletic director Harold McElhany requested that a bobcat paw print be developed as a logo. Bob Besuden came up with the current logo after finding a paw print in an encyclopedia and modifying it to its current appearance.

Toledo Rockets

University of Toledo
2801 West Bancroft
Toledo, OH 43606-3390

School Colors: Midnight Blue and
Gold
Year Founded: 1872
Basketball: Centennial Hall (9,000)
Football: Glass Bowl Stadium
(18,500)

WHEN THE UNIVERSITY of Toledo played the powerful Carnegie Tech in football in 1923, Pittsburgh sports writers were shocked to learn that Toledo still did not have a school nickname.

As the underdog Toledo team fought an uphill battle against Tech, Pittsburgh sports writers, for their own amusement, pressed James Neal, a Toledo student working in the press box, to come up with a nickname for his school.

Despite losing to Tech 32–12, Neal was impressed with Toledo's flashy performance against such a dominant force and dubbed his team the Skyrockets. The name was shortened to Rockets and has been in use as the official school nickname ever since.

Prior to 1923, the teams were often referred to as the Blue and Gold, Munies (municipal), and Dwyer's Boys (named after Coach Dwyer).

Other suggestions for nicknames were rejected. The Spanish theme of toreadors or bulls—harking back to Toledo's sister relationship with the city's namesake in Spain—was one that was considered. Commodores, Turtles, Bancroft Highwaymen, and Jeeps were others that never quite caught on with the Toledo student body.

In 1961, the U.S. Army missile program donated a genuine rocket for Toledo's Glass Bowl Stadium. The one-ton rocket, carrying two sets of fins and a propellant booster capable of guiding the missile to supersonic velocities, was donated because of the university's affiliation with the Ordinance Corps of the U.S. Department of Army in its training of officers. The rocket still stands in front of the stadium.

Toledo's mascot, Rocky the Rocket, wears a flashy blue and gold rocket suit and often carries an extinguisher full of carbon dioxide.

Western Michigan Broncos

Western Michigan University
B-206 Ellsworth Hall
Kalamazoo, MI 49008

School Colors: Brown and Gold
Year Founded: 1903
Basketball: Read Field House (8,250)
Football: Waldo Stadium (25,000)

Western Michigan University

IN 1939, the athletic board of Western State Teachers College, now known as Western Michigan University, adopted Broncos as its official school nickname.

The former name Hilltoppers was often confused with other universities such as Western Kentucky, which used the same nickname. School officials wanted a more unusual name, and many suggestions were turned in for consideration.

The Broncos' nickname was submitted by assistant football coach John Gill. School officials probably chose the name Broncos because it best described WMU athletes and added a little more kick to their athletic program.

North Carolina A&T Aggies

17

Mid-Eastern Athletic Conference

Mid-Eastern Athletic Conference
P.O. Box 21205
Greensboro, NC 27420-1205

Number of Schools: 9
Year Founded: 1970
Charter Members: Delaware State, Howard, Maryland Eastern Shore, Morgan State, North Carolina A&T State, North Carolina Central, and South Carolina State
Current Members: Bethune-Cookman, Coppin State, Delaware State, Florida A&M, Howard, Maryland Eastern Shore, Morgan State, North Carolina A&T, and South Carolina State
Division I Sports: Baseball, Basketball, Football, Swimming, Tennis, and Track and Field

Bethune-Cookman Wildcats

Bethune-Cookman College
640 Second Avenue
Daytona Beach, FL 32015

School Colors: Maroon and Gold
Year Founded: 1923
Basketball: Moore Gymnasium
       (2,500)
Football: Memorial Stadium (10,000)

BETHUNE-COOKMAN COLLEGE took on the nationally popular nickname Wildcats when a school official selected it during the school's first academic year.

According to retired professor of sociology Edward R. Rodriguez, who faithfully served Bethune-Cookman College for 46 years, the name originated from Leon C. James. The school's first football coach and dean of students, James dubbed his team the Wildcats during the team's inaugural 1923 season.

Coppin State Eagles

Coppin State College
2500 West North Avenue
Baltimore, MD 21216

School Colors: Blue and Gold
Year Founded: 1900
Basketball: Coppin Center (3,000)

COPPIN STATE COLLEGE was originally a female teachers institution with no intercollegiate athletic program. There is unfortunately no information regarding the origin of the school nickname.

Sports information officials believe the name originated sometime in the early 1950s when men were first admitted to the school. One school official explained his belief that the eagle was chosen as the official mascot because it represents excellent athletic qualities and is a very proud bird, as Coppin State College is one of the proudest black colleges in the nation.

Delaware State Hornets

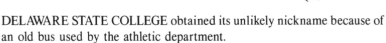

Delaware State College
1200 North DuPont Highway
Dover, DE 19901-2275

School Colors: Columbia Blue and
                    Red
Year Founded: 1891
Basketball: Memorial Hall (3,000)
Football: Alumni Stadium (5,000)

DELAWARE STATE COLLEGE obtained its unlikely nickname because of an old bus used by the athletic department.

Although there is no written history, old-timers believe the name was derived in the early 1940s from an old yellow bus used by the athletic department to transport Delaware State athletes. The athletes nicknamed the old bus the Hornet, which also reflects the campus location in an area where many hornets' nests are prevalent.

From that point on, the athletes, the student newspaper, and other college publications adopted the nickname Hornets. It was officially adopted by the students in 1942.

It should be noted that Delaware State's athletic dormitory, which bears the formal name Conwell Hall, has a very colorful Hornets' Nest sign at its front entrance.

Florida A&M Rattlers

Florida A&M University
P.O. Box 982
Tallahassee, FL 32307

School Colors: Orange and Green
Year Founded: 1887
Basketball: Gaither Athletic Center
          (3,855)
Football: Bragg Memorial Stadium
          (25,000)

THERE ARE TWO THEORIES about the origin of the Florida A&M University Rattlers' nickname.

The first account claims that when the land was cleared for the Tallahassee campus back in 1887, there was nothing on the site but palmetto trees and rattlesnakes. One source says the Rattlers' moniker was adopted because of all the rattlesnakes found in the area.

Another story says that former President Dr. J. R. E. Lee sought a name for the school's athletic teams that "would strike fear in the hearts of our opponents." As a result, he came up with the idea of a rattlesnake—and the name Rattlers.

Howard Bison

Howard University
Burr Gymnasium
Washington, DC 20059

School Colors: Navy Blue and White
Year Founded: 1867
Basketball: Burr Gym (3,900)
Football: William H. Green Memorial
          Stadium (7,500)

PEOPLE HAVE BEEN CONFUSED about Howard University's nickname, the Bison, for years. There are two possible explanations as to how the rare moniker originated.

A bison is a large, shaggy-maned animal most commonly recognized as the American buffalo. One theory explains that Bison was a nickname that Indians bequeathed to black regiments during the Indian Wars because these soldiers represented the very best when it came to a fighting spirit. The name Bison was eventually carried over to Howard, a predominantly black institution.

Another account stems from the research of Dr. W. E. Morrison, who also proposed the Indian War theory. According to the 1966 edition of *The H-Book*, the student handbook, Howard had previously been assigned to the federal government's Department of the Interior for budgetary purposes. The school eventually chose the symbol of that department, the bison, as its mascot.

It should also be noted that many professional and semiprofessional teams in all-black leagues used the nickname Bison before the integration of major-league baseball in 1947, when Jackie Robinson of the Brooklyn Dodgers broke the race barrier.

Maryland Eastern Shore Hawks

University of Maryland Eastern Shore
P.O. Box 1041 UMES
Princess Anne, MD 21853

School Colors: Maroon and Gray
Year Founded: 1886
Basketball: Tawes Gymnasium (2,500)

SCHOOL OFFICIALS AT the University of Maryland Eastern Shore had no clue as to why Hawks was chosen as the school's official nickname. But retired professor Richard Thomas, who was affiliated with Eastern Shore for 38 years, remembered the story.

Thomas, an industrial arts training professor, was recognized as a recruiter, information director, manager, and one of the best fans that ever watched the school's teams play. Each day after teaching, Thomas would walk over to the football field and watch the very successful teams scrimmage.

Thomas recalled that the Hawks' name emerged in 1947 or 1948 when he and a few others started thinking about a name that could be used to best describe the football teams. While looking for an animal or bird native to the shores of Maryland, someone suggested the moniker Hawks.

"We decided upon the Hawk because it is a vicious bird that is fearless and a great fighter," explained Thomas. "It described the ball club well."

Morgan State Bears

Morgan State University
301 Truth Hall
Baltimore, MD 21239

School Colors: Royal Blue and
                    Orange
Year Founded: 1867
Basketball: Hill Field House (5,500)
Football: Hughes Stadium (10,000)

ALTHOUGH NO ONE really knows for sure, it is believed the Morgan State University Bears' nickname was the brainchild of the school's colorful and spirited football coach, Talmadge Hill.

According to Daniel Clark, a five-year letter winner in football and a 1930 graduate, the name probably emerged from Coach Hill. A 1928 graduate of Morgan State, Hill became assistant football coach in the early 1930s.

Governor Hill, as he liked to be called, had a way with words. In fact, he nearly always was able to come up with colorful nicknames for everybody and everything. A smart, dedicated, leading figure in the Baltimore area, he was well liked by everyone. But the thing Hill was best known for was his ability to arouse the spirit of his boys while showing them how to have fun playing football.

So it is thought that Hill was the one who came up with the nickname Grizzly Bears for the Morgan State teams.

The teams were also called Golden Bears at one time because of the former team colors. Grizzly was eventually dropped, but the Bears moniker still represents Morgan State athletics.

North Carolina A&T Aggies

North Carolina A&T State University
1601 East Market Street
Greensboro, NC 27411

School Colors: Royal Blue and Gold
Year Founded: 1891
Basketball: E. F. Corbett Center
              (7,500)
Football: Aggie Stadium (16,500)

IT IS QUITE OBVIOUS that the nickname Aggies was chosen to represent
the school's athletes because the school's official name is North Carolina
Agricultural and Technical State University. However, the background
behind its fierce mascot, the bulldog, is a bit more exciting.

In Albert W. Spruill's book, *Great Recollections From Aggieland*, he
explains the origins of the nickname.

There was a student in school at the time named Ezra Pembleton who
had suffered the misfortune of having his legs cut off. Hailing from
Salisbury, Pembleton was a breeder of bulldogs and had some of the most
vicious dogs found anywhere. One of his dogs in particular, named Major
Brown, was his constant companion. Major Brown went to all Pembleton's
classes and trailed him everywhere. If anyone dared to touch his master,
that person would certainly feel the wrath of Major Brown.

One account relates that during the 1920s, unruly spectators at athletic
events were known to hit players and referees with sticks as well as fight
with teachers. During a close football contest with Virginia Union, referee
L. G. Gibson made a controversial call in A&T's favor. The Virginia
spectators did not like the ruling and wanted to jump the referee.

While the scuffle with the referee took place, Pembleton and his dog
were sitting near the scene. The dog probably thought someone was trying
to attack his master and tore into the fight. L. G. Gibson was somehow
singled out by Major Brown; the dog lunged at the referee and soon had him
on the ground fearing for his life. A&T was later severely reprimanded for
the incident.

It should also be noted that even after the game the Virginia Union
spectators still wanted to attack the referee, and two A&T fans, Cambell
and DeHughley, protected him. Cambell quickly went home and returned

with his pistol, daring anyone to come close to Gibson. DeHughley felt this was the incident that led the school to be called the Bulldogs.

The other version of the bulldog story states that an old shepherd dog that assisted in herding the college's cattle and other animals into shelter was frequently seen on campus. When a new herdsman was employed on the school farm in the 1920s, he brought along a bulldog.

The bulldog was brought on a leash to a big football game. During the game, the Aggies' fullback broke through the line time and time again to score touchdown after touchdown, only to have the referee call them all back on penalties. During the final few minutes, the bruising fullback ran up the middle and scored a touchdown. A big roar naturally thundered from the Aggies, but as the noise clamored to a hush, the referee signed the touchdown "no good."

"We can't win anyway," the boys concluded, "so we might as well admit it; but there's absolutely no fairness in the way the officiating has been done."

At that moment, someone untied the bulldog and he tore into the referee, wrestled him to the ground, and began to work him over.

It almost cost A&T membership from the CIAA, but it is also accepted as the day the Bulldog mascot was born. Over the years, A&T has become less "bullish" with the athletic referees.

South Carolina State Bulldogs

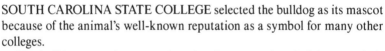

South Carolina State College
300 College Avenue
Orangeburg, SC 29117

School Colors: Garnet and Blue
Year Founded: 1896
Basketball: Smith-Hammond-
Middleton Memorial
Center (3,200)
Football: Oliver C. Dawson Bulldog
Stadium (14,000)

SOUTH CAROLINA STATE COLLEGE selected the bulldog as its mascot because of the animal's well-known reputation as a symbol for many other colleges.

The bulldog was chosen as the school's mascot in 1919 because it is known for its vigor and tenacity as well as equable disposition. The first logo was a stand-up bulldog holding a football in his paws since football was the first intercollegiate sport at the school. Numerous logos have been used since, but most common is the one portraying the bulldog with the letters *SC* across his sweater.

A compact, muscular, short-haired animal, the bulldog is a breed that was developed in England. It is very powerful and stubborn against resistance, and it attacks its foes with a methodical deliberation and fierceness.

Loyola Runnin' Ramblers

18

Midwestern Collegiate Conference

Midwestern Collegiate Conference
Pan American Plaza
201 South Capitol Avenue, Suite 500
Indianapolis, IN 46225

Number of Schools: 8
Year Founded: 1979
Charter Members: Butler, Evansville, Loyola, Oklahoma City, Oral Roberts, and Xavier
Current Members: Butler, Dayton, Detroit, Evansville, Loyola, Marquette, St. Louis, and Xavier
Division I Sports: Baseball, Basketball, Cross-Country, Golf, Indoor Track, Soccer, Swimming, and Tennis

Butler Bulldogs

Butler University
4600 Sunset Avenue
Indianapolis, IN 46208

School Colors: Blue and White
Year Founded: 1855
Basketball: Hinkle Fieldhouse (15,000)
Football: Butler Bowl (20,000)

BUTLER UNIVERSITY obtained its nickname through the relentless sarcasm of two student newspaper editors.

In the days before World War I, Butler played most of its football games against teams from the Indiana College Athletic League. Franklin, a neighboring institution, always provided a peppery brand of fight and was Butler's biggest rival.

The 1919 season was a tough one for Butler. The football team was without a regular coach following the 1918 season in which several teams who had never come close in previous years defeated Butler. But the defeats only seemed to pull the student body together and the "Butler Renaissance" soon began.

Butlerites were not only tired of the slaughter, but also of the name Christians for the football team. The name was undignified and not suited for the gridiron occasion.

Before the annual game with the Franklin Baptists, spirits were high. There was no love lost between Franklin head coach John Thurber and the Butler student body, and it was thought that any cuts on Thurber would be received with delight by the entire campus.

Alex Cavins was editor of the weekly student newspaper, *The Collegian*, at the time, and the talented George Dickson was the staff cartoonist. The staff felt something hot must be conceived for the weekly pep rally before the big game.

A Butler fraternity owned a bulldog named Shimmy who wandered into the newspaper office the night before publication. "Hey," said a staff member, "there's the idea!"

After the staff put their heads together, a big one-page cartoon by Dickson showed Shimmy the bulldog, labeled "Butler," taking a big bite out of the pants seat of a figure labeled "John the Baptist," referring to Thurber. The caption read, "Bring on That Platter, Salome."

The name Bulldogs stuck. Incidentally, Shimmy the bulldog did engage a Franklin mongrel in combat at halftime during the big game on Saturday. But nobody remembers who won.

Dayton Flyers

University of Dayton
300 College Park
Dayton, OH 45469

School Colors: Red and Blue
Year Founded: 1850
Basketball: UD Arena (13,500)
Football: Welcome Stadium (11,000)

THE STORY BEHIND the University of Dayton Flyers' nickname dates back to 1923, when three of the Catholic school's brothers took a stroll around the school's cinder track.

Prior to 1922, during the heyday of Dayton's initiation into big-time football, Dayton's athletic teams had been called the Hilltoppers, Red and Blue, Saints, School on the Hill, South Parkers, Varsity, and Daytonians. None of these monikers properly suited the faculty and students, and as Dayton entered the center ring of intercollegiate athletics, ideas for new nicknames were passed around.

One afternoon in 1923, three Dayton brothers, Charles Arns, Charles Belz, and Dr. Edgar Cullen, happened to be walking on the quarter-mile cinder track and were discussing their ideas for a new athletic title that could be easily incorporated into yells, songs, and newspaper articles.

Because Dayton is known for aviation, and especially for being the birthplace and home of the founders of flight, the Wright brothers, the three were contemplating nicknames relating to aviation. The Aviators and Daytonians were proposed by the group until Brother Arns suggested the nickname Flyers. It was short and could easily be worked into a yell. The name Flyers was officially adopted by the university in 1923, but actual use came slowly.

On November 20, 1980, Dayton's latest mascot was born. The new campaign, known as Flyerball, was intended to get fans "flyered up," according to Student Association director of entertainment Bill Coley. "We want fans to yell, scream, shout, and generally have a good time at a game," Coley said. "Fan enthusiasm has a positive effect on the team to play better basketball."

The Flyerball concept involved the introduction of a school mascot, which was developed over the course of the preceding year. The mascot, an exaggeration of a 1920s barnstormer, was portrayed by cheerleader Rick Cengeri. The barnstormer costume was designed by the same company that made the mascot attire for DePaul, Indiana, Duke, and many other schools around the country.

Detroit Titans

University of Detroit
4001 West McNichols Road
Detroit, MI 48221-9987

School Colors: Red and White
Year Founded: 1877
Basketball: Calihan Hall (8,837)

PRIOR TO 1919, University of Detroit athletic teams were known as the Tigers. Because the Detroit major-league baseball team went by the same name, things grew rather complicated in the Motor City.

In the fall of 1919, the Detroit *Free Press* assigned reporter Stan Brink to cover one of the school's Saturday football games. He was also told to come up with a nickname to use in the next day's wrap-up.

Since the members of the 1919 squad were exceptionally large, Brink thought a good nickname for the team would be Titans.

In Greek mythology, the Titans were a class of people who supposedly had almost perfect physiques. Whether Brink's comparison was correct or not, the name has remained with the University of Detroit ever since.

Evansville Purple Aces

University of Evansville
1800 Lincoln Avenue
Evansville, IN 47722

School Colors: Purple and White
Year Founded: 1864
Basketball: Roberts Stadium (11,096)
Football: Arad McCutchan Stadium
(4,000)

THE UNIVERSITY OF EVANSVILLE'S nickname, the Aces, was acquired after an opposing coach cracked a joke after losing.

Dan Scism, the sportswriter credited with first using the name Aces in headlines, said he did so at the suggestion of coach John Harmon in 1926. "Prior to that the Aces had been called Pioneers," Scism said. "But Coach Harmon suggested I call them the Aces because he was told by Louisville's coach that he didn't have four aces up his sleeve, he had five!"

In the late 1960s, Larry Hill, an artist for the Evansville *Press*, created the first mascot, Ace Purple, in the image of a turn-of-the-century riverboat gambler, which represented Evansville's location on the banks of the Ohio River.

To say the least, the first Ace was not a very likable guy, as he walked around brandishing a club with a spike through one end and possessed a penchant for pulling out a derringer pistol and blowing his enemies into the next card party. The university community was not pleased with this representation of the school, and Ace Purple soon vanished from the scene.

In 1977, when Evansville moved to Division I basketball, first-year sports information director Greg Knipping saw the need for a team mascot. He contacted Keith Butz, who is known for revamping the Purdue Boilermaker. Knipping provided Butz with pictures of the old Ace Purple, and his fertile imagination produced the current mascot.

Knipping's next task was to sell the idea to the school administration. Evansville is a United Methodist institution, and some trustees were concerned with the gambling image. However, Knipping quickly pointed out that qualities of the gambler are also used widely on the athletic field: cunning, daring, a quick wit, and shrewd judgment.

Knipping succeeded in reviving Ace Purple but never saw his dream mascot perform. He lost his life along with the entire Ace basketball team in the tragic December 13, 1977, plane crash. But when the Aces took the court the following autumn, Ace Purple was there, reviving the true spirit and legacy of the beloved Aces team.

Loyola Runnin' Ramblers

Loyola University of Chicago
6525 North Sheridan Road
Chicago, IL 60626

School Colors: Maroon and Gold
Year Founded: 1871
Basketball: International
            Amphitheatre (10,000)

LOYOLA'S NICKNAME dates back to the days when football was king of the campus.

Prior to the 1920s, all Loyola athletic teams were known by their school colors, thus they were called the Maroon and Gold. But in 1925, the school's football coach, along with the student newspaper, conducted a contest to find a livelier name for the football team.

The winning entry was the Grandees, which ties in to the Spanish origins of St. Ignatius of Loyola. However, this name apparently evoked little enthusiasm and did not catch on even after many months of use.

In 1926, school officials finally gave Loyola's teams their present nickname, the Ramblers. The school's football team used the name that season as they traveled over the United States, and it stuck. Even though football was dropped in 1930, the nickname is still proudly used by today's Loyola athletic teams.

Loyola recently added the prefix Runnin' to the nickname, and the teams are now known as the Runnin' Ramblers.

Marquette Warriors

Marquette University
1212 West Wisconsin Avenue
Milwaukee, WI 53233

School Colors: Royal Blue and Gold
Year Founded: 1881
Basketball: Bradley Center (18,600)

MARQUETTE UNIVERSITY represents the spirit, dignity, and strength of the name Warriors, which was first adopted by the Student Senate on May 13, 1954, after a 20-game search for a new name.

Warriors replaced the formerly used school nickname Golden Avalanche and Hilltoppers, which never seemed to quite fit the traditional style of the university.

The American Indian warrior was selected as the school mascot rather than a Spartan or Amazon warrior because the original inhabitants of North America were Indians and, more important, because the school was named after Father Jacques Marquette. Father Marquette came into direct contact with the American Indians during his North American explorations in the 17th century.

The suit of the First Warrior, Marquette's mascot, was chosen to represent six Wisconsin Woodland tribes: Chippewa, Menominee, Oneida, Winnebago, Stockbridge-Munsee, and Potawotami.

The current logo was developed over a two-year period and involved considerable thought and inspiration from students, administrators, and faculty alike. If you look carefully at the logo, you see key elements of the First Warrior's outfit, which, incidentally, can be worn only by a Marquette student of Indian descent: a wolf hood, worn by specific groups within Indian tribes and bearing an important spiritual meaning, and an eagle feather, held in place by a deer bone and representing special spiritual significance.

St. Louis Billikens

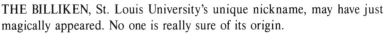

St. Louis University
3672 West Pine Boulevard
St. Louis, MO 63108

School Colors: Blue and White
Year Founded: 1818
Basketball: Kiel Auditorium (9,229)

THE BILLIKEN, St. Louis University's unique nickname, may have just magically appeared. No one is really sure of its origin.

In 1909, The Billiken Company of Chicago manufactured the Billiken— a little bullet-headed creature with pixie ears, grinning mouth, and rotund belly—in the form of savings banks and statuettes after the image was designed by a Kansas City art teacher.

The Billiken symbol of good luck also was turned into basque dolls, clay incense burners, marshmallow candies, metal banks, hat pins, watch fobs, salt and pepper shakers, belt buckles, pickle forks, and glass bottles. The Billiken was the rage of the nation for six months. But by 1912, the Billiken fad was for all practical purposes a memory.

Several theories link the odd name to St. Louis University. One involves Billy Gunn, who owned a drug store near Federal League Baseball Park, which was a hangout for writers and sports fans alike. According to a 1946 obituary, he was a "short, bespectacled man with a lively wit and an accurate memory for sports events and results, was friend and confidant not only to SLU players, but also to the coaches."

It was also written in the obituary that "Gunn gave the St. Louis University athletic teams their nickname. Coach Bender walked into Mr. Gunn's drug store one afternoon and was greeted by the proprietor with: 'Bender, you're a real Billiken!' Billy O'Connor, a noted sportswriter who was there, took up the name for Bender and eventually the university teams became known as the Billikens."

Another account indicates the nickname originated at football practice. One day at practice, as Charles McNamara and O'Connor looked on, the St. Louis squad executed its plays with such zest and finesse that Coach Bender was all smiles. Bender's sparkling broad grin and squinty eyes so impressed O'Connor that he exclaimed: "Why, Bender's a regular Billiken!"

McNamara later drew a cartoon of Bender in the form of a Billiken and posted it in Gunn's campus drugstore. Members of the football team were soon known as Bender's Billikens.

No one is sure exactly which story is accurate, but it is believed that the name Bender's Billikens was first seen in print during the 1910–11 football season.

One last note: buying a Billiken doll gives the buyer luck. Having one given to you leads to better luck. But the best luck comes to you if you stole the Billiken you have. St. Louis officials say they stole the Billiken from a world that forgot too soon about the "god of things as they ought to be."

Some schools have more trouble finding nicknames than others. Marquette University spent more than 20 years trying to dream up a replacement for its Hilltoppers' nickname.

Xavier Musketeers

Xavier University
3800 Victory Parkway
Cincinnati, OH 45207

School Colors: Blue and White
Year Founded: 1831
Basketball: Cincinnati Gardens
(10,400)
Schmidt Fieldhouse
(4,157)

THE XAVIER UNIVERSITY Musketeers' nickname was chosen by a faculty member because of the school's strong ties with France.

Following a directive from the school's Board of Trustees, Rev. Francis J. Finn, S.J., proposed the name Musketeers as the school nickname in 1925. It was immediately adopted and has been used ever since.

As Father Finn reasoned, the Musketeer, a dedicated guard to the king of France, was a fine symbol of the qualities that should inspire students and particularly the athletic teams at Xavier. Because of the university's long French history, he felt the name ideally suited both the students and faculty.

The Jesuit reverend Joseph Pierre de Bonnecamps, one of the school's first priests, was also one of the first Europeans to navigate past the Ohio River, in 1749. It is said that Ohio owes the first map of her state boundaries to him.

Among the first students at Xavier in the 1830s were French-speaking young men from Louisiana, who were forbidden by college officials to use their family tongue in recreational activities unless they first learned the English language.

The first Jesuit priest of Xavier, in 1840, was Father John Anthony Elet, a native of the French-speaking provinces of Belgium.

The great university patron, St. Francis Xavier, a native of Spain, received his formal education at the College of St. Barbe at the University of Paris. In 1540, he helped found the Jesuit Order in Paris.

Is it Broncs or Broncos? It really depends on which schools you are talking about. **Broncs** *is the correct spelling for Pan American and Rider (now there's a school that really goes with a horse name). However, the form* **Broncos** *is preferred by Boise State, Western Michigan, and Santa Clara.*

Witchita State Shockers

19

Missouri Valley Conference

Missouri Valley Conference
200 North Broadway, Suite 1905
St. Louis, MO 63102

Number of Schools: 8
Year Founded: 1908
Charter Members: Iowa, Kansas, Missouri, and Washington–St. Louis
Current Members: Bradley, Creighton, Drake, Illinois State, Indiana State, Southern Illinois, Tulsa, and Wichita State
Division I Sports: Baseball, Basketball, Cross-Country, Golf, Indoor Track, Tennis, and Track and Field

Bradley Braves

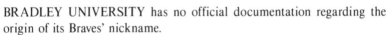

Bradley University
1501 West Bradley Avenue
Peoria, IL 61625

School Colors: Red and White
Year Founded: 1897
Basketball: Carver Arena (10,470)

BRADLEY UNIVERSITY has no official documentation regarding the origin of its Braves' nickname.

The private Peoria institution was founded in 1897 by Mrs. Lydia Moss Bradley, who wished to establish a lasting memorial to her husband and six children.

Bradley sports information department officials attribute the nickname Braves to Illinois's long history with the American Indians. When Illinois was a territory, the area was home to a large number of Indians. Sometime in the 1950s, the moniker Braves was chosen to represent the school's athletic teams.

Illinois, which is the Algonquin word for men or warriors, is also remembered for the Black Hawk War in 1832. Chief Black Hawk led the Sauk Indians in a two-year battle against the Illinois State Militia over land disagreements in which the Fox and Sauk Indians were forced to relocate west of the Mississippi River.

Creighton Bluejays

Creighton University
California at Twenty-fourth Street
Omaha, NE 68178

School Colors: Blue and White
Year Founded: 1878
Basketball: Civic Auditorium (9,373)

CREIGHTON UNIVERSITY OBTAINED its Bluejays' nickname through a 1924 newspaper contest. Prior to 1924, Creighton's athletic squads were known as the Hilltoppers. Feeling a need for a more colorful nickname, the Omaha *Bee* assisted the athletic board and alumni association in finding a new title by asking readers to send in suggestions. After reviewing more than 200 entries, the athletic board decided on Bluejays because of its close relationship to the school's blue and white colors.

The current Creighton logo, Billy Bluejay, was designed in 1941 by alumnus Joseph P. Murphy, who wanted to portray the bird with a more human stance and determined expression. Murphy's logo replaced the original Bluejay logo depicting a "birdwatcher's bluejay."

Drake Bulldogs

Drake University
Drake Fieldhouse
Des Moines, IA 50311

School Colors: Blue and White
Year Founded: 1881
Basketball: Veterans Memorial
            Stadium (11,679)
Football: Drake Stadium (18,000)

DRAKE UNIVERSITY acquired its current nickname from one of the early football coach's favorite pets. For Drake University's sake, they should be glad he wasn't crazy about guinea pigs.

When coach John L. Griffith arrived at Drake in 1908, he brought along two playful bulldogs that followed him everywhere—even out on the football field during afternoon practices.

Coach Griffith, who really couldn't look out for his dogs during games, allowed a willing student to parade them around on a leash during games. As a result, Art Gordon, sports editor of the Des Moines *Register*, dubbed the team "veritable Bulldogs."

The name Bulldogs was used at a pep rally before the 1909 Drake-Missouri football game, and both the students and fans liked it. Prior to 1909, Drake athletes were known as Ducklings, Drakes, Ganders, and Tigers.

Illinois State Redbirds

Illinois State University
Hovey Hall 401
Normal, IL 61761-6901

School Colors: Red and White
Year Founded: 1857
Basketball: Horton Field House
            (7,700)
Football: Hancock Stadium (15,000)

THESE DAYS, when school teachers are frequently walking the picket lines, it might be appropriate to call a team the Fighting Teachers. However, Clifford E. "Pop" Horton, physical education and health director, didn't think the name struck too fierce a note for Illinois State teams back in the early days.

When Horton arrived at Illinois State in 1923, the teams were known as the Teachers. He immediately wanted to change the name, and since the colors were cardinal and white, he wanted to call his teams the Cardinals.

The teams were known as the Cardinals for only a short time, since it was soon learned there would be a headline conflict between the St. Louis baseball Cardinals and Illinois State. Brick Young, sports editor of the Bloomington *Pantagraph*, was responsible for changing the name from the Cardinals to Redbirds to avoid further confusion.

"There was no trouble over dropping the name of Teachers," Horton said with a grin. "The fact of the matter is, I never heard a word about it. Everybody accepted the change. I thought it was right. In the long run, Redbirds has turned out to be a very desirable title. I'm very pleased about it."

Indiana State Sycamores

Indiana State University
Fifth and Chestnut
Terre Haute, IN 47809

School Colors: Columbia Blue and
White
Year Founded: 1865
Basketball: Hulman Center (10,200)
Football: Memorial Stadium (20,500)

INDIANA STATE UNIVERSITY obtained its Sycamores' nickname in 1921, when university officials sponsored a student body contest to name the athletic teams. To attract contestants, a three-dollar cash prize was offered to the student who submitted the winning nickname. The suggestions were narrowed down to three nicknames, and the students voted on ISU's Blue and White Day.

The students booed when the name Sycamores was placed on the ballot, but then apparently as a prank, voted for it in a landslide election.

When the name was first incorporated into ISU athletics, the Sycamore represented the common shade tree. However, somewhere along the line, someone told officials about the legendary Sycamore Indians. As a result, Indiana State soon adopted the athletic logo of an Indian head and headdress. However, studies have shown there was never any Sycamore Indian tribe. Years ago, the official university logo was changed to the outline of a Sycamore leaf.

The athletic department retained the Indian logo though. Officials simply did not believe a leaf could properly represent the ISU fighting teams.

Southern Illinois Salukis

Southern Illinois University
SIU Arena
Carbondale, IL 62901

School Colors: Maroon and White
Year Founded: 1869
Basketball: SIU Arena (10,014)
Football: McAndrew Stadium (17,324)

SOUTHERN ILLINOIS probably has one of the most confusing nicknames in the collegiate ranks. Jerry Isenberg, a perplexed reporter for the Newark *Star-Ledger*, wrote:

> Princeton has its Tiger; B.C. has its Eagle
> Rutgers is the Queensmen, a title truly regal
> But from frigid New York City to Kentucky's old Paduchee
> There's just one burning question—what the hell is a Saluki?

After 40 years of using the boring nickname Maroons, students at Southern Illinois wanted a more unusual nickname. Early in 1951, students began voting on various names, such as Knights, Egyptians, Marauders, and Rebels but could not reach a decision.

Finally, members of the athletic department, namely Abe Martin, Doc Lingle, Lynn Holder, Bill Waller, and Cecil Franklin, called a meeting of athletes and faculty representatives to introduce a new name—the Salukis.

Undoubtedly, there was a never-ending ordeal of explaining what a Saluki was and what relationship it truly held with SIU at that meeting. But some questions were cleared up. First of all, the saluki is a descendant of the famous aluki hunting dog, which dates back to ancient Egypt. The saluki, the world's fastest dog, is known for its speed and endurance, having reached speeds of 45 miles per hour. It is also the oldest pure breed in the world, existing as long ago as 3600 B.C.

Second, the name Saluki ties in with southern Illinois because the dog, which hails from Egypt, could represent the bottom third of the state of Illinois, known as Little Egypt. In Baker Brownell's *The Other Illinois*, he explains, "Although the legend probably was invented after the fact, it is persistent. There was a drought in the northern counties. . . . The wheat fields dried up, the streams died in their beds. But in southern Illinois rain fell and there were good crops, and from the north came people seeking corn and wheat as to Egypt of old. Thus the name, Egypt."

Southern Illinois's first mascot, King Tut, was killed by an automobile in 1954. At the 1956 homecoming football game, W. W. Vandemeer, an SIU alumnus, presented SIU with two pure-bred saluki pups.

The male, Burydown Datis, was whelped in England, and the female, Ornah Farouk, was a direct descendant of a champion from King Ibn Saud's own royal kennels in Saudi Arabia. Present mascots at SIU are the descendants of these first salukis.

Tulsa Golden Hurricane

University of Tulsa
600 South College Avenue
Tulsa, OK 74104

School Colors: Old Gold, Royal Blue, and Crimson
Year Founded: 1894
Basketball: Maxwell Convention Center (9,200)
Football: Skelly Stadium (44,210)

TULSA'S CURRENT NICKNAME, the Golden Hurricane, was the result of a football coach's enterprising scheme to gain the utmost publicity for his team.

The story behind Tulsa's nickname is described in Robert Rutland's 1952 book, *The Golden Hurricane—Fifty Years at the University of Tulsa.*

In 1922, football coach Howard Archer arrived in Tulsa with his knowledge of football, great optimism, and an eight-cylinder automobile. Any coach in those days who owned a high-powered automobile must be successful, wide-eyed Tulsans reckoned.

Oddly enough, it was during Archer's inaugural season that the team began playing under the tag Yellow Jackets. The origin of this name came from an innovative, energetic second-string squad member who was campus correspondent for a Tulsa newspaper. Since Tulsa was wearing new black and yellow jerseys instead of their traditional black and orange, the player-reporter dubbed the team Yellow Jackets in one of his articles.

After defeating Texas Christian 21–0 in the opening game of the season, Archer realized the potential of his team and was eager to publicize the outstanding efforts of his boys. The "name" affair had given him an idea: why not officially adopt a name and stick to it?

Since 1895, Tulsa athletic teams had been known by the term Kendallites, although they had also been referred to as Presbyterians, Tigers, Orange and Black, Tulsans, and now Yellow Jackets.

Archer, ecstatic with his new idea, wanted a more distinctive name for his team. He checked the records and after a remark about "roaring through opponents," he seriously considered the name Golden Tornadoes. But further research showed Georgia Tech already had chosen that tag in 1917.

Tulsa was in the process of preparing for an important game against Texas A&M, and Archer quickly wanted a new title for the Texas sportswriters to use. From the Tornado, he evolved the name meteorologically into Hurricane.

A few days before the team left for Dallas, he asked the squad to vote for the Golden Hurricane as their official nickname. Everyone on the team approved, except the second string player-reporter who felt his Yellow Jacket moniker was getting the raw end of the deal.

Tulsa, under the Golden Hurricane nickname for the first time, stormed over the favored Texas A&M in an exciting 13–10 triumph.

Wichita State Shockers

Wichita State University
Campus Box 18
Wichita, KS 67208

School Colors: Yellow and Black
Year Founded: 1895
Basketball: Henry Levitt Arena
(10,666)
Football: Cessna Stadium (31,500)

WICHITA STATE UNIVERSITY obtained its nickname differently from most other schools. The name was invented when a press agent told a team manager making posters to come up with a nickname on the spot.

In 1904, football manager R. J. Kirk (class of 1907) was helping post signs the week before Fairmount College (as Wichita State was then known) played Chilocco. Kirk tagged Chilocco with the nickname Indians on the posters, and a press agent for the Wichita Fall Festival, who was helping promote the event, demanded that Kirk come up with an appropriate moniker for Fairmount to balance the poster design. On the spot, Kirk wrote Wheatshockers on the poster. As a result, the football manager made his way into the athletic history books.

In those days when wheat was shocked, or headed, the majority of the football team earned college expenses by working all summer in the wheat fields or on threshing crews. In the fall, they came back tough enough to survive 60-minute games.

Although the name was never officially adopted, it caught on and survived until it was shortened to Shockers, as Wichita State teams are known as today. Kirk's nickname Shockers fits well, as Wichita State is located in the heart of the number one wheat-producing state in America.

When a nickname was being chosen for the University of Alabama at Birmingham teams, the Portland Trail Blazers reigned as champions of the National Basketball Association. Many folks figure that's where the school came up with their Blazer's nickname.

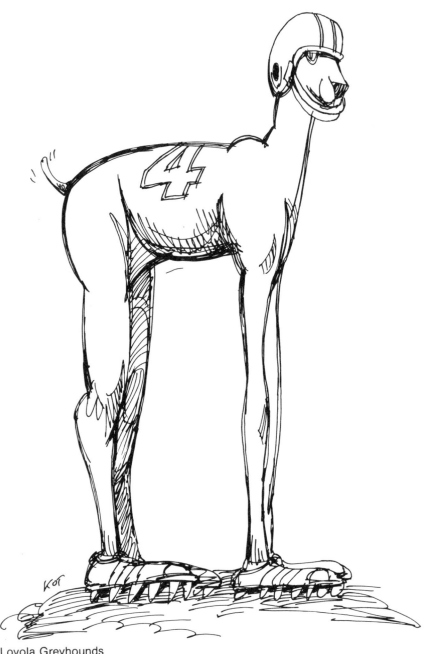

Loyola Greyhounds

20

Northeast Conference

Northeast Conference
900 Route 9
Suite 120
Woodbridge, NJ 07095

Number of Schools: 9
Year Founded: 1981
Charter Members: Baltimore, Fairleigh Dickinson, Long Island, Loyola College, Marist, Robert Morris, Siena, St. Francis (NY), St. Francis (PA), Towson State, and Wagner
Current Members: Fairleigh Dickinson, Long Island, Loyola College, Marist, Monmouth, Robert Morris, St. Francis (NY), St. Francis (PA), and Wagner
Division I Sports: Baseball, Basketball, Cross-Country, Golf, Indoor Track, Soccer, and Tennis

Fairleigh Dickinson Knights

Fairleigh Dickinson University
1000 River Road
Teaneck, NJ 07666

School Colors: Columbia Blue,
              Maroon, and White
Year Founded: 1942
Basketball: Rothman Center (5,000)

FAIRLEIGH DICKINSON UNIVERSITY'S athletes are called the Knights because of an old building situated on the school's original campus.

Fairleigh Dickinson was founded in 1942 in Rutherford, New Jersey, as a two-year college when founding father Peter Sammartino purchased an old building owned by one of his relatives. This building was an old French-style castle, complete with stained glass windows. Sammartino thought the Castle, as it was generally known, would make an excellent building for secondary education classes.

The Castle was the main building on the Rutherford campus. When the school became a four-year school in 1948 and the first basketball team was formed, Sammartino dubbed the squad the Knights, a takeoff on the notorious Castle.

Sam Convissor, a member of the school's first basketball squad and a 1953 graduate, recalled how he and other basketball team members worked as ushers as part of their scholarship agreements. Dressed in knight garb, the players worked at all school events.

Suits of armor now guard Fairleigh Dickinson's trophy case. Ironically, in 1961, Fairleigh Dickinson set up another school overseas in Wroxton, England, where the knight and castle traditions are also very prominent. The Wroxton campus also displays suits of armor.

Long Island Blackbirds

Long Island University
University Plaza
Brooklyn, NY 11201

School Colors: Blue and White
Year Founded: 1926
Basketball: Arnold Schwartz Athletic
Center (2,000)

LONG ISLAND UNIVERSITY'S story behind its Blackbirds' nickname goes back to the basketball team's ugly uniforms in the 1930s.

From 1926 until 1935, LIU sports teams were known either as the Blue Devils or the Beemen (after the legendary coach and author Clair F. Bee).

But in 1935, Long Island changed the color of its uniforms to stark black—no piping, stripes, or numerals to relieve the drabness. The sportswriters of the day, many with agricultural backgrounds, thought the basketball players resembled blackbirds, darting about tall and erect, yet making quick moves now and then to pick up grain and seeds from the ground. The name stuck, despite the change back to blue and white uniforms just a few years later.

Loyola Greyhounds

Loyola College
4501 North Charles Street
Baltimore, MD 21210-2699

School Colors: Green and Gray
Year Founded: 1852
Basketball: Reitz Arena (3,000)

DURING THE 1921–22 academic school year, members of the Loyola student body decided to come up with a new mascot and colors to signify the move of the campus to the Evergreens area in Baltimore.

When the nickname and color issue arose, Loyola's president, the Reverend Joseph A. McEneany, passed the responsibility to William Sweeney, president of the senior class. At that time, the senior class had fewer than 20 students.

Sweeney asked the students for input and it was decided the greyhound would be the official mascot and nickname. New school colors of green and gray were also adopted.

The greyhound is a logical choice for an athletic mascot. The tall, muscular, swift racing dog not only represents key athletic attributes but also school loyalty, because as you learned as a youngster, the dog is man's best friend.

Marist Red Foxes

Marist College
North Road
Poughkeepsie, NY 12601

School Colors: Red and White
Year Founded: 1946
Basketball: James J. McCann Center
                       (3,944)

A 1961 MEETING marked both the birth of Marist College's basketball team and the adoption of Red Foxes as the official nickname and mascot. Athletic director Brother William Murphy decided to organize a varsity basketball team to play scheduled games against other schools and thought a nickname and logo would be appropriate.

While glancing at a sports catalog, Brother Murphy noticed a reynard, more commonly known as a red fox, on the cover of the book. He decided this furry little creature was to be the logo of Marist College athletic teams.

The reynard comes from a great medieval cycle of stories that originated in the low countries, northern France, and western Germany. The rarity of the word prompted Brother Murphy to choose the general term Red Foxes. The wary animal, skilled at evading traps and dodging pursuers, is found in Eurasia, North Africa, and North America.

Monmouth Hawks

Monmouth College
Cedar Avenue
West Long Branch, NJ 07764

School Colors: Blue and White
Year Founded: 1933
Basketball: Alumni Memorial
Gymnasium (2,800)

MONMOUTH COLLEGE'S Hawks nickname originated in the early part of the 20th century, when the school was strictly a junior college.

Monmouth's nickname stemmed from the days when Monmouth was a two-year night school with classes held at Long Branch High School. According to a 1962 edition of the student newspaper, *The Outlook*, the 1934 sports editor suggested that the athletic teams of Monmouth Junior College be given a nickname. However, the idea never left the drawing board until the Press Club jumped into the campaign in 1939.

Students were asked to submit entries, and the Monmouth pupils were quick to respond. From a long list of names suggested by the student body and staff, about 15 were chosen for lines on the ballot. Some of these unusual nickname candidates included: Bearcats, Bees, Bisons, Commuters, Orange Fliers, Trojans, Elephants, EmJaCees, MaJiCians, MoJuCo, Blackhawks, and Nighthawks.

In the following week's *Outlook*, it was announced that EmJaCees, MaJiCians, and Nighthawks had been nominated. The judges, a basketball coach, a player, and a committee of student and faculty members, were to vote on the final nickname.

By the slim margin of six votes, the Nighthawks edged out the runner-up moniker, EmJaCees. The name Nighthawks fit Monmouth's students, who worked by day and studied by night.

Upon Monmouth's entry into the daytime ranks, the name was modified to Hawks, since Monmouth was no longer strictly an evening school.

The nickname Hawks also ties in with the environment of the area. Located in beautiful Monmouth County near the sea, the name gives special meaning to the nature and wildlife found in the community.

Robert Morris Colonials

Robert Morris College
Narrows Run Road
Coraopolis, PA 15108-1189

School Colors: Blue and White
Year Founded: 1921
Basketball: Sewall Center (3,056)

ROBERT MORRIS COLLEGE was originally founded in 1921 as a proprietary school of accountancy.

In 1935, the Pittsburgh School of Accountancy merged with a secretarial school and changed its name to Robert Morris School. The new school name was selected in honor of the historic Robert Morris (1734–1806), the financial hero of the American Revolution, a Pennsylvania signer of the Declaration of Independence, and a successful merchant who not only served in the Continental Congress but also gave of his own fortune to finance the noble causes of the patriots.

Following the revolution, Morris became superintendent of finance from 1781 to 1784 and organized a national bank, retrenched expenditures, and took steps toward establishing a national mint. Known for using his personal credit to raise funds for our "young republic, fledgling of the nations," he was often referred to as the most prominent merchant in America.

Since the Pennsylvanian business school was named after the financial hero who helped the colonies break away from England, it was natural that their athletic teams be called the Colonials.

St. Francis Red Flash

St. Francis College
Loretto, PA 15940

School Colors: Red and White
Year Founded: 1847
Basketball: Maurice Stokes Physical
           Education Building (4,000)
Football: The Pine Bowl (1,500)

ST. FRANCIS COLLEGE officials for many years did not actually know how their athletic teams came to be known as the Red Flash.

But recently, the mystery was solved. The nickname Red Flash dates back to 1927, when St. Francis boasted one of the swiftest ground attacks in Eastern football, headed by quarterback George Kunzler, right halfback Ed McLister, fullback Alphonse Abels, and left halfback Ralph Bruno. Because SFC wore predominantly red uniforms, the fans and the student newspaper, the *Loretto*, dubbed the backfield the Red Flashes.

The nickname soon spread to the entire squad, and the basketball team also took on the Red Flashes nickname that winter. Within 15 years, the name evolved into its present form of the Red Flash, with sports publicist Cy Bender credited for instituting the term.

Prior to 1927, the school's teams went by a number of unofficial nicknames, including Saints, Franciscans, and Frannies. Probably the most popular of the unofficial nicknames was the Frankies, a name that evolved from the Franciscan theme sometime in the 1930s.

St. Francis Terriers

St. Francis College
180 Remsen Street
Brooklyn Heights, NY 11201

School Colors: Red and Blue
Year Founded: 1884
Basketball: Physical Education
Building (3,000)

ST. FRANCIS COLLEGE, located in Brooklyn Heights, New York, selected the terrier as its mascot because of the dog's historical Irish roots.

St. Francis College was founded in 1884 by an Irish order of Catholic brothers, and its main purpose was to educate the children of working-class parents. During those early years, the school was filled mainly by students whose parents were Irish immigrants working in local factories and mills.

Over the years, someone came up with the nickname Terriers for the school. Since the school was founded by an Irish order, the terrier, an Irish dog breed, was most appropriate.

But the name Terrier also has a special meaning. The terrier is a scrappy, determined, little dog, just like the hardworking Irish immigrants who slaved day and night so their children could receive a college education.

The Terriers' nickname was officially adopted in 1933 and has been a loyal companion of St. Francis College ever since.

Wagner Seahawks

Wagner College
631 Howard Avenue
Staten Island, NY 10301

School Colors: Green and White
Year Founded: 1883
Basketball: Sutter Gymnasium (1,650)
Football: Fischer Memorial Field
(5,000)

WAGNER COLLEGE, like many other schools, obtained its nickname in a student-wide contest held after World War II. In 1947, when Wagner consisted of only a few hundred students, a contest was held to form a new nickname for the school's athletic teams. Apparently, school officials grew tired of the old, drab nickname Green Wave and wanted a more spirited, energetic mascot.

After a student panel screened all the suggestions, Wagner junior Ronnie Reynier's Seahawks entry was announced as the school's new official moniker. The Seahawks' name was selected because it tied in with the school's location on Staten Island as well as portraying an aggressive, fierce athletic symbol.

In 1982, as Wagner approached its 100-year anniversary, a professional design firm created a new school logo, which features a silhouette of the famous Wagner Seahawk. However, as real bird-watchers will quickly realize, the bird is actually a cross between a hawk and a falcon.

Eastern Kentucky Colonels

21

Ohio Valley Conference

Ohio Valley Conference
50 Music Square West, Suite 203
Nashville, TN 37203

Number of Schools: 8
Year Founded: 1948
Charter Members: Eastern Kentucky, Evansville, Louisville, Morehead State, Murray State, and Western Kentucky
Current Members: Austin Peay, Eastern Kentucky, Middle Tennessee State, Morehead State, Murray State, Tennessee State, Tennessee Tech, and Youngstown State
Division I Sports: Baseball, Basketball, Cross-Country, Football, Golf, and Tennis

IN 1948 the newly formed conference was named the Ohio Valley Conference, since the Ohio River touched the states from which the league drew, or hoped to draw, members.

Austin Peay State Governors

Austin Peay State University
College Street
Clarksville, TN 37044

School Colors: Red and White
Year Founded: 1927
Basketball: Dave Aaron Arena (9,000)
Football: Municipal Stadium (10,000)

THE REASONS BEHIND Austin Peay State's nickname is relatively
simple. In fact, it probably needs no explaining.

Tennessee governor Austin Peay, a favorite son of Clarksville, Tennessee,
signed a law establishing the school on April 26, 1927. The institution was
named Austin Peay Normal School, and the simple nickname Governors
was adopted in honor of the famous Clarksville native.

*No one knows exactly what Texas at Arlington's
Maverick mascot really is. It has been defined three
different ways—as cow, horse, and person.*

Eastern Kentucky Colonels

Eastern Kentucky University
Begley Building, Room 205
Richmond, KY 40475

School Colors: Maroon and White
Year Founded: 1906
Basketball: Alumni Coliseum (6,500)
Football: Hanger Field (20,000)

IN 1964, EASTERN KENTUCKY UNIVERSITY borrowed one of the state's most nationally renowned symbols, the colonel.

The school's first nickname originated in the 1920s as the Maroons, representing the official school colors. But in 1964, the moniker Colonels was unofficially adopted as the mascot. The Colonel, who made his debut in an October 1964 football game against Murray State, was portrayed by senior Roger Smith. He was dressed in southern attire and closely resembled the prominent figure Colonel Sanders, of Kentucky Fried Chicken fame.

At Georgia Tech, students refer to their teams by three different names: the Rambling Wrecks, Yellow Jackets, and Engineers.

Middle Tennessee State Blue Raiders

Middle Tennessee State University
Box 20
Murfreesboro, TN 37132

School Colors: Navy Blue and White
Year Founded: 1911
Basketball: Charles M. Murphy
          Center (11,250)
Football: Johnny ("Red") Floyd
          Stadium (15,000)

IN MIDDLE TENNESSEE STATE'S early days, the school football teams were known as the Teachers, Normalites, and Pedagogues. But in 1934 it was decided the school needed a more exciting nickname to describe the athletes. So during the football season, the Murfreesboro *Daily News* ran a contest to name the teams.

Charles Sarver, a football player on the team that season, was awarded the five-dollar prize for his winning Blue Raiders entry. Sarver admitted he borrowed the nickname from the Colgate Red Raiders, substituting the MTSU official color blue.

The symbol of Gen. Nathan Bedford Forrest on horseback was first used in 1945, when public relations director Gene Sloan began using the symbol along with the nickname. One of Tennessee's native sons, Forrest is recognized among the greatest Confederate generals in the Civil War.

In 1965, the school's student government organization established strict regulations regarding who could be selected to wear General Forrest's costume. The specification of the role is simply that the student must be a certain size as there is only one uniform available.

Morehead State Eagles

Morehead State University
UPO 1023
Morehead, KY 40351

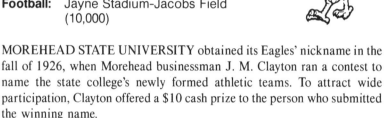

School Colors: Blue and Gold
Year Founded: 1923
Basketball: Ellis T. Johnson Arena
(6,500)
Football: Jayne Stadium-Jacobs Field
(10,000)

MOREHEAD STATE UNIVERSITY obtained its Eagles' nickname in the fall of 1926, when Morehead businessman J. M. Clayton ran a contest to name the state college's newly formed athletic teams. To attract wide participation, Clayton offered a $10 cash prize to the person who submitted the winning name.

The person who ended up with the $10 bill in her pocket was Miss Peaches Ellis of Morehead, who submitted the Bald Eagles entry. While not officially documented, it is believed an old restaurant in Morehead called the Eagle's Nest Restaurant inspired Miss Ellis's suggestion.

The name Bald Eagles represented Morehead State's athletic teams for a few years; then the name was shortened to Eagles.

Murray State Racers

Murray State University
Roy Stewart Stadium
Murray, KY 42071

School Colors: Blue and Gold
Year Founded: 1922
Basketball: Racer Arena (5,550)
Football: Roy Stewart Stadium
(16,800)

MURRAY STATE, which was founded as a teachers college in the early 1920s, was first known by the logical name of the Teachers.

Because Carlisle Cutchin coached basketball, baseball, and football at the school and was known as the father of athletics, most of his early teams were called the Cutchin Men.

The athletic teams went by both these unofficial nicknames until the early 1930s, when a sportswriter commented that one of Cutchin's teams played like thoroughbreds. Thus the nickname Thoroughbreds became synonymous with Murray State athletics.

Over the years, newspaper editors often substituted Racers as a shorter version of Thoroughbreds, and by the mid-1960s, Murray State teams had adopted the shorter nickname. The MSU baseball team is the last holdout, however, still preferring to be called the Thoroughbreds.

Tennessee State Tigers

Tennessee State University
3500 John Merritt Boulevard
Nashville, TN 37209-1561

School Colors: Blue and White
Year Founded: 1912
Basketball: Howard C. Gentry
          Complex (10,000)
Football: Hale Stadium (16,000)
          Vanderbilt Stadium (41,000)

TENNESSEE STATE'S story behind its nickname is a bit more "wild" than the normal stories. In 1959, a Bengalese tiger in India had turned into a savage killer and destroyed more than 40 domestic animals while ravaging local villages. Harold Jones, a former professor of agriculture at Tennessee State University, was on assignment with the U.S. Agency for International Development in India. Knowing of Jones's renowned ability as a big game hunter, government officials had asked him for help.

After waiting all night in a tree near a watering hole, Jones saw his prey come early in the morning. The slaying of the fierce Bengal made Jones an instant hero with the people of India. He personally skinned, salted, and stretched the tiger's skin. Then a Dutch taxidermy company was contacted to do the stuffing.

Jones, who realized the tiger could make an appropriate mascot for his alma mater, called Tennessee State's Dr. Leonard Archer, who immediately held a meeting with Student Council leader Gerald Durley. The two decided the school should purchase the tiger, which is now kept in a trophy case at Tennessee State. The proud mascot symbolizes what tenacity, self-determination, perseverance, and sacrifice can achieve.

Tennessee Tech Golden Eagles

Tennessee Technological University
Box 5057
Cookeville, TN 38505

School Colors: Purple and Gold
Year Founded: 1915
Basketball: Eblen Center (10,150)
Football: Tucker Stadium (16,500)

AFTER MORE THAN HALF A DECADE of using the same nickname, Tennessee Tech students grew tired of their Mountaineers' moniker.

On February 14, 1925, it was officially announced in the school newspaper, *The Oracle*, that the nickname Golden Eagles had prevailed over Mountaineers, which had faithfully represented Tennessee Tech for 56 years. Golden Eagles won by a landslide, defeating the old name by a vote of 139 to 18.

However, a Golden Eagle mascot didn't appear on the Cookeville campus until a private citizen proclaimed the university as the permanent home of a huge tin eagle statue that had earlier been stolen by students from the charred ruins of his resort hotel in Monteagle.

Leaving Cookeville, several Tech students bravely drove through a severe evening rainstorm to pilfer the metallic structure and return with it to the campus. Upon returning to University Gym, the creature with a 6'4" wing span was painted a glistening gold and suspended from the rafters for exhibition at the following day's basketball game.

Gov. Frank G. Clement, a lifelong friend of the hotel entrepreneur, promised the students he would work it out so the eagle could be retained as their mascot.

Clement's plan worked and the hotel owner sent Pres. Everett Derryberry a letter that officially declared the golden eagle as the school's property. The eagle statue proudly stands today atop Derryberry Hall, surveying the quad and the south part of campus.

Youngstown State Penguins

Youngstown State University
410 Wick Avenue
Youngstown, OH 44555

School Colors: Scarlet and White
Year Founded: 1908
Basketball: Beeghly Center (7,500)
Football: Stambaugh Stadium
    (16,000)

YOUNGSTOWN STATE UNIVERSITY is the only school on the college level that uses the unique nickname Penguins. The way the name originated is also unusual; five basketball players and the athletic director dreamed it up in a car on their way to play an opposing school.

Early Youngstown teams were referred to as Y College, YoCo, Wye Collegians, and many times as Locals. No one was proud of these names when they appeared in headlines. The name YoCo, an acronym for Youngstown College, was especially disliked because opponents found it adaptable for jeering by slurring YoCo to sound like yokel or loco. Youngstown State players and fans didn't find these names at all funny.

Members of the 1932–33 varsity basketball team used to occasionally sit in the cafeteria and discuss suitable names for the teams. But because they had no desire to adopt any nickname that was already in use, a consensus could never be reached.

It was in early February 1933 that Youngstown State made nickname history. Before the basketball squad traveled to West Liberty Teachers college, an intense snowstorm occurred, leaving drifts higher than two feet on the road. The team, which had traveled in a caravan of three cars, occasionally had to help push the cars out of ruts too deep to drive through.

Despite the terrible weather, the players' minds did not veer away from their search for a nickname. It was in athletic director Jack McPhee's car that the name Penguins was born. One of the passengers, which included players Bob Cole, Bob Schultz, Jimmy Rich, Fred McFarland, and newspaper editor Bennett Kunicki, suggested Penguins because of the cold, freezing weather conditions the team had to endure on their journey to West Virginia.

However, another version states that the players were dubbed Penguins on the game floor later that evening. Because of the cold weather, the gym was cold, and the spectacle of the players stomping about the floor and swinging their arms to keep warm prompted someone to remark, "They look like a bunch of penguins."

Either way, Youngstown State is noted as the only school to have Penguins as its official nickname.

Which school has a direct tie with dogsled trips to both the North and South Poles? It's the Connecticut Huskies, whose mascots have had direct ancestors who pulled sleds to both poles.

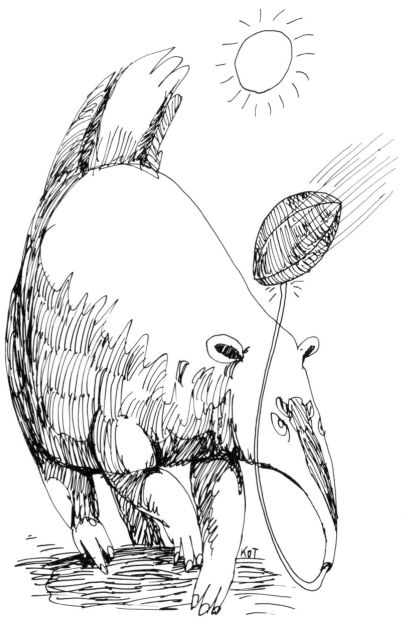

California-Irvine Anteaters

22

Pacific Coast Athletic Association

Pacific Coast Athletic Association
1700 East Dyer Road, Suite 140
Santa Ana, CA 92705

Number of Schools: 10
Year Founded: 1969
Charter Members: California–Santa Barbara, California State–Long Beach, California State–Los Angeles, Fresno State, Pacific, San Diego State, and San Jose State
Current Members: California-Irvine, California–Santa Barbara, California State–Fullerton, Fresno State, California State–Long Beach, Nevada–Las Vegas, New Mexico State, Pacific, San Jose State, and Utah State
Division I Sports: Baseball, Basketball, Cross-Country, Football, Golf, Soccer, Swimming, Tennis, Track and Field, and Water Polo

California-Irvine Anteaters

University of California, Irvine
Crawford Hall
Irvine, CA 92717

School Colors: Blue and Gold
Year Founded: 1964
Basketball: Bren Events Center
(5,000)

UNIVERSITY OF CALIFORNIA, IRVINE possesses one of the nation's unique nicknames. The name Anteaters usually brings plenty of chuckles and smirks from opposing teams.

When the school opened its doors in 1965 and the athletic program got underway, the search for an official mascot became a campus goal. UCI student Schuyler Bassett III is recognized as the main instigator behind the Anteater campaign. Inspired by Johnny Hart's well-known comic strip "B.C.," Bassett organized an all-out effort to promote the unusual name prior to the November 30, 1965, election. Bassett and his forces distributed bumper stickers, posters, and window decals depicting Peter the Anteater, a figure bearing a close resemblance to the Playboy bunny.

By the time the polls opened, only Anteaters, Eagles, Unicorns, Golden Bears, and Sea Hawks had obtained the necessary 100 signatures required to get a spot on the ballot. When school officials counted the votes, Anteaters had easily emerged as the official mascot and nickname, with a landslide 55.9 percent of the student vote.

UCI's new battle cry, "Give 'em the tongue. . . . Zot! Zot!" soon generated plenty of new spirit for UCI Anteater supporters and fans alike.

California–Santa Barbara Gauchos

University of California, Santa Barbara
Santa Barbara, CA 93106

School Colors: Blue and Gold
Year Founded: 1898
Basketball: Campus Events Center
(5,700)
Football: Harder Stadium (17,500)

WHEN INTERCOLLEGIATE ATHLETICS first began at California–Santa Barbara in 1915, the teams were immediately called the Road-runners. Roadrunner remained in vogue until 1934, when some students argued that a roadrunner was an unsuitable symbol of athletic skill. So in 1935, school officials switched to Gauchos and a legend was born.

The gaucho, a romantic, liberty-loving cowboy of the Old West, seemed an appropriate representative for the Santa Barbara area. The gaucho characterizes a unique combination of distinct Mexican and Indian flavor as well as the "ponderosa" spirit of the Old West.

The gaucho was always known as a happy-go-lucky dude. While frequently roaming the wide open land, he was associated with such questionable behavior as cattle rustling, drunkenness, and public disorder. Most people feared the gaucho, as his rebel-rousing antics could surface at any moment, but he was nevertheless respected. His ferocity and agility were never questioned, while his carefree attitude and sporadic behavior added to his colorful character.

California State–Fullerton Titans

California State University, Fullerton
800 North State College Boulevard
Fullerton, CA 92634

School Colors: Blue and Orange
Year Founded: 1957
Basketball: Titan Gymnasium (4,200)
Football: Santa Ana Stadium (12,000)

FOR YEARS, visitors at Cal State Fullerton have been confused—and for good reason. The official school nickname is the Titans, while the official mascot is an elephant. What's going on?

In the early 1960s, the Student Council sponsored an election to select the school's official nickname. More than a hundred names were suggested and were narrowed down to just a few before the election. The vote was close, with Titans narrowly prevailing over Aardvarks and Rebels.

"Even when it was decided that Titans would be the nickname, there was confusion as to what it represented," said founding dean of students Dr. Ernest Becker. "I was thinking of a large mythological figure from Greek history, not unlike Tommy Trojan (USC mascot), but with perhaps straighter, more modern lines. There were others, however, who related the name to the Titan missile then in prominence."

Since no one knew what to do about a mascot that would be representative of the name, nothing official was done. That is, until the "First Intercollegiate Elephant Race in Human History" was held.

What originated as a practical joke turned into the biggest happening on the Fullerton campus to this day. The gag attracted elephants from universities all across the nation and even an entry from Oxford University in England. More than 10,000 people turned out on a spring afternoon in 1962 to Dumbo Downs, a hastily graded field.

To promote the event, a drawing of a circuslike elephant called Tuffy the Titan, dressed in a sweater and beanie, was used as a logo. It soon appeared on sweatshirts and notebooks all over campus. The mascot easily outlasted the race, and a real elephant was soon seen at athletic events. In 1963, one elephant charged into the crowd, causing minor injuries, and the signs of a liability insurance crisis quickly halted the exciting living mascot tradition.

California State–Long Beach 49ers

California State University, Long Beach
1250 Bellflower Boulevard
Long Beach, CA 90480

School Colors: Brown and Gold
Year Founded: 1948
Basketball: Long Beach State
University Gymnasium
(2,200)
Football: Veterans Memorial Stadium
(12,500)

LONG BEACH STATE'S nickname, the 49ers, was selected as both the school name and mascot for two reasons. First, the name was adopted to commemorate the opening of the school's doors in 1949. Second, the nickname was appropriate because of the role played by pioneers in the heritage of the state of California. The California gold rush of 1849 brought thousands of settlers to the state from the East Coast, and the name 49ers serves as a memory of this great part of history.

Fresno State Bulldogs

Fresno State University
SID Office, NG153
Fresno, CA 93740-0027

School Colors: Cardinal, Blue, and
White
Year Founded: 1911
Basketball: Selland Arena (10,132)
Football: Bulldog Stadium (30,000)

FRESNO STATE UNIVERSITY obtained its nickname because of a little dog that waited day after day outside the school buildings until classes were out. Late in the initial 1921 football season, student body president Warren Moody and friends were continually greeted outside the main campus building by a small white bulldog. When the dog adopted Moody and his friends, they repaid the compliment by making their loyal companion the school mascot.

During a student body meeting, Ardis Walker recommended the adoption of Bulldogs as the official school nickname. On November 21, 1921, the *Morning Republican* first referred to Fresno State as the Bulldogs.

The school colors evolved out of a male-female argument when two schools were merged into Fresno State. The women from Fresno Normal School wanted blue and white as the school colors, while the men from Fresno Junior College demanded red and white. A compromise was finally reached with the school adopting red, white, and blue. Later, the red was changed to cardinal.

Nevada-Las Vegas Rebels

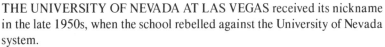

University of Nevada at Las Vegas
4505 Maryland Parkway
Las Vegas, NV 89154

School Colors: Scarlet and Gray
Year Founded: 1957
Basketball: Thomas and Mack Center
                 (18,500)
Football: Sam Boyd Silver Bowl
               (32,500)

THE UNIVERSITY OF NEVADA AT LAS VEGAS received its nickname in the late 1950s, when the school rebelled against the University of Nevada system.

UN system officials felt Reno should be the only major university in Nevada but lost the bid, and Nevada Southern, the original name of UNLV, was founded. However, officials attempted to keep Nevada Southern under their umbrella by giving the new university appropriations that could be defined as sparse at best. Someone dubbed the Nevada Southern athletic teams the Rebels since the school had rebelled from the Nevada system and set up their own university.

The students at NSU adopted a wolf as their mascot, the same as the

University of Nevada at Reno. Some NSU students from the southern states dressed their mascot in a Civil War Confederate uniform and named him Beauregard to further distinguish their southern roots. However, the wolf was last seen in a Rebel uniform in 1973, when black students objected to the Confederate uniform.

By 1982 UNLV had officially adopted the Hey Reb mascot seen today. The UNLV nickname underwent further change in the mid-1970s, when the name Runnin' Rebels was coined to describe the basketball team.

New Mexico State Aggies

New Mexico State University
Box 3145
Las Cruces, NM 88003-0001

School Colors: Crimson and White
Year Founded: 1888
Basketball: Pan American Center
(13,222)
Football: Aggie Memorial (30,343)

SINCE THE SCHOOL'S INCEPTION in 1888, its primary area of study has been agriculture. When the school was renamed New Mexico College of Agriculture and Mechanic Arts, the nickname of Aggies seemed most appropriate.

However, the story behind the name of the mascot, Pistol Pete, is a bit more exciting. It is named after Frank Eaton, a bigger-than-life veteran of the Old West.

In 1868, Frank Boardman, Eaton's Yankee father and a member of the Vigilantes (a gang of citizens interested in keeping law and order) was shot and killed by six members of a group called the Regulators. Following the shooting, Mose Beaman, an old cavalry scout and Boardman's friend, told eight-year-old Frank he would be cursed if he did not avenge his father's death. So under the tutoring of the old scout, Eaton became a quick-draw expert and an excellent marksman.

When he was 15, he traveled to Fort Gibson to learn more shooting skills from the cavalry. He outshot all the troopers at the fort and was nicknamed Pistol Pete by Colonel Copinger, the commanding officer.

By 17, Pistol Pete had killed four of his father's murderers—all in fair fights. A fifth murderer was already dead, and in 1881, Eaton heard that the last member still at large was living in Albuquerque, New Mexico. Eaton eventually found Wyley Campsey, the last Regulator, and shot him in a fair fight, although Eaton himself was seriously injured. He stayed in Lincoln County for some time recuperating from his wound, and today is considered by some to be a folk hero in Western lore.

In 1923, Pistol Pete agreed to the use of his photograph in a design of an NMSU college emblem. (Pistol Pete also played a leading role in the selection of the nickname Oklahoma State Cowboys, a member of the Big Eight Conference.)

Pacific Tigers

University of the Pacific
Stockton, CA 95211

School Colors: Orange and Black
Year Founded: 1851
Basketball: Alex G. Spanos Center
          (6,000)
Football: Pacific Memorial Stadium
          (30,000)

ALTHOUGH THE FACTS are inconclusive, it seems the University of the Pacific students and faculty are a bunch of renegade copycats.

All the evidence indicates that Pacific's nickname, the Tigers, along with the orange and black colors, were modeled after those used by Princeton University all the way out across the country in New Jersey. As a matter of fact, many of Pacific's charters, constitutions, and other academic framework were modeled after those used at Princeton.

It has also been suggested that since Pacific's size and general philosophy are quite similar to Princeton's, and since both institutions begin with a *P*, school officials chose to emulate Princeton's name and colors.

San Jose State Spartans

San Jose State University
One Washington Square
San Jose, CA 95192-0062

School Colors: Blue and Gold
Year Founded: 1857
Basketball: San Jose Civic
 Auditorium (2,412)
 Student Union Events/
 Recreation Center (4,500)
Football: Spartan Stadium (31,365)

THE NICKNAME of the San Jose State University Spartans was chosen by a student body election in 1924. Prior to that time, San Jose State teams were known as the Golden Raiders, a tag used by San Jose *Mercury* sportswriter Fred Merrick, who covered the school's athletic events in the late 1930s.

Utah State Aggies

Utah State University
UMC 7400
Logan, UT 84322

School Colors: Navy Blue and White
Year Founded: 1888
Basketball: The Spectrum (10,217)
Football: Romney Stadium (30,257)

THE REASON BEHIND the Utah State University Aggies' nickname is relatively simple. At one point in the school's history, the primary thrust was educating farmers. The school was founded as Utah State Agricultural College, and ever since the athletic program began, State athletes have been known as Aggies.

 The school mascot, Gus the Bull, obtained its name from the initials of the school cheer, "Go Utah State." Gus represents the great history of agricultural studies at Utah State University.

Arizona State Sun Devils

23

Pacific-10 Conference

Pacific-10 Conference
800 South Broadway, Suite 400
Walnut Creek, CA 94596

Number of Schools: 10
Year Founded: 1915
Charter Members: California, Oregon, Oregon State College, and Washington
Current Members: Arizona, Arizona State, California-Berkeley, UCLA, Oregon, Oregon State, Southern California, Stanford, Washington, and Washington State
Division I Sports: Baseball, Basketball, Crew, Cross-Country, Football, Golf, Gymnastics, Swimming and Diving, Tennis, Track and Field, Water Polo, and Wrestling

ODDLY ENOUGH, the Pacific-10 Conference actually began as the Pacific Coast Conference with only four schools in 1915. The number of schools in the conference varied many times, and in 1968 the name was changed to the Pacific-8 conference. Ten years later, on July 1, 1978, Arizona and Arizona State were admitted, creating the Pacific-10.

Arizona State Sun Devils

Arizona State University
University Activity Center
Tempe, AZ 85287

School Colors: Maroon and Gold
Year Founded: 1885
Basketball: University Activity Center
              (14,287)
Football: Sun Devil Stadium (70,491)

ARIZONA STATE UNIVERSITY selected its current nickname, Sun Devils, in 1946. Unique among American colleges, the name represents both climatic identification and an aggressive purpose.

In the early part of the century, the teams were called the Normals. But when the Normal School became a four-year institution in 1922, a sportswriter on the student newspaper urged a more combative school name be chosen—the Bulldogs. This name, highly popular among colleges, lasted at Arizona State for more than 20 years.

After the Sun Angel Foundation was formed in postwar 1946, a need for a new start in college athletics as well as a new nickname was recognized on the Tempe campus.

M. O. Best, a university regent and ASU supporter, is credited with choosing the name Sun Angels because of their unselfishness as benefactors of a reborn college in sun country. But soon after, ASU supporters were urging the student body to adopt a modification of this nickname—the Sun Devils—as it would represent their teams much better.

On campus, George "Pappy" Yates, Chuck Southern, Gilbert Cady, and a number of students began pushing for the name Devils. Bert Anthony, a staff artist for Walt Disney Studios, joined the cause and designed the Sun Devil logo still in use today.

On November 8, 1946, an election was held for adoption of the Sun Devils. There was a small campaign for a compromise name between Sun Devil and Bulldogs—the Sun Dogs. But the Sun Devils name sizzled by the Sun Dogs in an overwhelming victory.

Arizona Wildcats

University of Arizona
229 McKale Center
Tucson, AZ 85721

School Colors: Cardinal and Navy
Year Founded: 1885
Basketball: McKale Center (13,124)
Football: Arizona Stadium (51,952)

THE WILDCATS' NICKNAME became part of the Arizona tradition in 1914, when a student correspondent submitted his article to his newspaper boss.

Following the Arizona-Occidental football game at Occidental, Bill Henry, a student correspondent for the Los Angeles *Times*, penned the phrase, "The Arizona men showed the fight of wildcats."

When the student body back in Tucson read the dispatch of the game, they resolved that Arizona athletic teams would henceforth be known as the Wildcats.

Until the first University football game in 1899, the school colors were sage green and silver. However, the student manager that year, Quintus J. Anderson, was able to work some particularly crafty deal with a local merchant for game sweaters of solid blue with red trim. After seeing the combination, he requested that the colors be changed, and it's been cardinal and navy blue ever since.

California-Berkeley
Golden Bears

University of California, Berkeley
210 Memorial Stadium
Berkeley, CA 94720

School Colors: Blue and Gold
Year Founded: 1868
Basketball: Harmon Gym (6,700)
Football: Memorial Stadium (78,000)

THE UNIVERSITY OF CALIFORNIA, BERKELEY'S oldest active school tradition is the Golden Bear.

A 12-man track squad, which was the first UCB athletic team to compete outside the state, was sent to the East Coast in the spring of 1895 to run against the powerful eastern schools. Two silk banners accompanied the team, bearing the word California and the state emblem, a grizzly bear embroidered in gold.

The team was successful beyond its expectations, winning four and tying one out of six dual meets before winning the Western Intercollegiate Meet in Chicago. At the jubilant homecoming reception in Berkeley, the team's banners were proudly displayed and inspired English professor Charles Mills Gayley to compose the song "The Golden Bear." Students sung out this final verse:

> Oh, have you seen our banner blue?
> The Golden Bear is on it too.
> A Californian through and through
> Our totem he, the Golden Bear!

Since that time, the Golden Bear has been the mythical guardian of the university.

Oregon Ducks

University of Oregon
McArthur Court
Eugene, OR 97403

School Colors: Emerald Green and
Lemon Yellow
Year Founded: 1876
Basketball: McArthur Court (10,099)
Football: Autzen Stadium (41,099)

YOU MAY THINK it was natural for Oregon's original nickname, Webfoots, to evolve into Ducks. Many people feel that way, but actually the meaning of the original term has been totally misinterpreted.

The term webfoots was first used to describe fishermen off the coast of Massachusetts in the 1700s. In fact, it was the Webfoots of 1776, under the command of Gen. George Washington, that helped evacuate 10,000 troops across the East River to New York City. The Webfoots helped the colonists avoid a sure defeat and saved the war for the colonies.

When Oregon's Willamette Valley was being settled in the 1840s, the name Webfoots was given to new residents—partly because of the nonstop rain and partly because so many settlers hailed from the New England area.

When the university first opened in 1876, it did not take long for its athletic teams to be dubbed Webfoots. In the late 1890s, students voted the name in as their official nickname.

But as athletics got more news coverage, headline writers constantly searched for shorter names. Ducks, thought by writers to be the same thing as Webfoots, was installed by 1930 and was soon a popular name among fans.

During the early 1920s a real-life duck named Puddles was brought to football and basketball games. The duck lasted for many years but finally vanished from the Oregon sports scene after repeated complaints from the Humane Society.

In the late 1940s, athletic director Leo Harris capitalized on his friendship with Walt Disney and received permission to use Donald Duck as the official Oregon mascot. Disney's staff drew a series of special renditions of Donald, which made it the only college in the United States to have a Disney cartoon character as its official mascot.

However, the Donald Duck mascot was not the favorite with everyone. In 1978, a vote was held on the future of Donald Duck as mascot. Student editorial cartoonist Steve Sandstrom developed a mallard drake mascot and brought it up to challenge the Disney Duck. But the students voted in favor of the famous duck we all grew up with on Saturday mornings, and Sandstrom's mallard drake was told to go jump in the lake.

Oregon State Beavers

Oregon State University
Gill Coliseum
Corvallis, OR 97331

School Colors: Orange and Black
Year Founded: 1850
Basketball: Gill Coliseum (10,400)
Football: Parker Stadium (40,593)

OREGON STATE, like many other universities in the United States, is named after its home state's official animal.

In the early days, Oregon State's athletic teams were known as the Aggies. When orange uniforms replaced the drab sweatshirt-gray and tan jerseys, the teams were referred to as the Orangemen.

But in 1916, when the school yearbook was renamed *The Beaver*, the name Beaver became associated with the school. It is believed the press also had some influence in changing the name, particularly L. H. Gregorian of the *Oregonian*. At any rate, the name gained instant popularity among alumni and students.

Benny Beaver, OSU's mascot, was introduced by the school's rally squad to the student body on September 18, 1952, in an effort to pick up sagging school spirit.

"Benny Beaver, the rally squad's candidate for handsomest man in school, has never been on campus before," according to the *Barometer*, the student newspaper. "The animal stands six feet tall, wears vivid orange knicker-bockers, a black jersey, and his familiar orange and black rooters lid." Adopted as the official mascot in 1952, Benny Beaver still fires up the crowds at OSU athletic events today.

Southern California Trojans

University of Southern California
Heritage Hall
Los Angeles, CA 90089-0602

School Colors: Cardinal and Gold
Year Founded: 1880
Basketball: Los Angeles Sports Arena
           (15,509)
Football: Memorial Coliseum (92,516)

THE UNIVERSITY OF SOUTHERN CALIFORNIA Trojans' nickname
originated in 1912 when a sports editor was asked to select a new nickname. Prior to that time, teams were called the Methodists or Wesleyans,
neither of which university officials liked.

Because these names were not popular on campus, athletic director
Warren Bovard confronted Los Angeles *Times* sports editor Owen Bird and
asked him to come up with a nickname. The name Bird came up with was
Trojans, and he printed it in an article before the USC-Stanford game.

"At the time, the athletes and coaches of the university were under
terrific handicaps," Bird recalled later. "They were facing teams that were
bigger and better equipped, yet they had splendid fighting spirit. The name
'Trojans' fitted them.

"The term 'Trojan' as applied to USC means to me that no matter what
the situation, what the odds or what the conditions, the competition must be
carried on to the end and those who strive must give all they have and never
be weary in doing so."

One of the truly unique traditions in collegiate athletics is the performance of Tommy Trojan and his white horse, Traveler. Every time a USC
touchdown is scored, the band plays "Conquest" and Tommy and Traveler
explode out of the tunnel and gallop around the field, bringing all the fans to
their feet.

Stanford Cardinal

Stanford University
Stanford, CA 94305

School Color: Cardinal
Year Founded: 1885
Basketball: Maples Pavilion (7,500)
Football: Stanford Stadium (86,019)

STANFORD UNIVERSITY received its nickname from its bright red school color. When Stanford first admitted students in 1891, students voted on gold as the school color. However, a second student assembly was held soon after, and cardinal was selected as the school color.

A few days after the adoption of the color cardinal, local sportswriters picked up on it after Stanford defeated California in the school's first big game on March 19, 1891. The headlines the following day read, "Cardinal Triumphs O'er Blue and Gold."

However, Stanford officially adopted the Indians as its school nickname on November 25, 1930. The resolution passed by the Executive Committee of Students read as follows: "Whereas the Indian has long been unofficially recognized as the symbol of Stanford and its spirit, and whereas there has never been any official designation of the Stanford symbol, be it hereby resolved that the Executive Committee adopt the Indian as the symbol of Stanford."

Stanford dropped the Indian symbol in 1972 at the request of native American students in California colleges who found the Stanford mascot insulting to their culture and heritage.

After years of informal use, Cardinal was declared the official nickname for all athletic teams in November 1981. "While various other mascots have been suggested and then allowed to wither, the color has continued to serve us well, as it has for 90 years," said university president Donald Kennedy. "It is a rich and vivid metaphor for the very pulse of life."

UCLA Bruins

University of California, Los Angeles
405 Hilgard Avenue
Los Angeles, CA 90024-1639

School Colors: Blue and Gold
Year Founded: 1919
Basketball: Pauley Pavilion (12,583)
Football: Rose Bowl (104,000)

BACK IN 1919, when the university was formed, the football team was known as the Cubs because of the school's "younger" status in relationship to California-Berkeley's Bears.

Maybe that was an appropriate name for that first team, as the Cubs were defeated 74–0 by the Manual Arts High School squad. In fact, the school did not win its first conference football game until 1922.

In 1923, under the new direction of Jimmy Cline, the team won two games and sported a new name, the Grizzlies. UCLA was admitted to the Pacific Coast Conference in 1928. Since the University of Montana already used the nickname Grizzlies, UCLA had to find a new name. Staying with the bear tradition, school officials chose Bruins as their official nickname.

Live bear mascots were used until the early 1960s, when it was determined they grew too large and were too hard to control. Several male students played the part of UCLA mascot Joe Bruin in the mid-1960s. Then in 1967 the school received its first female mascot, Josephine Bruin. UCLA is one of only a few universities with both male and female mascots.

UCLA's friendly neighbor to the southeast—Disneyland—created and donated a new costume for the eight-foot Big Bear who leads the band at halftime. A year later, Joe and Josephine Bruin also received a face-lift, courtesy of a Disney designer. As a result, you can't find sharper-looking Bruins anywhere.

Washington Huskies

University of Washington
Graves Building, GC-20
Seattle, WA 98195

School Colors: Purple and Gold
Year Founded: 1861
Basketball: Heck Edmundson Pavilion
              (8,000)
Football: Husky Stadium (72,500)

THE FIRST NICKNAME of the University of Washington was the Sun-dodgers. But during the early part of the 20th century, people in the Pacific Northwest thought the name poorly represented the area. The name was dangerous to the tourist trade and led people to think the sun was never seen in Seattle.

So at the urging of the student body, a committee comprised of team captains, coaches, and faculty members was formed in 1921 to find a more appropriate name for the university. The committee searched for a proper name that could represent the spirit of the growing Northwest as the gateway to Alaska.

Three months later, the list of names was narrowed down to two, malamutes and huskies, which are breeds of Alaskan sled dogs. A debate took place to determine the official nickname of the school.

The committee finally decided upon Huskies, but not without strong disapproval by the student body. Many had never even seen a husky and wondered if perhaps another name should be chosen. To resolve the complicated situation, a campus fraternity obtained a real husky and showed the Alaskan sled dog off around campus, wiping out any doubts as to the value of the school's new nickname. The dog has been extremely popular for the past seven decades.

Washington State Cougars

Washington State University
Bohler M-8
Pullman, WA 99164-1602

School Colors: Crimson and Gray
Year Founded: 1890
Basketball: Friel Court (12,058)
Football: Martin Stadium (40,000)

WASHINGTON STATE'S nickname came off the drawing board of a California cartoonist after a big game.

Washington State went south to Berkeley to play the highly rated California team in 1919. WSU triumphed 14–0 in the contest, and following the game, an Oakland cartoonist portrayed the spoilers as cougars.

The name was officially adopted on October 28, 1919. *The Evergreen* covered the story and said, "For some weeks past, Washington State has been trying to get a fitting symbol for its football team. . . . Then the team went south and were dubbed Cougars by an enthusiastic Oakland cartoonist who wished to portray the Bear undone. The name has been formally adopted, it fits, and what could fit better?" Prior to the Berkeley game, Washington State teams were referred to as Farmers, Redskins, and Indians.

In 1927, Washington governor Roland Hartley presented a live cougar cub to the students at Washington State. This first cougar mascot was called Butch in honor of Herbert "Butch" Meeker, WSU's gridiron star at the time. Since then, the same name has been passed on from mascot to mascot.

The Cougars' monogram was designed by Randall Johnson, class of 1938. Originally used on campus trucks, the logo was later used on the side of the stadium, letterhead, and team pennants. This interesting logo features an open-mouthed Cougar with the three WSU initials inside the outline of the animal. The final letter *U* forms the cougar's mouth.

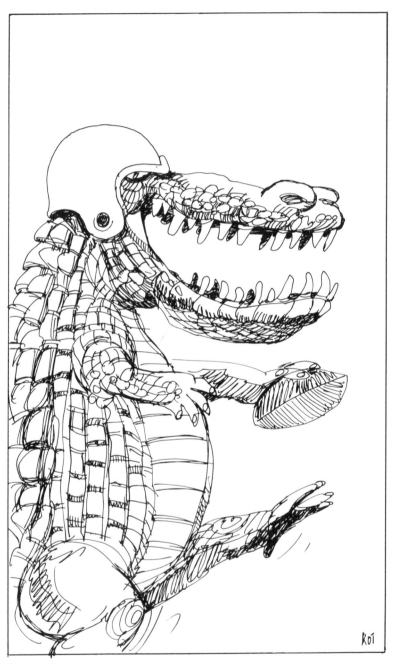

Florida Gators

24

Southeastern Conference

Southeastern Conference
3000 Galleria Tower, Suite 990
Birmingham, AL 35244

Number of Schools: 10
Year Founded: 1933
Charter Members: Alabama, Auburn, Florida, Georgia, Georgia
Tech, Kentucky, Louisiana State, Mississippi,
Mississippi State, South, Tulane, Tennessee,
and Vanderbilt.
Current Members: Alabama, Auburn, Florida, Georgia,
Kentucky, Louisiana State, Mississippi,
Mississippi State, Tennessee, and Vanderbilt
Division I Sports: Baseball, Basketball, Cross-Country,
Football, Golf, Indoor Track, Swimming,
Tennis, and Track and Field

Alabama Crimson Tide

University of Alabama
Box K
Tuscaloosa, AL 35486-9752

School Colors: Crimson and White
Year Founded: 1831
Basketball: Coleman Memorial Arena
(15,043)
Football: Bryant-Denny Stadium
(70,000)
Legion Field (75,808)

THE EARLY FOOTBALL teams at Alabama were originally known as the Varsity or simply the Crimson and White. The first popular nickname used by headline writers—the Thin Red Line—was seen in print in 1906 to describe Alabama's feeble football players.

However, it was not long before the name became outdated. The name Crimson Tide was believed to have come from Hugh Roberts, sports editor of the Birmingham *Age-Herald*, while covering the 1907 Alabama-Auburn contest. The Auburn powerhouse was the heavy favorite in the game, which was played in a sea of mud. But the Thin Red Line played a great game and left the flooded Birmingham field with a 6–6 tie. Thus the name Crimson Tide.

The story behind Alabama's red elephant mascot dates back to the 1930 football season when Coach Wallace Wade assembled the school's first truly great squad. On October 8, 1930, in Everett Strupper's Atlanta *Journal* coverage of the Alabama-Mississippi game, where Wade started his second team, Strupper wrote, "That Alabama team of 1930 is a typical Wade machine, powerful, big, tough, fast, aggressive, well-schooled in fundamentals, and the best blocking team for this early in the season that I have ever seen. When those big brutes hit you I mean you go down and stay down, often for an additional two minutes. . . .

"At the end of the quarter, the earth started to tremble, there was a distant rumble that continued to grow. Some excited fan in the stands bellowed, 'Hold your horses, the elephants are coming,' and out stamped this Alabama varsity."

Strupper and other writers continued to refer to the Alabama lineman as Red Elephants and the title eventually became Alabama's official mascot.

Auburn Tigers

Auburn University
P.O. Box 351
Auburn, AL 36831-0351

School Colors: Burnt Orange and
            Navy Blue
Year Founded: 1856
Basketball: Joel H. Eaves Memorial
          Coliseum (12,000)
Football: Jordan Hare Stadium
        (85,000)

THE AUBURN TIGERS' nickname comes from a line in Oliver Goldsmith's 1770 poem "The Deserted Village." The line of great importance to Auburn fans is "where crouching tigers wait their helpless prey."

Auburn's other nickname used in the early days was Plainsmen, which also came from a line in the same Goldsmith poem: "Sweet Auburn, loveliest village on the plains." Many Auburn athletes were from the plains; thus it was natural for sportswriters to dub the players Plainsmen.

The battle cry is "War Eagle" and is used in the same manner as Alabama's "Roll Tide" and Arkansas's "Whooo, Pig! Sooey!" The Auburn mascot is a live golden eagle named Tiger.

Florida Gators

University of Florida
P.O. Box 14485, Florida Field
Gainesville, FL 32604-2485

School Colors: Orange and Blue
Year Founded: 1853
Basketball: Stephen C. O'Connel
             Center (12,000)
Football: Florida Field (72,000)

THE UNIVERSITY OF FLORIDA's nickname originated when a young student in Virginia wanted to spice up a university pennant in order to put a few extra dollars in his father's pocket. The interesting thing is that the young man didn't even attend the school whose nickname he invented.

Austin Miller, a student at Virginia, was visited by his father, Phillip Miller, a Gainesville merchant who owned and operated a combination drugstore-bookstore on the Florida campus. While in Charlottesville, Austin's father decided to order University of Florida paraphernalia from the Michie Company. The father and son were given pennant samples of the Yale Bulldogs, Princeton Tigers, and other school emblems. When asked what Florida's emblem was, the Millers realized the school didn't even have one.

Austin Miller came up with Alligators as a suitable emblem, because the Michie manager said it had never been used and was native to Miller's home state. "I had no idea it would stick, or even be popular with the student body," Miller said. "We just wanted to get the Michie firm started on the pennants as quickly as possible so they would be available in time for the opening of the 1908 school term."

However, Miller was almost forced to choose another animal for the emblem. The Michie manager complained that he had never seen an alligator and didn't believe he could draw one. Austin Miller did not give up. After searching through books at the University of Virginia library, he returned with a picture of a 'gator . . . and the rest is history.

The first appearance of the emblem was in Miller's store in 1908. The Michie firm produced three-by-six-foot blue banners showing a large orange alligator, as well as smaller banners and pennants. The merchandise sold like hotcakes, and the name has stayed with the school ever since.

Georgia Bulldogs

University of Georgia
P.O. Box 1472
Athens, GA 30613-2199

School Colors: Red and Black
Year Founded: 1785
Basketball: Georgia Coliseum
(11,200)
Football: Sanford Stadium (82,122)

MANY OLDTIMERS say Georgia acquired its Bulldogs' nickname because of the strong relationship with Yale University, whose nickname is known far and wide as the Bulldogs. Georgia's first president, Abraham Baldwin, was a Yale man, and the early campus buildings were built from blueprints of Yale buildings.

But on November 3, 1920, Morgan Blake of the Atlanta *Journal*, wrote an article about school nicknames and stated, "The Georgia 'Bulldogs' would sound good because there is a certain dignity about the bulldog, as well as ferocity."

Three days following Blake's article, an Atlanta *Constitution* sportswriter used the name Bulldogs five times in his story covering a game against Virginia.

Georgia's first football mascot was introduced against Auburn in 1892. The first mascot was a goat that wore a black coat with red *UG* letters on each side. He also wore a hat with ribbons hanging down from his high horns. Auburn fans yelled throughout the game, "Shoot the billy goat."

Today, there may be no better known live college mascot in the country than the Georgia Bulldog, known as UGA, who has been owned by the Frank W. Seiler family of Savannah since 1956. UGA, the somber, fearless, bulldog who demands respect, has guarded the Georgia sideline with great dignity for many years.

Kentucky Wildcats

University of Kentucky
Memorial Coliseum
Lexington, KY 40506-0019

School Colors: Blue and White
Year Founded: 1865
Basketball: Rupp Arena (23,000)
Football: Commonwealth Stadium
          (58,000)

ODDLY ENOUGH, Kentucky's one and only nickname—Wildcats—originated in a campus chapel. In 1909 Commandant Corbusier, head of the university's military department, spoke to students in a chapel on campus. During his speech, he commented on the valiant showing of Kentucky's 6–2 football win over Illinois and declared, "They fought like wildcats!"

The Commandant's tag was soon popularized by word of mouth and the local press. All Kentucky athletic teams are known today as the Wildcats.

Louisiana State Fighting Tigers

Louisiana State University
P.O. Drawer V
Baton Rouge, LA 70894-9008

School Colors: Purple and Gold
Year Founded: 1855
Basketball: Maravich Assembly
Center (14,402)
Football: Tiger Stadium (78,882)

IN 1896, COACH A. W. JEARDEAU's Louisiana State University football squad went undefeated, which prompted school officials to adopt the nickname Tigers.

Although Tigers was a very common nickname among colleges at the time because of its color and athletic traits, the real reason behind using the Tigers' name dates back to the Civil War.

During the war between the states, a battalion of Louisiana soldiers comprised of New Orleans Zouaves and Donaldsonville Cannoners greatly distinguished themselves on the Confederate side at the Battle of Shenandoah. Southerners referred to this Confederate fighting band as the Louisiana Tigers.

When the LSU football teams entered the gridiron battlefields in only their fourth year of intercollegiate athletics, they tagged themselves the Tigers. In 1955, the courageous "fourth-quarter ball club," as the team was known, for its tradition of coming alive in the fourth quarter and pushing away defeat, helped the moniker grow to Fighting Tigers.

Mississippi Rebels

University of Mississippi
P.O. Box 217
University, MS 38677

School Colors: Cardinal Red and
                    Navy Blue
Year Founded: 1844
Basketball: C. M. ("Tad") Smith
                 Coliseum (9,000)
Football: Vaught-Hemingway Stadium
               (42,000)
               Mississippi Veterans
               Memorial Stadium (62,500)

OL' MISS HAS BEEN KNOWN as the Rebels since 1936, when the name was suggested by Judge Ben Guider. Rebels was among five final entries sent to southern sports writers for final selection from an original list of 200 nicknames. The selection process was part of a contest sponsored by the student newspaper, *The Mississippian.*

Of the 42 newsmen contacted, 21 responded. The name Rebels was the first choice of 18 journalists. Judge William Hemingway of the athletic committee announced the new name by stating, "If 18 sportswriters wish to use 'Rebels,' I shall not rebel, so let it go, Ol' Miss Rebels."

Two years later, the yearbook appeared as the *The Rebel Number*, with Colonel Reb making a new entrance in university publications. Colonel Reb has since become a nearly official university insignia.

Mississippi State Bulldogs

Mississippi State University
P.O. Drawer 5308
Mississippi State, MS 39762

School Colors: Maroon and White
Year Founded: 1878
Basketball: Humphrey Coliseum
            (10,000)
Football: Scott Field (41,000)

THE SOURCE OF the Mississippi State Bulldogs' nickname can be traced back to football parades in the early part of the century.

Following an 11–0 football win against rival Mississippi, excited students found a bulldog puppy and carried it through downtown Jackson as a part of their victory parade.

In 1926, 21 years after the puppy first took part in MSU activities, another bulldog appeared at a pregame rally as students prepared for their annual clash with Alabama.

Football coach Major Ralph Sasse provided the school with its first live-in mascot in October 1935, while in Memphis. "The boys sent me here to get a bulldog as a mascot, and they issued a warning that they wouldn't play against Alabama's Crimson Tide next Saturday in Tuscaloosa if I came back without one," Sasse said.

Sasse returned with Ptolemy, a gift from the Edgar Webster family. The team held up their end of the bargain, snapping a 20-year losing streak with a 20–7 victory over the Crimson Tide.

However, Ptolemy unfortunately died of food poisoning within the year. Prior to the Army games, Joe Rice Dockery, in a letter to the school's *Alumnus* magazine, promised Coach Sasse another bulldog to fill the vacancy if MSU triumphed over the Knights.

Following a 13–7 conquest over the highly rated and undefeated Army, Dockery drove up to Memphis and purchased Ptolemy's brother from the same litter and presented him to Sasse. The students named this dog Bully, and the name has been passed on over the years from mascot to mascot.

Early bulldog mascots were allowed plenty of freedom as they roamed from class to class and dormitory to dormitory. They were well fed, often feasting in the cafeteria due to the generosity of students.

Another unfortunate death occurred in 1939 when Bully's life was cut short by a campus bus. For days the entire campus mourned the death of their beloved mascot. He was laid in a glass-top casket following a half-mile funeral procession, complete with the 86-piece Maroon Band and three battalions of ROTC students.

Bully was buried under the player's bench at the 50-yard-line mark at Scott Field. It was such a touching experience that *Life* magazine was there to cover the event.

Tennessee Volunteers

University of Tennessee
P.O. Box 47
Knoxville, TN 37901

School Colors: Orange and White
Year Founded: 1794
Basketball: Thompson/Boling
          Assembly Center (24,535)
Football: Neyland Stadium (91,110)

THE UNIVERSITY OF TENNESSEE borrowed its nickname from the state's own name. The state of Tennessee acquired the nickname the Volunteer State in the early 1800s when Gen. Andrew Jackson mustered large armies from his home state to fight the Indians and later the British at the Battle of New Orleans.

The name became even more meaningful in the Mexican War when Gov. Aaron V. Brown issued a call for 2,800 men to battle Santa Ana and more than 30,000 volunteered. The cavalry uniform worn by Tennessee soldiers during the battle is still worn by the UT colorguard at school events.

In 1953, the student body developed a school mascot. Smokey, a rather pleasant blue tick coonhound, can be seen walking his post at all Tennessee football games. The dog is a native breed of Tennessee.

Vanderbilt Commodores

Vanderbilt University
P.O. Box 120158
2601 Jess Neely Drive
Nashville, TN 37212

School Colors: Black and Gold
Year Founded: 1873
Basketball: Memorial Gymnasium
(15,646)
Football: Dudley Field (41,000)

VANDERBILT UNIVERSITY received its nickname from a former quarterback writing for a local newspaper. The school was first dubbed Commodores in 1897 by Nashville *Banner* sportswriter William E. "Billy" Beard, a quarterback on the 1892 squad. Beard used the term in reference to Commodore Cornelius Vanderbilt, a man of tremendous will and self-reliance who donated more than $1 million in 1873 to build the university that still bears his name.

Vanderbilt's athletic logo, a single star and *V,* is an adaptation of the one-star naval rank insignia of a commodore. The official school colors, black and gold, were originally adopted by members of Vandy's first football team and have faithfully represented the school ever since.

Virginia Military Institute Keydets

25

Southern Conference

Southern Conference
10 Woodfin Street, Suite 206
Asheville, NC 28801

Number of Schools: 9
Year Founded: 1921
Charter Members: Alabama, Auburn, Clemson, Georgia, Georgia Tech, Kentucky, Maryland, Mississippi State, North Carolina, North Carolina State, Tennessee, Virginia, Virginia Tech, and Washington and Lee
Current Members: Appalachian State, Citadel, Davidson, East Tennessee State, Furman, Marshall, Tennessee-Chattanooga, Virginia Military Institute, and Western Carolina
Division I Sports: Baseball, Basketball, Cross-Country, Football, Golf, Indoor Track, Soccer, Tennis, Track and Field, and Wrestling

Appalachian State Mountaineers

Appalachian State University
Broome-Kirk Gymnasium
Boone, NC 28608

School Colors: Black and Gold
Year Founded: 1899
Basketball: Varsity Gymnasium
            (8,000)
Football: William J. Conrad Stadium
            (18,000)

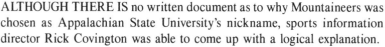

ALTHOUGH THERE IS no written document as to why Mountaineers was chosen as Appalachian State University's nickname, sports information director Rick Covington was able to come up with a logical explanation.

The Appalachian State campus is located in Boone, North Carolina, right in the heart of the Blue Ridge Mountains. The Boone campus is quite close to Mount Mitchell, which at 6,684 feet is the highest point east of the Rocky Mountains. So when Appalachian State athletic teams began competition in the midteens of this century, it was only natural for them to be called the Mountaineers.

Citadel Bulldogs

The Citadel
P.O. Box 7, Citadel Station
Charleston, SC 29409

School Colors: Light Blue and White
Year Founded: 1842
Basketball: F. Mitchell Johnson
            Center (3,052)
Football: Johnson Hagood Memorial
            Stadium (22,500)

THE CITADEL'S TEAMS ARE TAGGED with two nicknames: Cadets and Bulldogs. The Cadet title dates all the way back to the school's founding, when Citadel's full-time students were referred to as cadets.

The school's other nickname, Bulldogs, is more widely used today. No one is quite sure when this name first went into effect, but former Citadel athlete and coach Col. C. F. Myers explained, "When the Citadel started playing football, we didn't have real good teams. But the guys played hard and showed a lot of tenacity . . . like a Bulldog. The local paper started calling us Bulldogs and then the school picked it up."

The Citadel itself is named after the campus building that originally housed all of the school's first cadets and still stands in Charleston's Marion Square. Also referred to as Citadel Square, it is technically named for Gen. Francis Marion, a hero in the Revolutionary War.

The school's colors evolved after a team manager pulled the combination out of his hat on a road trip. In the spring of 1899, Cadet captain John W. Moore, manager of the baseball team, and a few friends decided to make team pennants. Since other schools had team colors, he decided the combination blue and white was most appropriate. The colors were readily accepted by the Corps of Cadets and are still in use today.

Davidson College Wildcats

Davidson College
P.O. Box 1750
Davidson, NC 28036

School Colors: Red and Black
Year Founded: 1837
Basketball: Charlotte Coliseum
(23,500)
Baker Sports Complex
(6,000)
Football: Richardson Field (8,000)

THERE ARE SEVERAL versions of how Davidson College athletic teams obtained their Wildcats' name. Although no one is quite sure which version is correct, everyone agrees the name is appropriate. Competing as a major college, Davidson, which has a small student body, generally plays schools much larger, and over the years has had a considerable degree of success.

The name was adopted sometime between 1917 and 1920. Some say the name came about following the Davidson–Georgia Tech football game when the Georgians said Davidson "fought like a bunch of wildcats."

Another explanation came from Albert S. Potts, a 1919 graduate, who went on to work in the sports departments for Charlotte and Atlanta papers. According to Potts, newspapers often referred to Davidson teams as the Preachers because of their affiliation with the Presbyterian church. Since he didn't feel this title correctly exemplified the team's fighting qualities and high spirits, he began to insert the name Wildcats into his articles.

However, Lacy McAlister, class of 1920, believes the Atlanta *Constitution* should receive credit for introducing the name. According to McAlister, the name first appeared after Davidson's 21–7 win over Auburn in 1917 when the headline read "Wildcats Twist Tigers' Tail." In the accompanying story, there was a reference to the Wildcats from Davidson.

East Tennessee State Buccaneers

East Tennessee State University
P.O. Box 21, 730A ETSU
Johnson City, TN 37614

School Colors: Blue and Gold
Year Founded: 1911
Basketball: Memorial Center (12,000)
Football: Memorial Center (12,000)

NO ONE AT East Tennessee State University really knows why their athletic teams are called the Buccaneers. But over the years a theory developed that just might provide the answer to this perplexing question.

As you probably already know, Johnson City is situated among the mountains in eastern Tennessee and is a great distance from the sea. So why on earth is the school nickname the Buccaneers?

Geologists and archaeologists teamed up and discovered an underground river in the vicinity of the university. Pirate Creek apparently weaves its way through many subterranean tunnels. It is believed the caverns at one time channeled all the way to the Atlantic Ocean.

After this discovery, the legend of the infamous buccaneer Jean Paul LeBucque was found in the history books. According to the legend, LeBucque was a real nuisance and terrorized the east coast of Florida as well as various ports in the Caribbean. Because things had become very dangerous for LeBucque in that area, he sailed north in search of a new home and a new hiding place for the vast treasures he had already acquired on the high seas.

He was apparently looking for an inland hiding place where he would be safe from the adversaries he had encountered. As the legend states, he discovered this underground river near Johnson City and called Pirate Creek his new home.

However, geologists believe the upheaval of the earth's crust, which now blocks the channel, probably killed LeBucque. This legend is generally accepted and is really the only possible explanation to why an inland school would have a pirate-type name.

East Tennessee State may also very well have the only athletic facility in the world that contains both a football field and a medical college. Memorial Center, which is the home for Buccaneer football, basketball, track, and tennis teams as well as the student recreation facility, also houses the Quillen-Dishner College of Medicine on its second floor.

Furman Paladins

Furman University
Poinsett Highway
Greenville, SC 29613

School Colors: Purple and White
Year Founded: 1826
Basketball: Greenville Memorial
                (6,000)
Football: Paladin Stadium (16,000)

PRIOR TO 1961, Furman University went by a number of different nicknames and did not use any single one as its official school name. The baseball team was known as the Hornets, the football team as the Hurricanes, and the basketball team as the Paladins.

The basketball team was named by a Greenville sportswriter who first used the Paladin name in the 1930s. But on September 15, 1961, by the majority vote of the entire student body, Paladins became the official school nickname for all the Furman athletic teams.

The name Paladin is derived from Count Palantine, who was one of 12 knights comprising the bodyguard and inner circle of the Emperor Charlemagne.

Marshall Thundering Herd

Marshall University
P.O. Box 1360
Huntington, WV 25715

MARSHALL UNIVERSITY

School Colors: Green and White
Year Founded: 1837
Basketball: Henderson Center Arena
         (10,250)
Football: Fairfield Stadium (17,312)

MARSHALL UNIVERSITY'S extravagant nickname, the Thundering Herd, was actually copied from the title of a novel.

In the early 1920s, Duke Ridgely, sports editor and columnist of the Huntington *Herald-Dispatch*, took the new nickname from the title of one of Zane Grey's famous Old West novels. Some 38 years later, in 1958, the student body voted on the school's nickname and instead chose Big Green.

But the name Thundering Herd refused to disappear, despite losing the election. In 1964, Pres. Stewart Smith formed a faculty-student committee to select a permanent nickname, and Thundering Herd stomped over Big Green and Rams.

Marshall University itself was named after John Marshall, the chief justice of the U.S. Supreme Court from 1801 to 1835.

Tennessee-Chattanooga Moccasins

University of Tennessee at Chattanooga
UTC Arena, Fourth and Marble
Chattanooga, TN 37403-2598

School Colors: Navy Blue and Old
                     Gold
Year Founded: 1886
Basketball: UTC Arena (11,218)
Football: Chamberlain Field (10,501)

THE MOCCASINS, the nickname of the University of Tennessee at Chattanooga, received their name from the Cherokee Indians who originally lived in the area.

In the city's earliest years, the central area of Chattanooga was located on an area of land along the banks of the Tennessee River. The Indians called this land Moccasin Bend. As the Indians looked down from nearby Lookout Mountain, they saw a stretch of land around the river was shaped like a moccasin.

The name Chattanooga was also provided by the Cherokees. When translated, it means "rock coming to a point," in reference to Lookout Mountain.

Virginia Military Institute Keydets

Virginia Military Institute
Lexington, VA 24450

School Colors: Red, White, and
Yellow
Year Founded: 1839
Basketball: Cameron Hall (5,029)
Football: Alumni Memorial Stadium
(10,000)

THE PROBLEM IN determining the source and significance of the Virginia Military Institute Keydets' nickname is that no definite meaning has been found for the word.

The United States Military Academy claims it was a word once used to denote the gray color found in the standard uniform of a cadet. Another explanation for the nickname is that due to the Southern drawl of some leaders of the VMI Corps, the term cadet was unintentionally modified to keydet.

VMI has had many different names throughout the years. The Flying Squadron was the longest-standing name to refer to VMI's teams. Originating in 1917 during the VMI–North Carolina football game, the name was used occasionally until the early 1950s, when Keydets was first used.

The school's mascot is a kangaroo. Back in 1947, two VMI cheerleaders recognized how rare the kangaroo was among colleges as a team mascot. After a live kangaroo was obtained as the school's mascot, a Name-The-Mascot contest was held, and the prize-winning name was T. D. Bound.

Western Carolina Catamounts

Western Carolina University
2517 Ramsey Center
Cullowhee, NC 28723

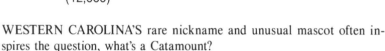

School Colors: Purple and Gold
Year Founded: 1889
Basketball: Liston B. Ramsey Activity
Center (7,826)
Football: E. J. Whitmire Stadium
(12,000)

WESTERN CAROLINA'S rare nickname and unusual mascot often inspires the question, what's a Catamount?

Catamount is a general term for wildcats, including the cougar, lynx, and bobcat. The Catamounts' name is very appropriate for Western Carolina since many cats of this variety roam the Appalachian Mountains, where the university is located.

The nickname evolved from a campus-wide contest held in 1933. At that time, the school was known as Western Carolina Teachers College, and its teams were called the Teachers. College officials were looking for an animal name rarely used in collegiate athletics as well as a name other schools would not copy. The contest eventually came down to Mountain Boomers, which is a small ground squirrel that scampers about the woods and is almost impossible to catch, and Catamounts.

Head football coach C. C. Poindexter really took a fancy to Catamounts, and the nickname was chosen. He wanted his players to be Catamounts with "fierce spirit, savage attacks, and lightning quick moves."

Western Carolina is the only college football team in the national playing under the name Catamounts. The University of Vermont also uses the name, but does not field a football squad.

McNeese State Cowboys

26

Southland Conference

Southland Conference
P.O. Box 863579
Plano, TX 75086-3579

Number of Schools: 8
Year Founded: 1963
Charter Members: Arkansas State, Arlington State, Evelyn
Christian College, Lamar Tech, and Trinity
Current Members: McNeese State, North Texas, Northeast
Louisiana, Northwestern State, Sam Houston
State, Southwest Texas State, Stephen F.
Austin State, and Texas-Arlington
Division I Sports: Baseball, Basketball, Cross-Country,
Football, Golf, Indoor Track, Tennis, and
Track and Field

McNeese State Cowboys

McNeese State University
P.O. Box A-10
Lake Charles, LA 70609

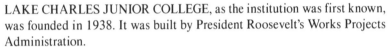

School Colors: Blue and Gold
Year Founded: 1938
Basketball: Burton Coliseum (8,000)
Football: Cowboy Stadium (20,000)

LAKE CHARLES JUNIOR COLLEGE, as the institution was first known, was founded in 1938. It was built by President Roosevelt's Works Projects Administration.

In 1940, the school's name was changed to John McNeese Junior College to honor the father of the Southwest Louisiana education system. McNeese had been the first superintendent of Calcasieu Parish Schools and also made the first cattle drive across the Sabine River.

In July 1950, the Louisiana legislature approved the school as a four-year college and renamed it McNeese State College. The name was changed to McNeese State University in 1970.

The Cowboys' nickname was selected because of John McNeese's longtime involvement in cattle drives as well as the cattlemen's association's involvement in building the school's arena.

North Texas Eagles

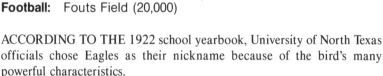

University of North Texas
P.O. Box 13917
Denton, TX 76203-3917

School Colors: Green and White
Year Founded: 1890
Basketball: The Super Pit (10,000)
Football: Fouts Field (20,000)

ACCORDING TO THE 1922 school yearbook, University of North Texas officials chose Eagles as their nickname because of the bird's many powerful characteristics.

As stated in the *Yucca*, the Eagle was an appropriate choice because "no other bird of the air and no beast of the field was ever so graceful, so swift, or so aggressive; there is no eye so keen, no talon so sharp or powerful. . . . An eagle is also independent and takes no food except that provided by his own power and skill. Furthermore, no other was ever so loyal to its kind. An eagle will die in defense of its nest."

The name was approved on February 1, 1922, and to the students and alumni of North Texas, the name has further significance. It suggests the esteem and loyalty for the school and for its soaring athletic program. As far as loyalty is concerned, a better mascot could not have been chosen.

Another unofficial nickname often used to tag the football team was the Mean Green. While Joe Greene was a sophomore with the team in 1966, the defensive squad was dubbed the Mean Green Defense because of their stingy play. The media and students soon picked up on the name. However, it wasn't until Greene's rookie season with the Pittsburgh Steelers that he was dubbed Mean Joe Greene, when a northern sportswriter confused Greene's alma mater's nickname with the defensive tackle's own name.

In May 1988, an administrative decision was made to change the school's name from North Texas State University to University of North Texas.

Northeast Louisiana Indians

Northeast Louisiana University
200 Stadium Drive
Monroe, LA 71209

School Colors: Maroon and Gold
Year Founded: 1931
Basketball: Ewing Coliseum (8,000)
Football: Malone Stadium (23,277)

NORTHEAST LOUISIANA'S athletic teams have been known as the Indians since the school began as Quachita Junior College in 1931. The school was named after the legend of the Quachita Indians, a particularly fierce tribe of warriors who roamed and raided homes and farms along the Quachita River basin. The name Indians naturally followed and has remained in use, despite considerable controversy.

Former assistant football coach and the university's first baseball coach, Woody Boyles, recalled that during his early days there was at least one athlete unhappy with the nickname. The captain of one of the early Northeast teams begged the student body to change the nickname. He claimed Northeast's opponents had been calling him a big fat squaw at recent events.

The school's mascot was the brainchild of former school services director Judy Kane. Working with designers from Walt Disney Studios, she devised the costume for the current Indian mascot, made by the same company that outfits the San Diego Chicken. A contest was held in the summer of 1980 to name the figure, and Michael Martin, the 12-year-old son of a longtime team trainer, won with his entry of Chief Brave Spirit. The Chief made his official debut on September 13, 1980, at Northeast Louisiana's football opener at Iowa State.

Northwestern State Demons

Northwestern State University
Prather Coliseum
Natchitoches, LA 71497

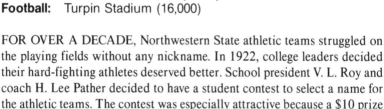

School Colors: Purple, White, and
                   Orange
Year Founded: 1884
Basketball: Prather Coliseum (3,400)
Football: Turpin Stadium (16,000)

FOR OVER A DECADE, Northwestern State athletic teams struggled on the playing fields without any nickname. In 1922, college leaders decided their hard-fighting athletes deserved better. School president V. L. Roy and coach H. Lee Pather decided to have a student contest to select a name for the athletic teams. The contest was especially attractive because a $10 prize was offered by the athletic department.

Some of the more entertaining entries included the Gridiron Knights, Daredevils, Boosters, Sharks, Cannons, Deers, Musketeers, Invincibles, Ground Hogs, Royalists, Cyclops, Bloodhounds, Professors, Cannon Balls, Wasps, and Rattlesnakes. From that group, a committee narrowed the suggestions down to only two names—Braves and Demons.

A student vote proved that Demons was the favorite name. The winners of the $10 prize were Aileen Ritter and Truett Scarborough, who split the prize money.

Sam Houston State Bearkats

Sam Houston State University
P.O. Box 2268
Huntsville, TX 77341

School Colors: Orange, White, and
                 Blue
Year Founded: 1879
Basketball: Bernard G. Johnson
             Coliseum (6,110)
Football: Bearkat Stadium (14,000)

THE ORIGIN OF THE BEARKATS' name remains a mystery at Sam Houston State University. Even after school officials called alumni, dug through old clippings, and flipped through pages of ancient yearbooks in hopes of finding an answer for this book, there was still no conclusive evidence to what a bearkat is or why it was ever selected to represent Sam Houston State.

However, it is known that student-mascot Sammy Bearkat was officially enrolled in school by Pres. Harmon Lowman in December 1959. His first appearance was before a home basketball game against Austin College.

During the 1970s, an unsuccessful attempt to bring a live bearkat mascot to the campus was made when a kinkajou was purchased from a Houston pet shop. Besides the fact that the exotic South American mammal doesn't look anything like a bearkat, there was one other minor problem with this version of Sammy. He kept biting the fans at athletic events. He was eventually thrown behind bars at the San Antonio Zoo so all visitors could admire this unusual animal . . . yet still keep their distance.

Southwest Texas State Bobcats

Southwest Texas State University
Jowers Center
San Marcos, TX 78666

School Colors: Maroon and Gold
Year Founded: 1899
Basketball: Strahan Coliseum (7,200)
Football: Bobcat Stadium (14,104)

SOUTHWEST TEXAS STATE chose its Bobcats' nickname simply because large numbers of this particular animal once inhabited the surrounding area.

During the university's inception, one of the most prominent types of wildlife found in central Texas was the bobcat. This made the nickname a popular choice, which has remained throughout the school's history.

The bobcat is a logical choice for an athletic nickname because it represents a fierce, sly, independent animal with great athletic qualities and a team that must be watched constantly because it is very dangerous.

Stephen F. Austin State Lumberjacks

Stephen F. Austin State University
Box 13010 SFA
Nacogdoches, TX 75962

School Colors: Purple and White
Year Founded: 1921
Basketball: Stephen F. Austin
          Coliseum (8,064)
Football: Homer Bryce Stadium
          (14,640)

STEPHEN F. AUSTIN STATE was founded by the 36th legislature of Texas in 1921 as Stephen F. Austin Teachers College.

Because the institution is located at Nacogdoches, in the piney woods commonly known as Deep East Texas, selection of a nickname was easy. Lumberjacks was a natural name for the school's mascot.

The legend of Nacogdoches has it that an old Caddo chief living near the Sabine River had twin sons, one with dark hair and swarthy skin, the other with blond hair and light skin. When it was time for them to become leaders of their own tribes, the father sent one brother on a three days' journey into the rising sun and the other brother on a three days' journey into the setting sun.

As the story goes, Nacogdoches, Texas, developed from the blond-haired brother's tribe. Natchitoches, Louisiana, developed around the dark-haired brother's descendants.

Texas-Arlington Mavericks

University of Texas at Arlington
Box 19079
Arlington, TX 76019

School Colors: Royal Blue and White
Year Founded: 1895
Basketball: Texas Hall (4,200)

THE TEXAS-ARLINGTON Mavericks' nickname replaced the Rebels in 1971. The school's teams are named in honor of one of the biggest landholders in Texas history.

Samuel Augustus Maverick was mayor of San Antonio in 1839 and was one of the signers of the Texas Declaration of Independence. He owned 340,000 acres of Texas land he purchased at only five cents an acre—a total of only $17,000. The Washington *Daily Globe* in 1854 called Maverick "the largest landholder in the world, and by far the wealthiest."

Mavericks is actually the school's fifth nickname. Other names include Hornets (1917–23), Junior Aggies (1923–49), Blue Riders (1949–51), and Rebels (1951–71).

After the selection of the name Mavericks in 1971, school officials began searching for a logo. Some folks say a maverick is a wild cow, others say it's a wild horse, and still others believe it is a free-thinking, independent-acting man. Actually, all three definitions are correct.

So a committee made up of representatives of the Student Congress began contacting artists in the area, asking for sketches of their personal interpretations of a Maverick.

All sorts of drawings came back: skinny cows, snarling cows, cows with long horns, and cows with steel-rimmed glasses and peace medallions. There were cowboys, too, smiling, frowning, drawing guns, shooting guns. And oh, yeah, a horse with horns.

A horse with horns? At first the committee members reactions were doubtful, to say the least. "You're the only university, as far as we know, having 'Mavericks' as a nickname," said Fort Worth artist Harry Bury, the creator of the unique creature. "A Maverick can be anything you say it is."

All the sketches were turned over to the Student Congress during the summer session so students could look over and decide upon the appropriate maverick. By a 65 percent vote, the unique, wild, spirited, untamed, and untamable horned horse was declared the official logo.

In 1982, the horned horse logo was replaced by a caricature of Sam Maverick, the historic landholder of Texas.

Arkansas Razorbacks

27

Southwest Athletic Conference

Southwest Athletic Conference
11300 West Mockingbird Lane, Suite 444
P.O. Box 569420
Dallas, TX 75356-9420

Number of Schools: 9
Year Founded: 1914
Charter Members: Arkansas, Baylor, Oklahoma, Oklahoma State, Rice, Southwestern, Texas, and Texas A&M
Current Members: Arkansas, Baylor, Houston, Rice, Southern Methodist, Texas, Texas A&M, Texas Christian, and Texas Tech
Division I Sports: Baseball, Basketball, Cross-Country, Football, Golf, Indoor Track, Swimming, Tennis, and Track and Field

Arkansas Razorbacks

University of Arkansas
Fayetteville, AR 72701

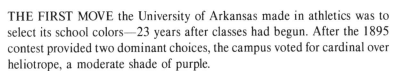

School Colors: Cardinal and White
Year Founded: 1871
Basketball: Barnhill Arena (9,000)
Football: War Memorial Stadium
(53,250)

THE FIRST MOVE the University of Arkansas made in athletics was to select its school colors—23 years after classes had begun. After the 1895 contest provided two dominant choices, the campus voted for cardinal over heliotrope, a moderate shade of purple.

The school played for 15 years without any school nickname. Then at a postseason rally following the 1909 undefeated football season, Arkansas coach Hugo Bezdek referred to his squad as "a wild band of Razorbacks" and the name quickly caught on. The famous yell, "Whooo, Pig! Sooey!" was added in the 1920s.

Arkansas received its first live mascot in the 1960s when Rib Red, a Duroc hog, was donated to the cause. Ragnar, a wild hog captured in South Arkansas by farmer Bill Robinson, served as mascot during the 1977 season. During Ragnar's reign, the beast killed a coyote, a 450-pound hog, and seven rattlesnakes—demonstrating the kind of aggressiveness that would have made Coach Bezdek mighty proud of his Arkansas boys.

Baylor Bears

Baylor University
CSB 393
Waco, TX 76798

School Colors: Green and Gold
Year Founded: 1845
Basketball: Ferrell Special Events
Center (10,000)
Football: Baylor Stadium (48,500)

BACK IN 1914, in an effort to highten student morale at Baylor University, Pres. Samuel P. Brooks allowed the student body to hold an election to select a new mascot. The five most popular names were all animals: Buffalos, Antelopes, Frogs, Ferrets, and Bears. The moniker Bears conquered the other four choices in the final balloting and a new mascot was born.

In 1916, Baylor received its first live bear from the Waco-based U.S. Army unit. Named Bruin, he was the first of many Baylor Bears to appear in the stadium on football Saturdays. Baylor, which still allows live mascots on the field, now receives its bears from Bear Country USA, a wildlife park in Rapid City, South Dakota.

Houston Cougars

University of Houston
3855 Holman
Houston, TX 77004

School Colors: Red and White
Year Founded: 1927
Basketball: Hofheinz Pavilion (10,060)
Football: The Houston Astrodome
(55,155)

THE UNIVERSITY OF HOUSTON received its nickname when the head coach felt a need for a team name.

John R. Bender, the university's first coach, named the Houston athletic teams the Cougars. Bender, who came from Washington State to accept the Houston job, gave the school the name in 1927 when it was still a junior college. The student newspaper assisted Bender in naming the team, and when Houston entered intercollegiate athletics in 1946, Cougars was officially declared the school nickname.

Rice Owls

Rice University
P.O. Box 1892
Houston, TX 77251

School Colors: Blue and Gray
Year Founded: 1891
Basketball: Autry Court (5,400)
Football: Rice Stadium (70,000)

RICE UNIVERSITY'S nickname, the Owls, emerged from the university's own heraldic shield. When looking over a number of ideas for the school's shield, the designer noted that several families with the surnames Houston and Rice both had chevrons and three avian charges on their coat of arms.

Working with this information, he adapted these same symbols for the university shield, on which a double chevron divides the field and the charges. The owls of Athena, which appear on an ancient Greek coin, are also part of the shield. When Rice's doors officially opened for classes in 1912, the athletic teams were called Owls because of the key role the birds played on the shield.

When former Rice guard Fred Curry was elected president of the school's Touchdown Club in 1974, he had big plans. When someone suggested some kind of winner-take-all award symbolic of the annual Rice-Houston football game, Curry went to work.

Purdue and Indiana fight each season for bragging rights to which team is the best in the state. The fierce rivalry is similar to the Rice-Houston game so he wanted to offer a trophy—a Bucket. When asked what the city of Houston is noted for, Curry replied, "Dirty Bayous—Bayou Bucket, a perfect name!" While on vacation that summer, Curry found a big, beat-up old bucket at an antique shop. He paid $60 for the bucket and had it mounted on a trophy in time for the 1974 game against Houston. Competing for the Bayou Bucket has become a tradition for this big game each fall.

Southern Methodist Mustangs

Southern Methodist University
Box 216
Dallas, TX 75275

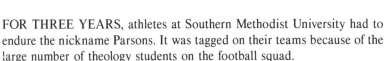

School Colors: Red and Blue
Year Founded: 1911
Basketball: Moody Coliseum (9,007)
Football: Ownby Stadium (24,000)

FOR THREE YEARS, athletes at Southern Methodist University had to endure the nickname Parsons. It was tagged on their teams because of the large number of theology students on the football squad.

Following the school's first athletic title, in which the women's basketball won state, sportswriters referred to SMU as one of the big three in basketball. It was then decided that the teams needed a more appropriate mascot to represent their wild, fighting spirit.

The Campus newspaper solicited ideas, and students submitted many fierce names including Bulls, Rams, Comanches, and Rattlers. One unnamed contestant valued honesty over ferocity: "Tadpoles signify we have left nothing behind and intend to develop for the future," he suggested.

The list was narrowed to three finalists. At a pep rally on October 25, 1917, the Mustangs, a nickname representative of the fleet-footed horses native to Texas, was selected over Bison and Greyhounds.

A common sight on football Saturdays today at SMU is a black pony racing across the football field following a Mustang score. This tradition dates back to 1932, the day on which Peruna I first took the field.

On November 4, 1932, a four-year-old pony was donated by T. E. Jones, the owner of Arlington Downs racetrack. The pony, named Peruna I, wore a red blanket donated by Jones. The blanket is still part of the Mustangs' mascot's football attire.

Unfortunately, Peruna I met tragedy in only the second year of his reign as mascot. Peruna I playfully ran out into Mockingbird Lane and was struck by a car and killed. Many students mourned his death, and Peruna I was buried outside Ownby Stadium, under a small statue of a mustang marking the grave.

Following the death of Peruna I, another proud tradition began. Each mascot to this day has been given to the school by the Cully Culwell family, owner of Culwell and Sons men's store. Thanks to the Culwells, the Peruna legend of the SMU Mustang lives on today.

Texas A&M Aggies

Texas A&M University
College Station, TX 77843

School Colors: Maroon and White
Year Founded: 1876
Basketball: G. Rollie White Coliseum
            (7,500)
Football: Kyle Field (72,387)

MOST EARLY-DAY STUDENTS at Texas A&M University were farmers. As a result, Aggies is the only nickname the school has ever used.

Founded in 1876, Texas Agriculture and Mechanical University was a school devoted primarily to the education of students interested in agriculture. The Aggies' nickname was used to describe those early students and has stayed with the school ever since.

Texas A&M University is one of the few big schools in the nation to retain A&M in its proper title.

Texas Christian Horned Frogs

Texas Christian University
Box 32394
Fort Worth, TX 76129

School Colors: Purple and White
Year Founded: 1873
Basketball: Daniel-Meyer Coliseum (7,166)
Football: Amon G. Carter Stadium (46,000)

TEXAS CHRISTIAN UNIVERSITY'S unique name, the Horned Frogs, was born when the school was still located in Waco, Texas. Both the name and mascot were installed for the 1897–1898 school year. Two stories are given for the origin of the nickname.

The first explanation credits two literary societies that were appointed to select a title for the school's yearbook. They decided upon *The Horned Frog* because the animal was commonly sighted in much of Texas. The name Horned Frog eventually became synonymous with TCU students and became the official school nickname.

But what Texans really see out on the range is not a frog but rather a Texas horned lizard. Long ago, Texans coined the term horned frog. At any rate, Texas Christian has the only iguana mascot in the nation.

The second story describes how fans challenged the football team to take on the tough nature of these abundant little creatures that inhabited the football field.

The horned frog is not really a fierce, dangerous creature. In fact, after many successful years of TCU athletics, a fan wrote to the *TCU Daily Skiff* complaining that the mascot was too passive for such a fiercely competitive team. The editor replied, "A name comes to mean what you make it mean."

Texas Longhorns

University of Texas
P.O. Box 7399
Austin, TX 78712

School Colors: Burnt Orange and White
Year Founded: 1881
Basketball: Erwin Center (16,231)
Football: Austin Memorial Stadium (77,809)

THE LONGHORNS, the nickname of the University of Texas, came to life one day when a newspaper editor simply took it upon himself to name the school's teams.

According to D. A. Frank, sportswriter for the Dallas *Texan*, one day in the fall of 1903 editor-in-chief Alex Weisburg approached him and said, "D. A., hereafter in every sports article, call the team Longhorns, and we'll so have it named." Frank obeyed the instructions of his boss, and when he took over Weisburg's job later in the year, he continued to instruct his writers to use the name Longhorns.

In 1906 the name became official, and the teams have been known as the Longhorns ever since. The school has one of the most famous collegiate sports gestures on record, the famous "Hook 'em Horns" salute, which is achieved by extending the forefinger and little finger in an upward position.

The Texas longhorn is a breed of beef cattle that first arrived in America from Spain on the second voyage made by Columbus, in 1493. These cattle are characterized by a great array of colors and proved their value during extremely dry periods on the Texas ranch land. With their long spreading horns, they were part of the long trail drives of cattle moving to market for many years. However, by 1900 the Texas longhorn was driven to near extinction. But the longhorn has made a comeback in the last decade, and you can once more see them dotting the countryside.

Texas Tech Red Raiders

Texas Tech University
P.O. Box 4199
Lubbock, TX 79409

School Colors: Scarlet and Black
Year Founded: 1923
Basketball: Lubbock Municipal
            Auditorium (8,174)
Football: Jones Stadium (47,000)

TEXAS TECH UNIVERSITY received its original nickname from a coach's wife who didn't like the name a newspaper had suggested. The first suggestion for Tech's nickname appeared in the Fort Worth *Star-Telegram* in 1925 when the athletic teams were referred to as the Dogies.

However, Mrs. E. V. Freeland, the head coach's wife, didn't think the name was very complimentary and offered her own suggestion. She recommended the team be called Matadors because of the extravagant Spanish architecture at Tech. She also suggested the school use the colors scarlet and black, which represented the matador's red cape and black costume.

The first mascot at the school was a black calf, donated after Tech's first football victory in 1925. Branded with the winning score, the calf was later killed and barbecued for the team with the idea that the hide would be tanned and placed in the trophy room. However, the hide would not retain its hair and was therefore ruined.

One accomplishment this calf did achieve in its one-year reign was that no opposing fan ever rode it without getting thrown off. This became a regular performance at halftime during that inaugural season.

Yet the name Matadors did not last too long. During the 1930s, Collier Parrish, sports editor of the Lubbock *Morning Avalanche* was inspired by Tech's coast-to-coast schedule and entirely red uniforms to call the team the Red Raiders. Since head coach Pete Cawthon and the team also liked the name, Red Raiders soon became both the official mascot and name.

Prior to the 1954 Gator Bowl, Bert Eades, a member of the Hockley County Sheriff's Posse, came up with the idea of a horse leading the football team onto the field. A black stallion was donated for the parade, and Joe Kirk Fulton, a Tech agriculture student, was chosen as the rider.

In describing Fulton's procession around the field, the Atlanta *Journal* said, "No team in any bowl game ever made a more sensational entrance." Tech went on to "lasso" the Auburn Tigers 35–13 in that game.

The two most popular nicknames among Division I basketball and football teams are the Bulldogs and Tigers, tied with a dozen schools each. Flying closely behind are the Eagles, used by 10 schools, and the Wildcats, representing nine campuses.

Mississipi Valley State Delta Devils

28

Southwestern Conference

Southwestern Conference
1500 Sugar Bowl Drive
New Orleans, LA 70112

Number of Schools: 8
Year Founded: 1920
Charter Members: Bishop College, Paul Quinn College, Prairie View A&M, Sam Houston College, Texas College, and Wylie College
Current Members: Alabama State, Alcorn State, Grambling State, Jackson State, Mississippi Valley State, Prairie View A&M, Southern, and Texas Southern
Division I Sports: Baseball, Basketball, Football, Golf, Tennis, and Track and Field

Alabama State Hornets

Alabama State University
Montgomery, AL 36195

School Colors: Black and Gold
Year Founded: 1874
Basketball: C. J. Dunn Arena (3,200)
Football: Cramton Bowl (24,600)

ALABAMA STATE was tagged the Hornets in the 1920s when the football team fielded a team of younger players. During the 1923–24 football season, Alabama State's football team consisted of high school and junior college students. When the youngsters played Talladega College, a wise Talladega player commented, "those little boys sure play like a nest of hornets." Ever since, the athletic teams of Alabama State University have been known as the Hornets.

Associate professor of education Dr. Robert B. Stone described the significance of the Hornets nickname in "The Hornet Mystique." One passage explains: "Hornets are a different kind of species. They are among the most social animals on earth, which means they get along well together. They are goal-oriented, meaning they know what they're doing before they start. They don't begin an operation until they are all ready, each knowing its particular role and responsibility. Once they begin their mission they are driven to see it completed. Hornets have a back-up system that replaces each fallen Hornet with a fresh Hornet equally dedicated to the completion of the Hornet's goal. Nothing stays the Hornets from completion of their appointed goal."

Alcorn State Braves

Alcorn State University
P.O. Box 510
Lorman, MS 39096

School Colors: Purple and Old Gold
Year Founded: 1871
Basketball: Scalping Grounds (7,000)
Football: Henderson Stadium (10,000)

BECAUSE THERE IS no document on file explaining the origin of Alcorn State University's nickname, no one really knows why it was adopted.

However, because of the history of the area surrounding the Lorman campus, a logical theory can be formed. According to university public relations director Ralph Payne, many years ago the Natches Indians roamed the land where the campus was eventually set up. It is quite possible that when ground breaking took place in 1871, remnants of Indian and heritage were still very prevalent in the area.

So when it came time to pick a nickname, people submitted many names that dealt with Indians and Indian tribes. Out of all the suggestions, school officials decided upon Braves as their official nickname and mascot.

Grambling State Tigers

Grambling State University
P.O. Box N
Grambling, LA 71245

School Colors: Black and Gold
Year Founded: 1901
Basketball: Memorial Gymnasium
               (4,500)
Football: Robinson Stadium (22,500)

THE GRAMBLING STATE UNIVERSITY Tigers' moniker originated in 1936 when Pres. Ralph Waldo Emerson Jones selected the school's nickname.

According to Fred Hobdey, Associate Athletic Director and former basketball coach, Jones chose the nickname Tigers because he thought it would make an excellent symbol for Grambling State's athletic squads.

Similar to how many other nicknames were selected, it is Hobdey's belief that Grambling State chose the Tiger because of the prominence of Louisiana State's Tiger in the southeastern part of the state.

Jackson State Tigers

Jackson State University
P.O. Box 17490
Jackson, MS 39217

School Colors: Blue and White
Year Founded: 1877
Basketball: Lee E. Williams Athletics
& Assembly Center
(10,000)
Football: Mississippi Veterans
Memorial Stadium (62,517)

IN 1923, JACKSON STATE formally selected Tigers as the official nickname of its athletic teams. However, there is no document that explains how or why the name was selected.

The tradition of courageous football at Jackson State began in 1920, when only 13 men went out for the team. When Coach Bragg resigned from the head coaching position the previous term, Jackson State found itself with only six players.

Despite university president Hubert's fondness for the game, he told the players they should forget about football. The determined students, however, continued to practice daily on their own until their number reached 13.

The team selected Ernest Richards, a French teacher who had never played football, as their coach. The team went undefeated and went on to be honored as the Mississippi state champions of intercollegiate football.

These 13 players, known as the Iron Thirteen, were never beaten in a football contest for three consecutive years.

Mississippi Valley State Delta Devils

Mississippi Valley State University
P.O. Box 743
Itta Bena, MS 38941

School Colors: Green and White
Year Founded: 1946
Basketball: Harrison Gymnasium
            (6,000)
Football: Magnolia Stadium (10,000)

WHEN MISSISSIPPI VALLEY STATE opened its doors in 1946, it was without a mascot. Athletic director Cleotha Hatchett wanted to quickly find one and wanted to somehow find one that related to the nearby Mississippi River.

Itta Bena, the city where the campus is located, records very high temperatures in the peak of summer. The common phrase "hot as a devil," which is often hollered around town, played a role in the naming of the teams.

So in 1950, Hatchett took the name Devils and added Delta to it, creating the unique nickname Delta Devils. The name is appropriate to the campus geography, since Itta Bena is located along the flatlands of the Mississippi Delta.

Prairie View A&M Panthers

Prairie View A&M University
P.O. Box 097
Prairie View, TX 77446

School Colors: Purple and Gold
Year Founded: 1876
Basketball: Baby-Dome (6,500)
Football: Blackshirt Stadium (6,000)

NO ONE AT PRAIRIE VIEW A&M University really has any idea why Panthers was selected as their official school nickname. In fact, the only documentation anyone could find at all on the name is on the back of an old calendar.

Angela A. Williams, special collections/archives assistant at the university library, headed the three-week search for the answer to the Panther nickname mystery done exclusively for this book. After much diligent work, the only clue Williams discovered was the 1974–75 Prairie View A&M activities calendar, which briefly mentioned the Panther nickname on the back.

The passage said: "Prairie View's athletic teams are known as the Panthers. The name is descriptive of the fierce, blood-thirsty manner in which the Panthers enter into athletic competition."

Southern Jaguars

Southern University
P.O. Box 9942
Baton Rouge, LA 70813

School Colors: Blue and Gold
Year Founded: 1880
Basketball: F. G. Clark Activity Center
          (7,500)
Football: A. W. Mumford Stadium
          (24,000)

NOBODY—STAFF MEMBER, STUDENT, nor alumnus—seems to have any idea as to why Southern University teams are known as the Jaguars. No records were kept on the subject, and most early leaders in the athletic department have now passed away. However, it is known that at one time Southern's nickname was the Jaguar Cats.

The swift, fierce jaguar is defined as a large feline mammal of tropical America having a tawny coat spotted with black rosettelike markings.

Lacumba, the school's live Jaguar mascot, was a gift of Southern's class of 1961 and is kept at the Baton Rouge Zoo when not appearing at campus activities. Lacumba is not a tame cat by any means and is always treated with caution at all school functions.

Texas Southern Tigers

Texas Southern University
3100 Cleburne
Houston, TX 77004

School Colors: Maroon and Gray
Year Founded: 1946
Basketball: Adams Gym (3,500)
Football: Jefferson Stadium (18,000)
                    Rice Stadium (70,000)

AS FAR AS COACH Robert Moreland can tell, there is no special meaning at all behind Texas Southern University's adoption of the nickname Tigers. The school was formed in 1946. It is believed the Tigers nickname originated in 1947 or 1948 when the athletic program got underway.

"They probably reached into a bag and pulled out the Tigers nickname," commented longtime coach Moreland. "I don't think there was any reason behind it at all. Prairie View was the Panthers and Southern was the Jaguars, so maybe they thought that Tigers would fit well with the other schools."

It should be noted, however, that even before intercollegiate athletics were formed at the school, some club teams on campus unofficially called themselves the Tigers.

Jacksonville Dolphins

29

Sun Belt Conference

Sun Belt Conference
Suite 1010
1408 North Westshore Boulevard
Tampa, FL 33607

Number of Schools: 8
Year Founded: 1976
Charter Members: Georgia State, Jacksonville, New Orleans, North Carolina–Charlotte, South Alabama, and South Florida
Current Members: Alabama-Birmingham, Jacksonville, North Carolina–Charlotte, Old Dominion, South Alabama, South Florida, Virginia Commonwealth, and Western Kentucky
Division I Sports: Baseball, Basketball, Cross-Country, Golf, Soccer, and Tennis

Alabama-Birmingham Blazers

University of Alabama in Birmingham
University Station
Birmingham, AL 35294

School Colors: Green and Gold
Year Founded: 1966
Basketball: UAB Arena (8,500)

THE ATHLETIC PROGRAM at the University of Alabama in Birmingham didn't begin until the late 1970s. The program obtained its nickname via a UAB "Name Our Team Contest" in 1978. The UAB student newspaper, *The Kaleidoscope* sponsored the contest, and students, faculty, and staff were all invited to propose possible nicknames for the university.

After narrowing the list to four—Blazers, Barons, Titans, and Warriors—the name Blazers was announced on January 13, 1978, as the official nickname. In fact, the nickname was so popular that out of almost 2,000 votes, Blazers received 1,147.

"The Blazers' nickname was chosen because it flowed well with University of Alabama in Birmingham," recalled sports information director Grant Shingleton. "To this day, we still are trying to find out exactly what a Blazer is."

Shingleton also pointed out that the contest took place the same year the Portland Trail Blazers won the National Basketball Association title. Apparently, the name was very popular with the student body.

Oddly enough, the school mascot is a student dressed in a chicken costume. After experimenting with other mascots, the chicken emerged from the popularity of the famous San Diego Chicken. The mascot's name is Beauregard T. Rooster and can be seen at many athletic and university functions.

Jacksonville Dolphins

Jacksonville University
Jacksonville, FL 32211

School Colors: Green and Gold
Year Founded: 1934
Basketball: Jacksonville Coliseum
(10,000)

JACKSONVILLE UNIVERSITY received its rare nickname from a campus election. Some 13 years after the school got its start, it was still without a nickname. In order to keep up with other schools, a student-body contest was held in 1947 to give Jacksonville sports teams a distinctive nickname.

The leading suggestions were Green Raiders, Buccaneers, Juggernauts, Green Dragons, and Dolphins. Dolphins was the most popular name and came out the winner.

Because of the campus's close proximity to the Atlantic Ocean, and since dolphins actually swim in the St. John's River, which flows along the Jacksonville campus, the name Dolphins seemed appropriate.

In 1971, Jacksonville University adopted Nellie, the prize dolphin at the Daytona Marineland, as its official mascot.

North Carolina–Charlotte 49ers

University of North Carolina at Charlotte
University Boulevard
Charlotte, NC 28223

School Colors: Green and White
Year Founded: 1946
Basketball: Charlotte Coliseum
(23,000)

UNC-CHARLOTTE'S athletic symbol and mascot, the 49er, has a unique origin. Many people erroneously believe the 49er nickname originated for one of two possible reasons: Some think the name emerged because the campus is located on North Carolina's Highway 49. Others incorrectly believe the campus is located atop an abandoned gold mine.

However, both reasons are false. In 1946, the state legislature established a Charlotte extension of the UNC system for returning veterans of World War II. After the extension center served its purpose, funds for the Charlotte campus were to be cut off. A group of concerned Charlotteans successfully dissuaded the lawmakers, however, and after a long legislative battle, the group hailed the birth of Charlotte College in 1949.

Feeling it was the centennial pioneer spirit of 1849 gold rushers and the we-will-not-be-defeated attitude of the Charlotte group that saved the school, students adopted the 49ers' nickname. A grizzled old miner was selected as the official mascot.

Old Dominion Monarchs

Old Dominion University
H&PE Building/Room 232
Norfolk, VA 23529-0197

School Colors: Slate Blue and Silver
Year Founded: 1930
Basketball: Norfolk Scope (10,253)

FOR MANY YEARS, athletic teams of the Norfolk Division of the College of William and Mary (as Old Dominion was formerly called) were known as the Braves. The name was derived from William and Mary's Indians' nickname to mean little Indians.

When Old Dominion reached four-year status, they no longer found it suitable to be known under William and Mary's fatherly nickname. The Monarchs' sobriquet also serves as a link between the traditions of the past and the realities of the present.

On October 16, 1986, the school's official board of visitors approved a new logo and color change for the campus. The new logo features a crown on a lion's head, representing a historic past and a strong future.

South Alabama Jaguars

University of South Alabama
1107 HPELS Building
Mobile, AL 36688

School Colors: Red, White, and Blue
Year Founded: 1963
Basketball: Mobile Municipal
              Auditorium (10,000)

INFORMATION REGARDING the University of South Alabama's nickname, Jaguars, like a few other nicknames, is scarce. Ever since the athletic program began at South Alabama in 1965, the team nickname has been Jaguars. According to former director of athletics Dr. Mel Lucas, Jaguars was one of several nicknames on the ballot in a 1965 vote, and it won by a landslide in the student election.

The jaguar is an appropriate symbol because it is a fierce hunter known to be one of the fastest animals on earth.

South Florida Bulls

University of South Florida
4202 East Fowler Avenue
Tampa, FL 33620

School Colors: Green and Gold
Year Founded: 1956
Basketball: Sun Dome (10,300)

IF YOU THINK THIS is a cock and bull story, you're absolutely right. As reported in South Florida's *Sundry,* in October 1962 students were faced with the task of selecting a school nickname. After a student vote, Buccaneers was declared the winner.

However, after a quick phone call to Pensacola Junior College, it was found the name Bucs was the same as that school's mascot. Therefore, the second-place entry, Golden Brahmas, was said to be the winner.

But the committee decided the Pensacola conflict really wasn't serious enough to warrant a switch to Golden Brahmas. After all, the students voted Buccaneers as their mascot, and Buccaneers it should be.

Brahma backers soon became bullish about being beaten, and a petition was circulated to hold a new election. The result this time: the Golden Brahmas butted the Bucs out of first place—prompting one observer to suggest the mascot should be a peg-legged bull with a patch over his eye.

A bull? Now the mascot situation was really "fowled up." As the cattle industry quickly pointed out, a brahma is not a bull at all but a chicken—a *brahman* is a bull. So the students, who thought they had grabbed a bull by the horns, had really picked a chicken. Or you might say they laid an egg with the selection of their mascot.

"Since the American brahman has been the salvation of Florida's cattle industry, I think it would be fitting that a Florida college should adopt this noble animal as its symbol," said the secretary of the Eastern Brahman Association.

The Golden Brahman name stuck until the 1981–82 school year, when school officials shortened the name to Bulls because the media was having problems fitting the full name into headlines. At any rate, they didn't have to worry about spelling errors anymore.

Virginia Commonwealth Rams

Virginia Commonwealth University
Box 2003
Richmond, VA 23284-2003

School Colors: Black and Gold
Year Founded: 1838
Basketball: Richmond Coliseum
          (10,716)

VIRGINIA COMMONWEALTH'S father schools were Richmond Professional Institute and the Medical College of Virginia, which merged in 1968.

Prior to 1968, Richmond Professional Institute's athletes were known as the Green Devils and donned the colors of yellow and green. However, the faculty committee at the newly formed Virginia Commonwealth University decided to change both the image and the colors. School colors became black and gold, and the nickname Rams was selected.

The Ram's mascot first appeared in Richmond in the early 1950s when athletic director Ed Allen conducted a vote of Richmond Professional Institute students on the Running Ram. The ram symbol was not officially installed until 1968, though, when the full-scale merger took place.

Western Kentucky Hilltoppers

Western Kentucky University
Bowling Green, KY 42101

School Colors: Red and White
Year Founded: 1906
Basketball: E. A. Diddle Arena
                   (12,370)
Football: L. T. Smith Stadium (19,250)

ANYONE WHO HAS VISITED the Western Kentucky University campus will agree Hilltoppers is a logical choice for the school nickname.

On February 4, 1911, the Western Kentucky State Normal School was moved from the site of its forerunner, Southern Normal School, to southwestern Bowling Green. The move was completed when the entire student body marched to the new site, carrying desks, chairs, and other sorts of school equipment.

Since the summit of "the Hill" rises 232 feet above nearby Barren River and surrounding low plains, it was only natural that athletes who represent the school centered on the crest should be known as Hilltoppers. The name was not formally introduced until the 1925–26 school year when the name was first sewn on the basketball team's jerseys. Prior to that time, the teams were known as the Pedagogues or Teachers.

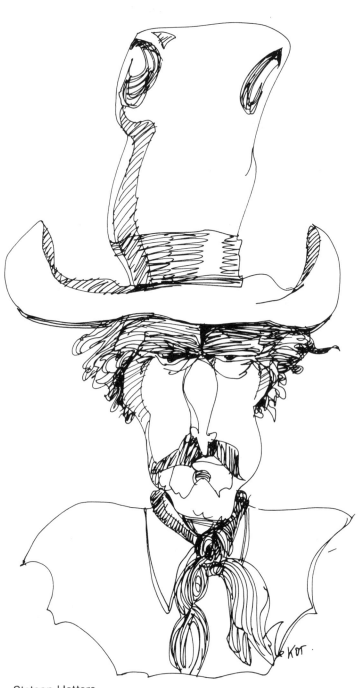

Stetson Hatters

30

Trans America Athletic Conference

Trans American Athletic Conference
Butler Building, Suite 215
237 South Milledge Avenue
Athens, GA 30605

Number of Schools: 10
Year Founded: 1978
Charter Members: Centenary, Hardin-Simmons, Houston Baptist, Mercer, Northeast Louisiana, Oklahoma City, Pan American, and Samford
Current Members: Arkansas–Little Rock, Centenary, Georgia Southern, Georgia State, Hardin-Simmons, Houston Baptist, Mercer, Samford, Stetson, and Texas–San Antonio
Division I Sports: Baseball, Basketball, Cross-Country, Golf, Soccer, and Tennis

Arkansas–Little Rock Trojans

University of Arkansas at Little Rock
2801 South University
Little Rock, AK 77204

School Colors: Maroon and White
Year Founded: 1927
Basketball: Barton Coliseum (8,303)

AT A RECENT LUNCHEON, 1930 Arkansas–Little Rock class president Bill Normal revealed the deep, dark, secret of how the school became known as the Trojans. During his presidency, the students decided a nickname should be developed for the new basketball program. Norman told the story this way. "We needed a name, so a meeting was called to choose one. After quite a discussion, the suggestion was made to write some names on the blackboard. The board was full of names. I wrote the name 'Trojans,' realizing that no other college team in this part of the country had that name.

"The only one I knew of was the Trojans of the University of Southern California, who were getting national recognition on the radio at that time. Slips of paper were passed around and the students were asked to write on the slip one of their choices. Trojans received a majority of the votes."

The first track team at Little Rock was known as the Trojan Warhorses. One year later, in 1931, the first football team was organized, with Coach Longstreth at the helm, and he chose to call his team the Trojans, which has lasted throughout UALR athletic history.

Centenary Gentlemen

Centenary College
P.O. Box 4188
Shreveport, LA 71134-0188

School Colors: Maroon and White
Year Founded: 1825
Basketball: Gold Dome (4,000)

THE UNIQUE NICKNAME of Gentlemen was first established on the Centenary campus in the fall of 1922. Because the majority of Centenary men were also soldiers, the moniker Gentlemen (Gents for short) was a name carried with pride and was a logical choice.

The new nickname was first mentioned in the 1923 Centenary *Yoncopin* yearbook in that season's football summary: "The boys were beginning to round into pretty good form by this time and as several recruits had been recently added, we were beginning to resemble a real college football team.

"Yet there was some doubt on the eve of the first game. Reports from the Marshall camp had them recruiting from the boiler factories and we were made to believe that the Marshall team was coming to Shreveport to mop-up with the 'Gentlemen.' (You see we had just taken the name of 'Centenary Gentlemen' and far be it from us to start a dispute at that time.)

"Well, we put on our best manners but just couldn't help from running up a 77–0 score."

It should be noted that the women's athletic nickname is, you guessed it, the Ladies.

Georgia Southern Eagles

Georgia Southern College
Landrum Box 8082
Statesboro, GA 30460

School Colors: Blue and White
Year Founded: 1906
Basketball: Hanner Fieldhouse (5,500)
Football: Allen E. Paulson Stadium
(18,000)

GEORGIA SOUTHERN COLLEGE'S current nickname, Eagles, was adopted in January 1960, when the school's name was changed from Georgia Teachers College. The Eagles' nickname was chosen by a faculty committee that screened many suggestions made by students and faculty. The eagle was selected because it is indigenous to Georgia. At one time, the king of the birds could be found in great numbers in the coastal region of the state not far from Statesboro.

Prior to being known as the Eagles, Georgia Southern was known by two other nicknames. From the school's founding in 1906 until 1950, its athletic teams were known as the Blue Tide. However, in 1950, when the school was known as Georgia Teachers College, the nickname was Professors.

Georgia State
Crimson Panthers

Georgia State University
Atlanta, GA 30303-3083

School Colors: Red and Gray
Year Founded: 1913
Basketball: GSU Sports Arena (5,500)

GEORGIA STATE UNIVERSITY obtained its original nickname from the grounds on which the sports teams play and it had nothing to do with animals.

The original nickname of the University was Panthers. This name emerged because the athletic fields on the urban campus are located on the outskirts of Atlanta in an area known as Panthersville. Thus the nickname was logical.

In the spring of 1988, the Georgia State athletic department introduced its new logo and nickname. The athletic teams now play under the name Crimson Panthers. Although the official athletic team colors are sky blue and royal blue, the university colors are red and gray, and the official logo appears in crimson. The new logo, which should provide greater flexibility in the development of future uniforms, publications, and so forth, was designed by art major Emanuel Toles.

Hardin-Simmons Cowboys

Hardin-Simmons University
Drawer H-HSU Station
Abilene, TX 79698

School Colors: Purple and Gold
Year Founded: 1891
Basketball: Mabee Complex (3,003)

KEEPING UP WITH the great Cowboy tradition of Texas, Hardin-Simmons's original nickname was the Wranglers. However, sometime between 1915 and 1920 school officials changed the name to Cowboys. The name is a logical choice as there were still many cowboys living near Abilene, in the heart of cowboy country in western Texas. Both names represented the great number of men who settled in Texas during the Civil War.

When football was still part of the school's athletic program, a cowboy decked out in chaps, ten-gallon hat, and lariat would perform on football Saturdays, givin' a hoot 'n holler for old Hardin-Simmons.

Houston Baptist Huskies

Houston Baptist University
7502 Fondren Road
Houston, TX 77074

School Colors: Royal Blue and
                    Orange
Year Founded: 1963
Basketball: Sharp Gym (1,800)

IN 1964. APPARENTLY for no reason, the Houston Baptist University president changed the school nickname on his own. When the school opened its doors in 1963, the athletic teams were known as the Spartans. However, after only one year under this name, Dr. William Hinton changed it to Huskies. For what reason, nobody really knows.

Since Hinton has retired and left the country, sports information director

Paul Walters has searched for the significance behind the Huskies' moniker. After contacting coaches, students, and faculty, Walters came up with the conclusion that President Hinton changed the name to Huskies simply because he preferred it over Spartans.

After the student body approved the nickname, a white Siberian husky was announced as the official mascot.

Mercer Bears

Mercer University
Macon, GA 31207

School Colors: Orange and Black
Year Founded: 1833
Basketball: Macon Coliseum (9,000)

IT IS BELIEVED BY Mercer University officials that their Bears' nickname may have come from the taunting of an opposing football player. In the late 1800s, before helmets were worn on the gridiron, many football players chose to grow their hair long for protection. During a football game against Georgia, as one of the Mercer running backs approached the line, a Georgia lineman yelled, "Whence cometh the bear." The nickname Bears was born from this statement.

Some people claim the name was borrowed from Baylor. Since Baylor and Mercer are both Baptist schools that share the same colors, that may be. But would a Baptist school swipe a nickname?

Samford Bulldogs

Samford University
800 Lakeshore Drive
Birmingham, AL 35229

School Colors: Crimson and Blue
Year Founded: 1841
Basketball: Siebert Gym (4,000)
Football: Siebert Stadium (6,000)

NO ONE REALLY KNOWS how or why Bulldogs was selected as Samford University's nickname.

The institution began as Howard College in 1841, as a Southern Baptist–affiliated campus in Marion, Alabama. In 1887 the school was moved to East Lake, Alabama. The school moved once again to Birmingham in 1957 under the financial help of an Alabama insurance man, Frank Park Samford. Samford was the chairman of the board of trustees and in 1965 the school was renamed Samford University in his honor.

Although there is no document written on the name, Alf Van Hoose, sports editor of the Birmingham *News*, recalled the name was first used by the media around 1930. Van Hoose believes school officials were searching for an appropriate nickname for their athletes and selected the traditional nickname Bulldogs, which has justly represented many collegiate programs for many years.

Stetson Hatters

Stetson University
Campus Box 8317
DeLand, FL 32720-3756

School Colors: Green and White
Year Founded: 1883
Basketball: Edmunds Center (5,000)

STETSON WAS FOUNDED in 1883 as DeLand Academy by Henry A.
DeLand, who also founded the city in which the campus is located.

In 1884, a severe freeze hit Florida and wiped out much of the orange
crop. This seriously affected DeLand's financial status and the future of the
city and academy. DeLand turned to his longtime friend, Philadelphia hat
manufacturer John B. Stetson, for financial help. Stetson responded, and
because he saved the school and community, DeLand in return changed the
name of the school to John B. Stetson University.

When the school began to develop an intercollegiate athletic program in
the early 1900s, it was only logical that the team's nickname be Hatters. As
you might say, the name truly fits.

Texas-San Antonio Roadrunners

University of Texas at San Antonio
San Antonio, TX 78285-0691

School Colors: Orange and White
Year Founded: 1969
Basketball: Convocation Center
(5,100)

LIKE MOST TEXAS SCHOOLS, the University of Texas at San Antonio selected its school nickname to represent some of the great animals and birds found in the local area.

In the 1977 campus-wide election for a school nickname, the Road-runner sped away from the pack of suggestions including Armadillo. A bird representative of the Texas hill country and the entire southwest, the Roadrunner was officially adopted as the school name early in 1978. The name signifies speed, endurance, and all-around athletic ability. The name, as team officials hope, will give their athletes an edge on the court, field, and track.

KoT.

San Diego Toreros

31

West Coast Athletic Conference

West Coast Athletic Conference
5421 Geary Boulevard
San Francisco, CA 94121

Number of Schools: 8
Year Founded: 1952
Charter Members: Pacific, St. Mary's, Santa Clara, San Francisco, and San Jose State
Current Members: Gonzaga, Loyola Marymount, Pepperdine, Portland, St. Mary's, San Diego, San Francisco, and Santa Clara
Division I Sports: Baseball, Basketball, Cross-Country, Golf, Soccer, and Tennis

Gonzaga Bulldogs

Gonzaga University
East 502 Boone Avenue
Spokane, WA 99258

School Colors: Blue, White, and Red
Year Founded: 1887
Basketball: Martin Centre (4,000)

TODAY, IT WOULD NOT be difficult to match the nickname Fighting
Irish to the proper school in a trivia game. However, if one went back to the
early 1900s, the Fighting Irish team one would be talking about might well
be Gonzaga University in Spokane.

The school's early nickname was the Fighting Irish, after the great Irish
tradition on campus. However, the name was changed in 1921, in a special
tribute to the school's great football team.

Coach Gus Dorais, the man who with Notre Dame's Knute Rockne is
credited with inventing the forward pass, had a spirited bunch of players
during that outstanding 1921 season. A local sportswriter praised Gonzaga's "bulldog-like tenacity" on the gridiron, and Bulldogs became the pet
name for the squad.

The Bulldogs' cognomen was officially used for the first time in Gonzaga's only postseason bowl apppearance in the East-West Classic against
West Virginia on Christmas Day, 1922. Although football was discon-
tinued after the 1941 season, the name Bulldogs has been synonymous with
Gonzaga athletics ever since.

Loyola Marymount Lions

Loyola Marymount University
Loyola Boulevard at West Eightieth Street
Box 345
Los Angeles, CA 90045

School Colors: Crimson, Gray, and
Columbia Blue
Year Founded: 1911
Basketball: Albert Gersten Pavilion
(4,156)

NO ONE AT Loyola Marymount University really knew how the Lions nickname originated until sports information director Barry Zepel did some deep digging. After talking to Jesuit priests in the school's infirmary, Zepel discovered that when the campus was moved to its present location on a bluff in 1927, an abundance of mountain lions roamed the area. The area had not been settled and there was a lot of wildlife, primarily lions. School officials adopted the Lions as their official nickname simply because the animals inhabited the campus area when ground was broken for the school's new buildings.

Zepel added that mountain rats also were found in great numbers and are still around the Los Angeles area. "I'm sure glad they didn't choose Rats as the nickname," commented Zepel.

Pepperdine Waves

Pepperdine University
24255 Pacific Coast Highway
Malibu, CA 90265

School Colors: Blue and Orange
Year Founded: 1937
Basketball: Firestone Fieldhouse
(3,104)

IN 1937, A NEW SCHOOL on California's west coast opened its doors to 167 excited students from 22 states and two foreign countries. When the students arrived at the freshly built campus, they found the concrete floors were still a bit wet. As a result, they were treated by the Pepperdine family to an all-expense-paid, week-long stay at the nearby William Penn Hotel.

During their stay, George Pepperdine kept students busy with tours and diversions, including a visit to the seashore. Many midwesterners had never seen the ocean before, and, captivated by it all, some particularly impressed students from Tennessee suggested the nickname Waves. Ever since the seaside field trip, the Waves' name has been rolling right along with Pepperdine athletics.

The selection of the school's colors is also quite simple. According to University president Batsell Baxter, blue was selected to represent the sea and orange was chosen because of the abundance of California oranges grown in the area.

Portland Pilots

University of Portland
5000 North Willamette Boulevard
Portland, OR 97203-5798

School Colors: Purple and White
Year Founded: 1901
Basketball: Earle A. Chiles Center
(5,000)

THE UNIVERSITY OF PORTLAND Pilots' nickname came about because of the unique environment in which the campus is located, on a beautiful, dramatic bluff overlooking the Willamette River and the city of Portland. The Pilots' nickname was chosen as a tribute to the ship pilots who daily steer their cargo past the University of Portland en route to the Pacific Ocean or into the nearby dock areas at the Port of Portland.

The nautical theme is prevalent on campus as the student newspaper, *The Beacon*; the yearbook, *The Log*; and the bookstore-restaurant, the Pilot House, were all named to signify the proximity of the campus to Portland's river and ocean life.

St. Mary's Gaels

St. Mary's College
Drawer A
Moraga, CA 94575-1101

School Colors: Red and Blue
Year Founded: 1863
Basketball: McKeon Pavilion (3,500)
Football: St. Mary's Stadium (3,500)

ACCORDING TO *Webster's Dictionary*, Gael is defined as the Celtic peoples, especially the Irish. But how does that fit in with St. Mary's College?

Prior to 1926, the college football team was known as the Saints and the baseball squad was called the Phoenix, a name still used to identify baseball boosters at the school. During the very successful 1926 football season, St. Mary's upset arch rival California-Berkeley for the first time in school history, winning 26–7. The win was keyed by an outstanding sophomore running back, Boyd "Cowboy" Smith, who scored on runs of 80 and 55 yards.

In the following day's San Francisco *Call-Bulletin*, sportswriter Pat Frayne saluted Smith's performance by printing a roster that resembled a Dublin phone directory page with a lead sentence reading, "The Lone Horseman and the Galloping Gaels trampled the Golden Bears of California in a flurry of speed and strength."

Smith's Lone Horseman tag was soon forgotten, but the Galloping Gaels identification stuck. Within a year, head coach Ed "Ship" Madigan applied for a copyright. St. Mary's finished the season with nine wins, no losses, and one tie and received national recognition and, thanks to a young sports reporter, a new nickname for its athletic teams.

San Diego Toreros

University of San Diego
Acala Park
San Diego, CA 92110

School Colors: Blue and White
Year Founded: 1949
Basketball: USD Sports Center
              (2,500)
Football: Torero Stadium (4,000)

SAN DIEGO UNIVERSITY acquired its nickname via the founding father's budding interest in Mexican heritage. The university's original nickname was Pioneers. In 1962, the school's athletic department changed its nickname to Toreros.

A torero is a Mexican bullfighter. The exact origin of USD's nickname is unknown, but the school's founding father, Bishop Buddy, was quite fascinated with Mexican history and culture. It is believed the unique nickname was a result of his influence.

San Francisco Dons

University of San Francisco
Ignatian Heights
San Francisco, CA 94117-1080

School Colors: Green and Gold
Year Founded: 1855
Basketball: Memorial Gymnasium
              (5,300)

PRIOR TO 1930, when the University of San Francisco was known as St. Ignatius College, the school nickname was the Grey Fog. It was an appropriate although not very elegant moniker for teams from the city by the Golden Gate Bridge.

In 1930, as St. Ignatius was celebrating its 75th anniversary, school officials, with the approval of the city's leading citizens, changed its name to the University of San Francisco. With the change, the city's Chamber of Commerce thought it might be a good time to dispose of the nickname that referred to the wispy cloud that often drifted in from the Pacific. University authorities were asked to come up with a new nickname for their athletic teams.

Studies showed the early history of California and San Francisco had been marked by the exploits of the adventuresome and swashbuckling Spanish dons. Because of the parallel growth of the city and the school from those early gold rush days, the name Dons became the choice of the committee in charge of finding a new moniker.

Santa Clara Broncos

Santa Clara University
Leavy Activity Center
Santa Clara, CA 95053

School Colors: Bronco Red and White
Year Founded: 1851
Basketball: Toso Pavilion (5,000)
Football: Buck Shaw Stadium (10,000)

THE SANTA CLARA UNIVERSITY Broncos' nickname originated from the philosophical mind of one of the school's faculty members. The Reverend Hubert Flynn, S.J., professor of philosophy, is credited with creating the name on November 5, 1923.

"The Bronco is a native westerner, a chunk of living dynamite. He's not very big, but he's game to the core. He can kick. He can buck," wrote Father Flynn in his letter suggesting adoption of the nickname. "And if you turn him loose in open spaces, his speed outstrips the wind. The Bronco's distinctive traits typify all Santa Clara could wish for in an athletic program."

Hawaii Rainbow Warriors

32

Western Athletic Conference

Western Athletic Conference
14 West Dry Creek Circle
Littleton, CO 80120

Number of Schools: 9
Year Founded: 1962
Charter Members: Arizona, Arizona State, Brigham Young, New Mexico, Utah, and Wyoming
Current Members: Air Force, Brigham Young, Colorado State, Hawaii, New Mexico, San Diego State, Texas–El Paso, Utah, and Wyoming
Division I Sports: Baseball, Basketball, Cross-Country, Diving, Football, Golf, Gymnastics, Indoor Track, Swimming, Tennis, Track and Field, and Wrestling

Air Force Falcons

United States Air Force Academy
HQ USAFA/AHI
Colorado Springs, CO 80840-5461

School Colors: Silver and Blue
Year Founded: 1959
Basketball: Cadet Fieldhouse (6,007)
Football: Falcon Stadium (52,137)

WHEN THE AIR FORCE Academy opened its doors in 1959, the first freshman class was given the responsibility of coming up with a distinctive nickname for the new institution.

On September 25, 1959, the cadets chose the Falcons as their official nickname and mascot. They selected the soaring falcon because the bird best represents the combative role of the United States Air Force.

Cadets evaluated the many qualities of the fierce falcon and decided there was a definite correlation with the tradition of the air force. The falcon can soar at great speeds, sometimes reaching 180 miles per hour. The courageous bird also has great power, graceful flight, and keen eyesight and is alert at all times.

Brigham Young Cougars

Brigham Young University
Smith Fieldhouse
Provo, UT 84602

School Colors: Royal Blue and White
Year Founded: 1875
Basketball: Marriott Center (22,700)
Football: Cougar Stadium (65,000)

THE BRIGHAM YOUNG Cougars' nickname dates back to 1915 when coach and physical education director E. L. Roberts began using the name in sports columns he wrote for Salt Lake City's *Deseret News*.

Roberts started most intercollegiate sports at the Mormon university, including the first gymnastics team west of the Mississippi River. He resumed football in 1920 after it had been banned for two decades due to the unfortunate death of the son of a Latter-Day Saints church leader.

Roberts came up with the Cougars' name from his extensive hiking and nature walks in Provo Canyon where he encountered packs of cougars. In 1911, he also started an annual hike up Mount Timpanogos—an event that became a huge and highly popular tradition in Utah for 60 years.

Colorado State Rams

Colorado State University
Moby Gym Complex
Fort Collins, CO 80523

School Colors: Green and Gold
Year Founded: 1870
Basketball: Moby Gymnasium
(10,000)
Football: Hughes Stadium (30,000)

COLORADO STATE'S mascot, the ram, was officially adopted in 1946, joining a long list of school mascots. The first was Peanuts, an English bulldog, who accompanied the Colorado State football and basketball teams to all contests. Replacing Peanuts was a black bear cub in 1919. However, the cub's reign lasted only until 1921, and the school went without a mascot until 1946.

The original Rocky Mountain Bighorn Sheep, named Cam the Ram, was donated by a student organization in 1946 to serve as the team mascot. Cam's name was derived from the initials of the College of Agriculture and Mechanical Arts.

The ram ties in well with Colorado and the Rocky Mountains. It is a strong, dangerous animal of the mountains that will defend his territory at all costs. Colorado State, who hopes to be the king of the mountains, wants its athletes to take on the aggressive nature of the ram.

Hawaii Rainbow Warriors

University of Hawaii
1337 Lower Campus Road
Honolulu, HI 96822-2370

School Colors: Green and White
Year Founded: 1907
Basketball: Neal S. Blaisdell Arena
(7,575)
Football: Aloha Stadium (50,000)

THE RAINBOW tradition began in 1924 when the Hawaii football team was hosting Oregon State at old Moiliili Field. Late in the game, with Hawaii defending a 7–0 lead, a magnificent rainbow arched over Manoa Valley.

Encouraged by the wondrous sight and the cheering crowd, Hawaii held Oregon State scoreless with a last-second goal line stand. It was thought the university would not lose any games if a rainbow appeared in Manoa Valley during a contest. Since atmospheric conditions are conducive for rainbows in late fall, Hawaii's 1924 and 1925 undefeated seasons certainly enhanced this tradition.

The student newspaper, *Ka leo O Hawaii*, developed a logo for the teams. A fierce-looking yet comical malo-clad figure, Hu-Hu, the Rainbow Warrior, was designed and officially adopted as the student body emblem.

In 1924, head football coach Larry Price and Dick Grimm, of KITV radio, created a mascot. Wearing an oversized plastic head, clad in malo and cape, and armed with a spear, the mascot was modeled after the Hawaiian demigod Kupua, who displayed magical powers in battle, speech-making, and partying.

Early Hawaiian teams went by a number of different nicknames. They were first called the Pilipili Boys, since Pilipili is the Hawaiian name for where the campus is located. They were later known as the Green simply because of the colors of their uniforms. They were also referred to as the Aggies, after the school's original name of College of Agriculture and Mechanic Arts of the Territory of Hawaii.

The team was known as the Deans or Fighting Deans from 1922 to the 1930s. The name referred to the popular and respected university president, Dr. Arthur L. Dean, who served from 1914 to 1927. The name was used interchangeably with Rainbows until just before World War II.

New Mexico Lobos

University of New Mexico
Albuquerque, NM 87131

School Colors: Silver and Cherry
Year Founded: 1889
Basketball: The Pit (17,136)
Football: University Stadium (30,646)

AFTER SERVING IN World War I, Roy W. Johnson headed out West from his Michigan home to assume the position as leader of the University of New Mexico's athletic program.

Those early years at UNM were tough for Johnson. For the entire 1920s, Johnson labored as athletic director, coach for all sports, groundskeeper, athletic business manager, equipment custodian, and teacher.

One of Johnson's first accomplishments was finding a more formidable name for the school's athletic teams. The teams were previously known under the dull names Varsities or Universities. In the fall of 1920, the extensive search for an exciting team name was successful. After reviewing reams of ancient New Mexican anthropological history, Johnson found that prehistoric natives of New Mexico believed and worshipped certain gods, in the same manner as the Greeks and Romans had done centuries ago.

One of the chief gods worshipped by the ancient inhabitants was Kujo the wolf, a war god of extreme prominence. Kujo was admired for his power, courage, and shrewdness.

Johnson found this wild and ferocious timber wolf of the Southwest to be a perfect symbol for New Mexico's athletic teams. The Spanish word for this feared and hated animal is *lobo*; the name has been synonymous with the school ever since.

The Weekly, the student newspaper, reported on October 2, 1920, "Eureka! At last, a real name for the University teams [The Lobos]. A name with a wallop in both fists (or paws)—a name that will make you sit up and take notice."

San Diego State Aztecs

San Diego State University
San Diego, CA 92181

School Colors: Scarlet and Black
Year Founded: 1897
Basketball: San Diego Sports Arena
(13,741)
Football: Jack Murphy Stadium
(60,049)

LOCATED ON A BLUFF overlooking Mission Valley, San Diego State University had been commonly referred to as Montezuma Mesa, home of the Aztecs, for more than 50 years.

The unique name Aztecs was adopted by the school in 1925. Prior to its adoption, San Diego State teams were unofficially dubbed Skaters and Professors by area sportswriters. The Aztecs, proposed by school newspaper and yearbook editors Fred Osenberg and Lewis Schellbach, was unanimously approved by school officials.

At the time of approval, school colors were purple and gold. But as time went on, these colors became unpopular with the students. Whittier College, San Diego's rival 100 miles to the north, also wore purple and gold. So did St. Augustine High in San Diego, making lettermen's jackets worn on El Cajon Boulevard quite indistinguishable.

An election for new school colors was held on January 18, 1928, and students voted to adopt scarlet and black. Three years later, the university moved from Normal Street in San Diego to its current location in East San Diego, and Montezuma Mesa became the home of San Diego State.

Texas-El Paso Miners

University of Texas at El Paso
El Paso, TX 79968

School Colors: Orange, Blue, and
White
Year Founded: 1913
Basketball: Special Events Center
(12,222)
Football: Sun Bowl (52,000)

THE UNIVERSITY OF TEXAS AT EL PASO began as the tiny Texas School of Mines and Metallurgy. In the 1930s, when officials felt it was time the school had a nickname, Miners was chosen simply because the institution trained students for the mining industry.

The school was renamed Texas Western, and later the current name, University of Texas at El Paso, was selected. The school's athletic teams still fight for victory under the nickname Miners.

Utah Utes

University of Utah
Special Events Center
Salt Lake City, UT 84112

School Colors: Crimson and White
Year Founded: 1850
Basketball: Jon M. Huntsman Center
                (15,000)
Football: Rice Stadium (35,000)

THE UNIVERSITY OF UTAH'S current nickname was chosen because of
the local Indian tribe, which the state of Utah was also named after.

Since the early 1900s, Utah athletic teams were referred to as either the
Redskins or Utes. The Utes' name was derived from the Shoshone tribe
called the Utes that inhabited the area. Even today the name fits the school,
as there is a Ute Indian reservation in Vernal, only 170 miles away from the
Salt Lake City campus.

The state of Utah's name is also derived from the Indian tribe. The
Spanish form of the word is Utta, which evolved into the English form of
Utah. In its Navajo translation, it means upper or higher up.

Government officials also proposed that the state be named Deseret,
meaning land of the honeybees, from the Book of Mormon, but it was
rejected by members of Congress who favored the Utah name.

In the 1970s, when many Indian organizations were upset with the
commercial use of their names for school mascots, university officials
dropped the moniker Redskins and adopted Utes as the sole nickname of
the school.

Wyoming Cowboys

University of Wyoming
Box 3414, University Station
Laramie, WY 82071

School Colors: Brown and Yellow
Year Founded: 1886
Basketball: Arena-Auditorium (15,000)
Football: War Memorial Stadium
            (33,500)

THE UNIVERSITY OF WYOMING received its school nickname as a result of some hecklers in the stands at a pickup game—two years before the first official collegiate athletic event was ever held.

The story is that an 1891 Wyoming pickup football team appealed to a 220-pound ex-Harvard cowpuncher, Fred Bush, for help against their bitter rivals, the Cheyenne Soldiers. Bush agreed to play, then signed up for a course or two at the school.

When Bush first trotted onto the field decked out in a checkered shirt and Stetson hat, someone yelled, "Hey, look at the cowboy!" Since many of the team members were also ex-cowboys, the name stuck.

The first team mascot, a white pinto Shetland pony named Cowboy Joe, was given to the school by the Farthing family and the Cheyenne Quarter-back Club in 1950. Joe retired to the University Farm in 1965 for a well-deserved rest after 15 years of rooting the Cowboys on to victory.

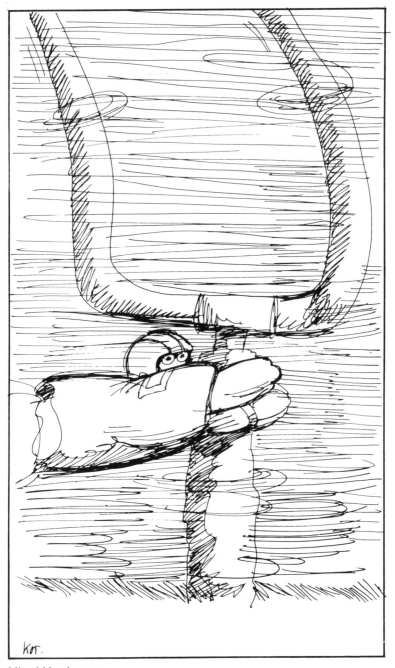

Miami Hurricanes

33

Independents

THE NINETEEN SCHOOLS listed here play as independents in Division I basketball. There are 24 schools that play as independents in football.

Only five teams—Akron, Miami, Northern Illinois, Notre Dame, and Tulane—play as Division I independents in both sports.

University of Akron
Brooklyn College
Central Connecticut
    State University
University of Central Florida
Chicago State University
DePaul University
Florida International University
University of Maryland–
    Baltimore County
University of Miami

Mount St. Mary's College
Nicholls State University
Northern Illinois University
University of Notre Dame
Oral Roberts University
Southeastern Louisiana University
Tulane University
U.S. International University
University of Wisconsin–
    Milwaukee
Wright State University

Akron Zips

University of Akron
JAR 76
Akron, OH 44325

School Colors: Blue and Gold
Year Founded: 1870
Basketball: JAR Arena (7,000)
Football: Rubber Bowl (35,482)

ONE OF THE UNIQUE nicknames in college athletics belongs to the University of Akron, which owes its moniker to a female student who tried on a pair of Zipper shoes.

When athletics began at Akron in 1925, the university found itself without a nickname. A contest was conducted on campus to fill the void, and many potential names were submitted by students, faculty, and alumni. A large number of suggestions were entered, including Golden Blue Devils, Tip Toppers, Rubbernecks, Hillbillies, Kangaroos, and Cheveliers, to name just a few.

After a vote by the students, Akron lettermen, local sportswriters, and faculty was conducted, Akron had itself a new nickname on January 15, 1926. Margaret Hamlin, a freshman, found the answer with the moniker Zippers and received a $10 cash prize.

Hamlin's idea emerged from a six-dollar pair of rubber shoes called Zippers, which her father had given to her. What made the name even more appealing has that the shoes were a product of the Akron-based B. F. Goodrich Company.

On September 13, 1950, athletic director Kenneth "Red" Cochrane announced that the nickname had been officially shortened to Zips. Some say this happened because of the vulnerability to puns when the zipper became a popular addition to men's trousers. Others say it was shortened because it was easier for the press to use, especially in headlines.

In 1953, Student Council member and all-American diver Bob Savoy satisfied the university's need for a mascot. As chairman of the search committee, he evaluated all possible mascots and came up with Zippy the Kangaroo. It was chosen because it was an animal that was "fast, agile, and powerful with undying determination—all the necessary qualities of an athlete."

Brooklyn Kingsmen

Brooklyn College
Bedford Avenue and Avenue H
Brooklyn, NY 11210

School Colors: Maroon and Gold
Year Founded: 1930
Basketball: Roosevelt Gymnasium
                            (1,700)
Football: Roosevelt Field (3,000)

ALL THE KING'S horses and all the king's men . . .

Since Brooklyn College is located in Kings County, school officials didn't have to look too far for a nickname for their sports teams. When the school was founded in 1930, the teams were immediately referred to as the Kingsmen. Since the state of New York itself is named after Dutch royalty, the name Kingsmen fits well with the state, campus, and surrounding community.

Central Connecticut State Blue Devils

Central Connecticut State University
1615 Stanley Street
New Britain, CT 06050

School Colors: Blue and White
Year Founded: 1849
Basketball: Kaiser Hall (4,500)
Football: Arute Field (8,000)

ACCORDING TO A longtime coach at Central Connecticut State, the Blue Devils' nickname was chosen in a contest. Retired basketball coach Bill Detrick recalls that in either 1947 or 1948 the students grew restless and wanted a new team moniker. A student body election was held and Blue Devils was declared the winner.

The name is significant because it ties in well with the school colors while giving the squads a mischievous, dangerous image on the athletic fields.

When Central Connecticut entered the Division I ring of collegiate athletics in 1986, a new logo was developed featuring a burly demon sporting a trident and clenched fist, ready to blaze by opposing teams.

Central Florida Knights

University of Central Florida
Orlando, FL 32816-0555

School Colors: Black and Gold
Year Founded: 1963
Basketball: UCF Gymnasium (2,456)
Football: Florida Citrus Bowl (50,000)

ONE YEAR AFTER intercollegiate athletics began at the University of Central Florida, then known as Florida Technological University, students felt their athletes deserved a team nickname. In the summer of 1970, the students approached university president Charles Millican for suggestions. "Operation Mascot" was soon aided by suggestion boxes located on campus and a committee comprised of students, staff, and faculty members.

In December 1970, the winning entry, Knights (based on the Knights of Pegasus), was announced. Voters elected the Knights of Pegasus and allied the mascot with the university's seal, which prominently features Pegasus, the winged horse of Greek mythology.

Chicago State Cougars

Chicago State University
Ninety-fifth Street and King Drive
Chicago, IL 60628

School Colors: Green and White
Year Founded: 1867
Basketball: CSU Physical Education
and Athletics Building
(2,500)

CHICAGO STATE UNIVERSITY'S current nickname, the Cougars, was adopted in the early 1970s as a result of possible unfavorable racial interpretations.

The school began primarily as a teachers college in 1867. However, in 1897, the school became Chicago Normal School, due to the assistance of Col. Francis Wayland Parker. When Chicago State's athletic program was founded, school officials decided upon the nickname Colonels in honor of its founding father, Colonel Parker.

However, during the civil rights movement of the 1960s, school officials questioned the Colonels' moniker, believing the nickname's connection with southern plantation owners would possibly promote offensive racial connotations. When the school moved in 1971 and became Chicago State University, school officials did not wish to be connected with racism in any way. So they changed the name.

The student government held an election on nine potential nicknames. The nickname Cougars eventually was declared the winner, squeaking past such other popular names such Bisons and Lions. It is possible the Cougars' name received such great acceptance because there was a popular hockey team in town at the time called the Chicago Cougars.

DePaul Blue Demons

DePaul University
1011 West Belden Avenue
Chicago, IL 60614-3205

School Colors: Scarlet and Royal
            Blue
Year Founded: 1898
Basketball: Rosemont Horizon
            (17,500)

DEPAUL UNIVERSITY inadvertently obtained its nickname from the school's early basketball uniforms. In 1900, when the first athletic team was formed to represent DePaul, the monogram D, for DePaul, was selected for use on the uniforms. Perhaps it would have cost too much money to have D-E-P-A-U-L sewn across the jersey.

The nickname D-men originated from these early uniforms and eventually evolved into Demons. Blue was added to the Demons' nickname by student approval to signify the loyalty to the school in 1901.

Florida International
Golden Panthers

Florida International University
Tamiami Trail
Miami, FL 33199

School Colors: Blue and Gold
Year Founded: 1972
Basketball: Sunblazer Arena (3,600)

AFTER FLORIDA INTERNATIONAL UNIVERSITY opened in 1972, its athletic teams were known by newspaper reporters as the No-Names. In Rafe Gibbs's book, *Visibility Unlimited*, he explained this anonymity was troublesome, and suggestions for a mascot to represent the school were solicited from the public.

"Cartoonists in the Miami *Herald* depicted Teddy Bears and Leapin' Lizards as possible mascots. On campus, more than 60 suggestions were submitted. Finally, it was decided that the Sunblazers name would carry the banner for FIU."

The name Sunblazers served the young and growing university faithfully, but with growth sometimes comes the need for change. In the spring of 1987, university president Dr. Mitch Maidique felt a mascot that would more accurately portray the pride and dignity of the school was needed. He wanted a name people could identify with anywhere, one that would indicate the school's close ties with Florida's natural environment.

At a kick-off gala for the university's first fundraising Cornerstone Campaign, President Maidique said, "The University is taking a more visible, aggressive, and determined stance in all areas—academic quality, community involvement, student recruitment, fundraising, and attracting dollars for sponsored research and training.

"The image of the Panther focuses on an easily explainable, shared value. All people can identify with the motion and strength of the Panther."

On July 8, 1987, Maidique's appointed Panther implementation task force recommended the adoption of the Golden Panther as the new mascot. The term golden reflects the school colors, adds distinction to an already regal image, and serves to clearly distinguish the university from all other Panther mascots.

Maryland–Baltimore County Retrievers

University of Maryland, Baltimore County
Baltimore, MD 21228

School Colors: Old Gold and Black
Year Founded: 1966
Basketball: UMBC Fieldhouse (4,024)
Football: UMBC Stadium (4,500)

WHEN ATHLETICS FIRST BEGAN at the University of Maryland, Baltimore County in 1966, the school selected its nickname from the state mascot. The Chesapeake Bay Retriever is the state mascot of Maryland, and school officials quickly adopted the retriever as their own. The retriever is an appropriate choice to represent an athletic team because it is a strong, quick hunter as well as the most loyal of animals.

Famous cartoonist Jack Davis created Baltimore County's unique school logo of a dashing retriever in uniform. Later, a bronze statue of the Retriever was erected on campus. It has become a custom for students to rub the dog's nose on exam days for good luck.

Miami Hurricanes

University of Miami
P.O. Box 248167
Coral Gables, FL 33124

School Colors: Orange, Green, and
                     White
Year Founded: 1925
Basketball: James L. Knight Center
                  (5,020)
Football: Orange Bowl (75,500)

THE DEVASTATING HURRICANE of September 16, 1926, postponed the opening of Miami's doors until October 18. Just five days later, on Friday, October 23, the new university's football team played its first game.

The night before the game, against Rollins College, reporter Jack Bell came out to practice and asked Porter Norris, a member of the Miami team, what he should call the team in the next day's issue. He told Norris that local dignitaries and school officials wished to name the team after a local flower or bird.

Porter blew up and replied that he and his teammates would not stand for their team's being named after any local flora or fauna. Since the game had been postponed by a hurricane, he suggested, "Why not name the team the Miami Hurricanes?"

Bell agreed with Norris's logic and called the team the Hurricanes. The story has it that Ev Sewell, head of the Miami Chamber of Commerce, was displeased with the name because he felt it would be detrimental to the city, which was trying to shake its hurricane image.

Bell campaigned and made a bargain with Sewell that if the team won under the name Hurricane, then the name would stay. The team rose to the occasion by going undefeated in its eight games that inaugural season.

In the 1930s and 1960s, campaigns were made to get rid of the name, for fear it would harm the city's tourism and development. But the name was retained, and, as one spokesman said, "Does anyone think Chicago is full of bears just because the town has a football team by that name?"

And just think: if Bell hadn't asked a player who would speak his mind, University of Miami teams today could be known as the Orange Blossoms or the Mockingbirds, Florida's state flower and bird, respectively.

Mount St. Mary's Mountaineers

Mount St. Mary's College
Route 15
Emmitsburg, MD 21727

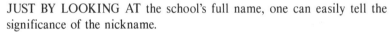

School Colors: Blue and White
Year Founded: 1808
Basketball: Knott Athletic
Convocation Complex
(3,500)

JUST BY LOOKING AT the school's full name, one can easily tell the significance of the nickname.

In 1792, Rev. John DuBois, a French émigré priest, was transferred to a pastorate in Frederick, Maryland, which included missions in Emmitsburg and the chapel maintained by the Elder family, who had settled south of town on land called St. Mary's Mount.

In 1808, Father DuBois bought land on the mountain to build a new church and school. By 1809, the school had quickly grown into three sections—a preparatory school for young boys, a college, and a seminary. Mount St. Mary's College, now the oldest independent Catholic college in the United States, was thus founded.

The first college publication, which appeared on campus on June 8, 1830, referred to the people of the area as Mountaineers due to the location and name of the school. Students and athletes have been known ever since as the Mount, Mountaineers, or Mounties.

Nicholls State Colonels

Nicholls State University
P.O. Box 2032
Thibodaux, LA 70310

School Colors: Cardinal and Gray
Year Founded: 1948
Basketball: Stopher Gym (3,800)
Football: John L. Guidry Stadium
(12,800)

NICHOLLS STATE WAS founded as Francis T. Nicholls Junior College in 1948. The first athletic teams at Nicholls Junior College were fielded in 1950 and were known as the Buccaneers because of the school's location on the bayou. However, after only two years of competition, the athletic program was dropped.

When the school became a four-year institution in 1956, the Student Government Association selected a Confederate colonel as the official nickname and mascot. The Colonel was chosen because Francis T. Nicholls, after whom the school is named, served as a colonel for the Confederate Army during the Civil War.

Northern Illinois Huskies

Northern Illinois University
112 Evans Field House
De Kalb, IL 60115-2854

School Colors: Cardinal and Black
Year Founded: 1895
Basketball: Chick Evans Field House
(6,076)
Rockford MetroCentre
(9,000)
Football: Huskie Stadium (20,257)

ALTHOUGH THE HUSKIES' nickname is popular on Northern Illinois University's campus today, there were many other cognomens to describe "old NI's" athletic teams.

Profs, an obvious expression of the institution's mission as a teachers college, was a moniker used in the early days. The name Cardinals, borrowed from the school colors, was popular in the 1920s. The tag Evansmen was used in the 1930s, as a reverent recognition of athletic pioneer George G. "Chick" Evans. Other terms used to describe NI teams were Northerners and Teachers.

In 1940, a four-man committee made up of members of the Varsity Club—which included Evans, Harold Taxman, Walter Lorimer, and Harry Telman—was appointed to find a term with "a trifle more dash."

After much debate and research, a final decision on the name Huskies was reported in the January 25, 1940, edition of the *Northern Illinois* student newspaper. "Not only does the term have color and meaning, but it is particularly apt as in regard to NI's varsity teams," the article noted. "From now on the word 'Huskies' will be used constantly in this paper and in other papers to indicate our athletic squads."

As a further note, Evans made reference in that 1940 story to a huskie dog, not husky. So ever since, when talking about the individual, the correct form at the De Kalb campus is Huskie.

Notre Dame Fighting Irish

University of Notre Dame
Convocation Center
Notre Dame, IN 46556

School Colors: Gold and Blue
Year Founded: 1842
Basketball: Joyce Athletic and
Convocation Center
(11,418)
Football: Notre Dame Stadium (59,075)

THE FIGHTING
■ IRISH

THERE ARE A NUMBER of explanations as to how Notre Dame acquired its proud Fighting Irish nickname and tradition. No one knows for sure which theory is most accurate, so take your pick.

One story suggests the name was born in 1887, Notre Dame's first season of football. With Notre Dame leading Northwestern 5–0 in Evanston, Illinois, the Wildcat fans began to chant, "Kill the Fighting Irish, kill the Fighting Irish," as the team trotted back onto the field at halftime.

Another tale has the nickname originating at halftime of the fierce Notre Dame–Michigan football contest in 1909. With his team trailing, one Notre Dame player yelled to his teammates to get them going—players who happened to have names like Dolan, Kelly, Glynn, Duffy, and Ryan. "What's the matter with you guys? You're all Irish and you're not fighting worth a lick!" he hollered. Notre Dame came back and won the game, and the press, who overheard the remark, reported in their articles "a victory for the Fighting Irish."

The most widely accepted explanation of the moniker is that the press dubbed the teams while trying to characterize their never-say-die fighting spirit and their Irish qualities of grit, determination, and tenacity. However, it is very likely that the name emerged as an abusive expression tauntingly directed toward the athletes from the small, private, Catholic institution in South Bend. It was Notre Dame alumnus Francis Wallace who popularized the nickname in his New York *Daily News* columns in the 1920s.

The 1929 Notre Dame *Scholastic* printed its own version of the story: "The term 'Fighting Irish' . . . first attached itself years ago when the school, comparatively unknown, sent its athletic teams away to play in another city. . . . At that time the title 'Fighting Irish' held no glory or prestige.

"The years passed swiftly and the little school began to take a place in the sports world. . . . 'Fighting Irish' took on a new meaning. The unknown of a few years past has boldly taken a place among the leaders. The unkind appellation became symbolic of the struggle for supremacy of the field. . . . The term, while given in irony, has become our heritage. . . . So truly does it represent us that we are unwilling to part with it."

Notre Dame had previously competed under the nickname Catholics during the 1800s. The team was more popularly known during the early 1920s as the Ramblers, after the immortal backfield known as the Four Horsemen.

In 1927, Notre Dame president Matthew Walsh officially adopted the Fighting Irish as the nickname of the university.

Oral Roberts Titans

Oral Roberts University
7777 South Lewis Avenue
Tulsa, OK 74171

School Colors: Blue, Gold, and White
Year Founded: 1965
Basketball: Mabee Center (10,575)

THE TITANS' NICKNAME has been with Oral Roberts University since the school's inception in 1965. At the time, there were less than 1,000 students. By a popular-vote election, Titans was announced as the official nickname.

The nickname Titans was introduced for its definition of being one who overachieves. Since Oral Roberts is such a small school, it is looked upon as one of the less than powerful sports foes by many other schools. Therefore, an overachiever image is just fine for ORU.

The nickname was popularized in 1972, when the Titan basketball team moved into the new Mabee Center Arena. The students who sat in the student section developed a popular cheer called the Titan Train. In 1980, puppetmaker Judy Collins designed a huge engineer named Casey Titan as the school mascot.

Southeastern Louisiana Lions

Southeastern Louisiana University
P.O. Box 880
Hammond, LA 70402

School Colors: Green and Gold
Year Founded: 1925
Basketball: University Center (7,500)

SOUTHEASTERN LOUISIANA went without a nickname until the 1930s when the student body held an election to choose a team mascot. Many suggestions, some serious and some amusing, were received.

However, it was the entry of Elmer Sanders, the center on the football team, who provided the winning nomination. The name Lions proved very popular on campus and was quickly adopted.

Yet in the early 1960s, the fierce king of the jungle almost didn't survive in Hammond. Because the school could not locate a live lion to lead student cheers and roars at athletic contests, student Jim Corbett suggested that Southeastern change its name to Ponies. His reasoning was that a live pony mascot would be much easier to obtain.

But that's when Clifford Ourso, a Baton Rouge businessman, stepped into the picture and offered to donate a lion cub to serve as SLU mascot. At last, in 1962, the school had a live mascot! In 1963, students voted to name the cub Lobo. But in 1964, the tiny lion was renamed Roomie in honor of the late Hollis R. "Roomie" Wilson, a longtime member of the school's biological sciences faculty and a strong supporter of intercollegiate athletics.

Tulane Green Wave

Tulane University
Monk Simons Complex
New Orleans, LA 70118

School Colors: Olive Green and Sky
                     Blue
Year Founded: 1834
Basketball: Tulane Arena (5,000)
Football: Superdome (74,966)

THERE IS A LONG HISTORY of Tulane University nicknames, so pay close attention.

Prior to 1919, Tulane's athletic teams were known as the Olive and Blue, after the school colors. In 1919, the Tulane newspaper, *The Hullabaloo* began calling the football team the Greenbacks.

Only one year later, on October 20, 1920, Earl Sparling, the editor of the student newspaper, wrote a football song that appeared in the paper. The song, entitled "The Rolling Green Wave," began to receive student acceptance, and a newspaper reporter covering the Tulane–Mississippi A&M

game referred to the squad for the first time as the Green Wave. By the end of that 1920 season, the name seemed to be accepted by the *Hullabaloo* and other daily papers, although as late as 1923 the name Greenbacks was still used interchangeably with the Green Wave.

At one time, Tulane's mascot was a pelican riding on a surfboard while slashing through the waves of the Gulf of Mexico. Later in 1955, the Greenie, created by cartoonist John Chase, was adopted as mascot.

When Dr. Rix Yard became Tulane's athletic director in 1963, he and others felt Tulane need a more virile symbol for its teams. Working with Elton Endacott, the manager of the Tulane Bookstore, several sketches were submitted by Art Evans, who created Purdue's Boilermaker, USC's Trojan, and many other collegiate mascots.

The angry-looking Green Wave logo finally came into being in 1964 and has been Tulane's official athletic symbol ever since.

U.S. International Soaring Gulls

U.S. International University
10455 Pomerado Road
San Diego, CA 92131

School Colors: Columbia Blue and
             Gold
Year Founded: 1952
Basketball: Golden Hall (5,000)

U.S. INTERNATIONAL UNIVERSITY received its current nickname from people who sent in a novel whose morals closely depicted the university's own goals.

The school was first known as California Western University and played under the nickname Westerners. However, when the name was changed to U.S. International in the late 1960s, the name no longer fit the institution.

When the school was in search of a new name in 1973, dozens of people sent in copies of Richard Bach's book *Jonathan Livingston Seagull.* Many people thought the book represented the high educational standards set by U.S. International, including motivating people to reach their full potential and working toward doing their absolute best in everything they set out to do.

After receiving such large numbers of the book, school officials decided to adopt the Soaring Gull's name. In 1979, U.S. International's logo showing a white seagull flying into a rainbowed sunrise was released.

Wisconsin-Milwaukee Panthers

University of Wisconsin–Milwaukee
P.O. Box 413
Milwaukee, WI 53201

School Colors: Black and Gold
Year Founded: 1956
Basketball: Klotsche Center (4,000)

UNIVERSITY OF WISCONSIN–MILWAUKEE evolved from the merger of the Wisconsin State College of Milwaukee and the University of Wisconsin system in 1956. Prior to the merger, Wisconsin State College was known as the Green Gulls, a takeoff on the campus' location near the shores of Lake Michigan.

Following the merger, UWM was officially nicknamed the Cardinals and played under the colors red and white. However, university officials, wanting a more exciting name for their athletes, held a student contest to select a new moniker and school colors in 1965. The winning entry was Panthers, and the university adopted the nickname as well as new colors of black and gold.

The original Panther logo was a silhouette of the dangerous jungle feline. In 1974, a prancing panther symbol was adopted, which featured the animal dancing the whirling dervish with the letters *UWM* on his chest. However, the logo was changed again in 1985 to the more modern panther used today.

Wright State Raiders

Wright State University
Dayton, OH 45435

School Colors: Green and Gold
Year Founded: 1964
Basketball: Physical Education
             Building (2,750)
             Ervin J. Nutter Center
             (11,000)

THERE IS ABSOLUTELY no significance whatsoever behind the Wright State University nickname and mascot. A few years after Wright State fielded its first athletic team in 1968, a student election was held to determine the school's nickname. A vote was held on a list of names nominated by a committee of staff, students, and faculty members; the winning name was Raiders.

However, Wright State's first athletic director, Don Mohr, wasn't particularly fond of the name. "Because our founders were the Miami University and Ohio State, I wanted some kind of a name that would tie in with those schools. However," Mohr said with a chuckle, "Raiders was the name the kids wanted, and in those days, they got what they wanted."

The color combination of green and gold was also adopted via the student election. These colors were not Mohr's first choice either, but hey, you can't win 'em all!

Index

STORIES BEHIND the nicknames of all 293 NCAA Division I football and basketball teams are included in this book. Of these schools, 274 are listed according to the conference in which they play basketball. The remaining 19 schools are included in an Independents chapter following the 32 Division I Conference chapters.

There are 19 independent schools in basketball and 24 in football. For example, Penn State plays as an independent in football yet plays basketball in the Atlantic 10 Conference.

Only five teams—Akron, Miami of Florida, Northern Illinois, Notre Dame, and Tulane—play as Division I independents in both sports.